D0914126

Texas & Northeastern Mexico, 1630–1690

University of Texas Press   Austin

• TEXAS &

by *Juan Bautista Chapa*

NORTH-

Edited with an introduction

EASTERN

by William C. Foster

MEXICO •

Translated by Ned F. Brierley

1630–1690

Translation of *Historia del nuevo reino de León de 1650 a 1690*

Copyright © 1997 by William C. Foster
All rights reserved
Printed in the United States of America

First edition, 1997

Requests for permission to reproduce material from this work should be sent to Permissions, University of Texas Press, Box 7819, Austin, TX 78713-7819.

⊗ The paper used in this publication meets the minimum requirements of American National Standard for Information Sciences—Permanence of Paper for Printed Library Materials, ANSI Z39.48-1984.

Library of Congress Cataloging-in-Publication Data

Chapa, Juan Bautista, 1630 or 31–1695.
   [Historia del Nuevo Reino de Leon de 1650 a 1690. English]
   Texas and northeastern Mexico, 1630–1690 / by Juan Bautista
Chapa ; edited with an introduction by William C. Foster ; translated by Ned F. Brierley. — 1st ed.
     p.   cm.
   Includes bibliographical references and index.
   ISBN 0-292-71188-3 (alk. paper)
   1. Nuevo Leon (Mexico : State)—History.   2. Texas—History—To 1846.   3. Mexico—History—Spanish colony, 1540–1810.
4. Indians of Mexico—Mexico—Nuevo Leon (State)—History.
I. Foster, William C., 1928- . II. Title.
F1316.C4613   1997
972'.13—dc 20   96-25202

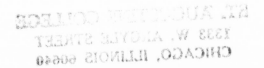

To my grandchildren:

William Chandler
Kalle Marie
Annika Kirsten
Jenner Lindh

Contents

Contents

❧

MAPS

FIGURES

Preface

IN compiling source materials for *Spanish Expeditions into Texas, 1689 – 1768*, I recognized that a number of significant Spanish and French diaries and journals, which seemed to me critical to an appreciation of Texas history, had not been translated into English. Within the past three years, Jack Jackson and I, as coeditors and collaborators, have worked to have translated—with comprehensive introductions, full annotations, and detailed route maps—the diaries of Governor Gregorio de Salinas Varona's 1693 expedition, Brigadier Pedro de Rivera's 1727 inspection tour, and the Marqués de Rubí's 1767 expedition, which followed the Camino Real from San Antonio across Texas to the Spanish capital of the Province of Texas in present-day Louisiana. This book—the translation and annotation of two additional seventeenth-century Spanish classics that have been cited repeatedly by American and Mexican scholars as among the most authoritative documents of the Spanish colonial period in Texas—is an extension of that effort.

The first and more significant work is Juan Bautista Chapa's *Historia del Nuevo Reino de León*, a history of Texas and northeastern Mexico covering the period 1630 to 1690. This narrative covers the history of Texas from the establishment of Luis de Carvajal's kingdom (1579), which included northeastern Mexico and most of Texas south and west of Austin. The second work is Governor Alonso de León's previously unpublished revised diary of the 1690 expedition from Monclova to East Texas. Manuscript copies of these two works are held in the Beinecke Library of Yale University, which graciously made copies available for this study.

Chapa's *Historia*, supplemented by Captain Alonso de León's (the elder's) *Discourses*, records the earliest colonization of Nuevo León, a geographically identified Spanish kingdom or province that included all or part of approximately forty present-day South and West Texas counties. Areas north of the lower Rio Grande were explored, and mining and slaving settlements were established from present-day Monterrey north to the lower Rio

Grande in the 1580s, decades before Jamestown was founded in Virginia (1607) and the Pilgrims landed in New England (1620). There is no comparable systematic history for other areas in northern New Spain written in the seventeenth century by a contemporary senior official.

This work required the careful translation of the two seventeenth-century Spanish documents, one of which is found only in manuscript form. These translations were skillfully accomplished by Ned F. Brierley, who specializes in translating Spanish colonial documents and who assisted in the translations of the diaries of Governor Salinas Varona, Brigadier Rivera, and the Marqués de Rubí. Adela Pacheco Cobb of Washington, D.C., again provided valuable assistance as a translator and editor. The maps were prepared by John V. Cotter, a highly regarded cartographer who was responsible for the excellent maps in *Spanish Expeditions into Texas, 1689–1768*. Jack Jackson served again not only as the principal scout and guide but also as the expedition sketch artist and skillfully depicted scenes and personalities with exacting detail and an artistry that brings the reader and viewer directly into the story. Christina Jackson (who served as *redactora anónima* for our earlier works) provided the critical review that a manuscript requires in draft form. The principal academic review of the work was performed admirably by historian and professor emeritus Oakah L. Jones, whose numerous comments helped us remain on track and avoid deep potholes. Despite this outside aid, the study required the highly professional touch and driving enthusiasm of the University of Texas Press's assistant director, Theresa J. May.

Those of us who have toiled on the project may, I believe, now rest with some assurance that significant parts of the rich historical record compiled by Alonso de León (the elder), Juan Bautista Chapa, and Alonso de León (the younger) will be available to a broader contemporary reading public, as the authors would have wished.

W.C.F.

Introduction

THREE hundred years ago, an anonymous author living quietly and alone near Monterrey, Mexico, completed a rich and detailed history of present-day Texas and Nuevo León covering the years 1630 to 1690. The manuscript, which describes not only the Spanish leaders of the period but also the native population and natural environment of northeastern Mexico and Texas, went unpublished for over two hundred years, and it was not until 1961 that the author's identity was revealed. That author was Juan Bautista Chapa, a man who was fearful of the Spanish Inquisition, but whose experience during the period as secretary to several governors of Nuevo León gave him the ability and the knowledge necessary to write such an insightful account. He was a close companion of Captain Alonso de León (the elder), whom he accompanied on numerous military actions against Indian tribes near Monterrey and the lower Rio Grande, and he served under Governor Alonso de León (the younger) on the 1686 and 1689 expeditions in search of the French settlement at present-day Matagorda Bay on the Central Texas coast. No comparable history was ever written by a resident Spanish official about other parts of northern New Spain.

This book is the first annotated English rendition of both Chapa's *Historia* and Governor Alonso de León's revised 1690 expedition diary. Scholars of the Spanish colonial period and the general public interested in Texas history will find the translations clear and easy to read and will have the opportunity to enjoy a seventeenth-century Spanish classic, the earliest systematic history of Texas.

This introduction will track the publication of Chapa's work and unfold the mystery of authorship. A full review of each of Captain Alonso de León's *Discourses* on the history of Nuevo León from its inception in 1579 to 1650 is included to provide background for Chapa's account. The *Discourses* highlight the efforts by Luis de Carvajal y de la Cueva in the 1580s to settle the kingdom of Nuevo León (which included most of South Texas) and the

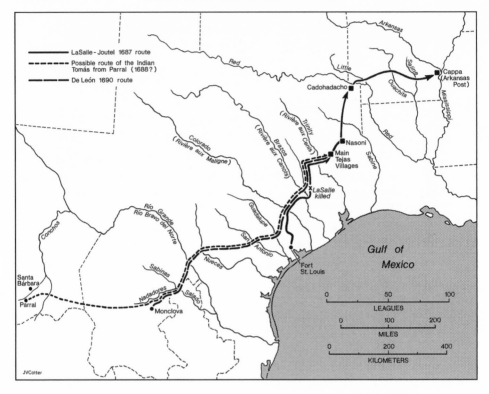

MAP 1. *French, Spanish, and Indian routes to East Texas and the Mississippi River, 1687–1690.*

lifeways and customs of the Indian population. Finally, a brief examination of the significance of Chapa's contribution to the understanding of the period will introduce his *Historia.*

In 1909 the highly respected Mexican bibliographer Genaro García included the chronicle or *Historia* written by Chapa (then known only as *autor anónimo*) in the *Historia de Nuevo León con Noticias sobre Coahuila, Texas y Nuevo México, por el Capitán Alonso de León, un Autor Anónimo y el General Fernando Sánchez de Zamora.*[1] García's compilation also included three *Discourses* on the history of Nuevo León before 1650 authored by Captain Alonso de León and a short, one-chapter history of the Río Blanco area—located in the southern part of the province—prepared by General Fernando

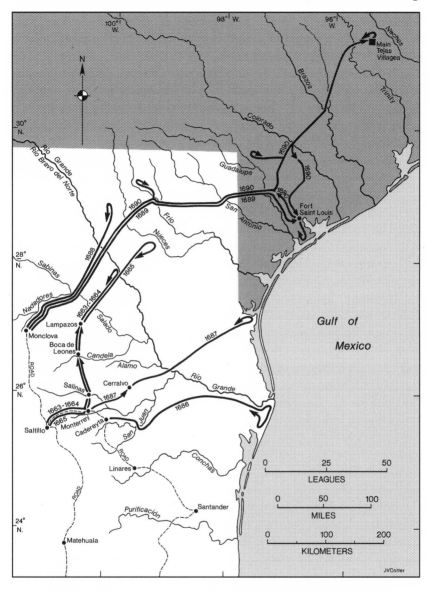

MAP 2. *Spanish expedition routes in Northeastern Mexico and Texas, 1663–1690. Light area is Nuevo León.*

Sánchez de Zamora. Excluded from García's *Historia de Nuevo León* was the revised copy of Governor Alonso de León's 1690 expedition diary, which was a part of García's larger collection.

The history of Chapa's manuscript is very sketchy. Genaro García tells us only that José Mariano Beristáin de Sousa referenced a manuscript history of Nuevo León written by Captain Alonso de León that Beristáin had found in the library of the Royal University of Mexico.[2] García obtained the manuscript from Canon D. Vicente de P. Andrade's private library.

Carl L. Duaine, a South Texas historian and descendant of Juan Bautista Chapa, prepared the only known English translation of Chapa's *Historia*.[3] Duaine added his own historical essays and material relating to his family to the translated but unannotated text of De León's *Discourses* and Chapa's history. The work was privately printed in 1971. Duaine apparently had a copy of the manuscript used by Genaro García, which is presently held in the Beinecke Library at Yale University. While Duaine's translation gives most of the history with general accuracy, it is inexact in many details.

Herbert E. Bolton reviewed García's edition of the *Historia de Nuevo León* for the *American Historical Review* (vol. 15:640–642) in 1912, three years after the initial publication of the work. In his complimentary assessment, Bolton emphasizes that the chapters written by the "anonymous author" contain significant material relating to the history of Texas, including the only published report of Spanish raids conducted in the 1660s against the highly mobile Cacaxtle Indians, who lived along the lower Rio Grande and in South Texas. In commenting on Chapa's history in his 1916 *Spanish Exploration in the Southwest, 1542–1706*, Bolton adds, "It is of highest importance, for, besides throwing additional light on De León's early career, it contains a diary of the expedition of 1686, and accounts of the four remaining journeys of De León into Texas in 1687, 1688, 1689, and 1690."[4]

In *Spanish Exploration in the Southwest*, Bolton includes an annotated English translation of Governor Alonso de León's first edition of his 1690 diary, which he concluded before the expedition was completed.[5] However, in his annotations, Bolton relies heavily on De León's revised version for footnote material to correct and complete the barren parts of the translated version. The professor added that the complete García collection, including the unpublished 1690 revised De León diary, had been purchased by Yale University, which recently made a microfilm copy of the manuscript available for this study.

Texas and Mexican authorities on Spanish Texas and the history of northeastern Mexico have frequently cited Captain De León's *Discourses* and Chapa's *Historia*. As mentioned, Bolton gives the chronicles high praise in both his review in 1912 and in his introduction to Governor De León's 1690 diary translation in *Spanish Exploration in the Southwest*. William E. Dunn cites García's edition of the *Historia* extensively in his 1917 study, *Spanish and French Rivalry in the Gulf Region of the United States, 1678–1702*. Carlos E. Castañeda refers to the *Historia* repeatedly in annotations to his English translation of Fray Juan Agustín de Morfi's *History of Texas 1673–1779*, and Vito Alessio Robles and Eugenio del Hoyo rely on Chapa's accounts in their histories of seventeenth-century Nuevo León and Texas.[6] More recently, Thomas N. Campbell and Robert S. Weddle have used García's version of the *Historia* (or a translation of parts of it) in their studies of the native population of northeastern Mexico and South Texas and of Spanish expeditions from northeastern Mexico to Texas during the 1665–1690 period.[7] Finally, the significance of Chapa's history is summarized in Peter Gerhard's conclusion that the *Historia de Nuevo León* is "the key contemporary document" to any historical study of the region.[8]

In 1961 the second edition of the *Historia de Nuevo León* was published with a comprehensive introduction by highly regarded Mexican historian Israel Cavazos Garza. Cavazos identifies several manuscript copies of the *Historia de Nuevo León* but follows the 1909 García imprint in his second edition. In the introduction, Cavazos adds a biographical study of the authors of the three chronicles included in the volume: the *Discourses* of Captain Alonso de León, covering the period before 1648; the *Historia* by the anonymous author (identified for the first time as Juan Bautista Chapa), covering the period 1630 to 1690; and the relatively brief "Discovery of the Río Blanco" by General Fernando Sánchez de Zamora.

Cavazos declares that he assumed the responsibility of determining the identity of the anonymous author and after careful analysis of Chapa's history and numerous documents available to Cavazos in the Monterrey archives, he concludes that the *autor anónimo* is indeed Juan Bautista Chapa. Since 1961, other scholars, including Lino Gómez Canedo, in the bibliography of *Primeras exploraciones y poblamiento de Texas (1686–1694)*, have given Cavazos credit for first identifying the *autor anónimo*. The 1961 edition of the *Historia* was followed quickly by a third edition in 1975, a fourth in 1980, and a fifth in 1985.

In 1990 Cavazos prepared an even more exhaustive study of the *autor anónimo* and a history of Chapa's life for the tricentennial commemorative edition of Chapa's *Historia del Nuevo Reino de León*.[9] Cavazos invited Alejandro H. Chapa, a descendant of Juan Bautista Chapa and a resident of Monterrey, to write the preface. In his introduction Cavazos stresses the historical value of Chapa's work, which registers chronologically and systematically the outstanding events that occurred in the Kingdom of Nuevo León (which then included all or part of about forty Texas counties south and west of Austin)[10] during the sixty-year period between 1630 and 1690. Cavazos's 1990 study is rich in detail concerning the information available and the analysis that led him (and others) to the conclusion that the *autor anónimo* was Juan Bautista Chapa.

Chapa, the son of Bartolomé Chapapría and Batestina Badi, was baptized in Albisola, near Genoa, on November 16, 1627. He arrived in New Spain in 1647 and perhaps studied in Mexico City before arriving in Nuevo León around 1650. By 1652 Chapa was secretary to the village of Cadereyta, where Alonso de León (the elder) served as the local militia captain. In 1653 the chronicler married Beatriz de Treviño, the daughter of a wealthy early settler whose residence in Nuevo León predated Governor Martín de Zavala's arrival in 1626. By 1662 Chapa had become secretary to Governor Zavala and had initiated in the municipal archives of Monterrey over three hundred files comprising court cases, reports, wills, land grants, inventories, and other handwritten documents. As his appointment as *secretario perpetuo* survived the death of Governor Zavala, Chapa subsequently served as secretary to Governor León de Alza, Zavala's successor, and later to Governor Azcárraga.

The fact that Chapa served these governors, according to statements made in his will and other documents, supports the conclusion that he was the anonymous author, and Governor De León's apparent reference to Chapa as "el autor" in his 1689 expedition diary adds additional weight.[11] At age sixty-three, one year after returning from his last expedition, Chapa completed his *Historia*; he was by then a widower, in poor health, and living alone near his five children, who resided in Cerralvo and Monterrey. He prepared a will in January 1694, and died in Monterrey on April 20 of the following year.

The 1990 commemorative edition of Chapa's *Historia* was published as a separate work rather than as part of a larger volume, as initially published in

1909. Although Chapa's work stands alone as a comprehensive and systematic historical account, the importance of his chronicle can best be appreciated after reviewing some of the significant observations made by Captain Alonso de León in *Discourses on Nuevo León* before 1650. De León's detailed observations on the geography, climate, fauna, flora, and native population of Nuevo León provide the background for Chapa's account, which begins with events that occurred in the early 1650s but includes reports from the 1630s.

DE LEÓN'S *DISCOURSES*

Captain Alonso de León divided his account into three parts, called *Discourses*. Unlike Chapa, who constructed his *Historia* chronologically, De León presents his comments topically, in chapters with general subject headings. This review of the *Discourses* will follow De León's topical approach.

In one discourse De León identifies the pre-1650 geographic area of Nuevo León and notes that the realm extended from Monterrey south to the Province of Huasteca (south of the Río Blanco), west to Nueva Vizcaya, east to the Gulf coast, and north into present-day Texas to a point 200 leagues north of Pánuco, or the bay and modern port of Tampico. This distance north is the same as that identified in 1579 as Luis de Carvajal y de la Cueva's jurisdiction in northeastern Mexico and present-day Texas. As seen on Map 2, Nuevo León included a major part of the lower Texas Gulf Coast, Central Texas, and West Texas. The eastern boundary line extended generally along the coast north from Tampico at approximately 97°48′ west longitude (the approximate longitude at Tampico Bay) to intersect with a northern boundary at approximately 29°45′ north latitude (approximately 200 leagues, or 520 miles, north of Tampico Bay). This northern boundary line extended from a point about 30 miles southwest of Austin west across Texas toward modern-day Chihuahua.[12]

De León describes the climate in Nuevo León in the 1640s as being extremely hot in the summer and harshly cold in the winter. The temperature dropped below freezing in November, the streams froze hard in February and March, and it snowed regularly from December through January. In the countryside the trees were covered with snow for a day or more, and in the mountains the snow remained for more than two months. De León's report on weather conditions in Nuevo León is also consistent with the climate described in the region by Padre Isidro Félix de Espinosa in the early 1700s,[13] but is inconsistent with the warmer and drier weather recorded in the area during the past one hundred years.

León's description of Nuevo León was given in the middle of the Little Ice Age, a period that occurred in Europe and North America generally between 1550 and 1850. As Jean M. Grove explains, the climate in Europe and North America from the eighth century to the twelfth century was much warmer and drier than today (it permitted grain to be grown in Greenland), but by the thirteenth century, the climate had changed sharply, culminating in the Little Ice Age.[14] During this period, Texas and northeastern Mexico experienced a cooler and wetter climate, which helps explain Chapa's reports of large bison herds on grassland prairies south of the Rio Grande near Eagle Pass, where today the brush would not support such herds.

De León carefully records not only the native trees, bushes, and cacti in Nuevo León, but also the domesticated fruit trees and vines planted in the province by the Spaniards. His list of native trees includes the familiar cottonwood, willow, cypress, mulberry, mesquite, and live oak. He also identifies several less familiar ones: the ebony (*ébano*), a thorny short evergreen with heavy crescent-shaped bean pods; the brazil (*brasil*), a small colorful shrub with black berries in the fall; and the laurel (*laureles*), which is today called a Texas laurel (*Sophora secundiflora*), with small pods that hold rock-hard red beans used by Indians to prepare intoxicating drinks.[15] He mentions the familiar cacti *cocolmecate* and prickly pear and also includes unspecified wild fruit trees and berry bushes (dewberry or blackberry) as well as medicinal plants and herbs.

The Spaniards, De León says, had introduced their own domesticated fruit trees, fig trees, grapevines, and melons. Although he describes the natives in Nuevo León as nonagricultural, neighboring tribes to the south in Huaxteca and to the west along the Conchos River in Nueva Vizcaya had cultivated maize, beans, melons, and cotton for years, perhaps centuries, before the Spaniards introduced their domesticated plants.

De León also gives one of the earliest lists of the wild animals found in northeastern Mexico and Texas—deer, antelope, jackrabbits, coyotes, cottontails, prairie chickens, javelina, armadillos, raccoons, "spotted cats without tails," and wild or feral cattle and hogs. He further describes the bobtail spotted cat as a large animal capable of downing a three-year-old horse, which suggests that the cat was perhaps a lynx rather than the smaller bobcat. It is significant that he does not mention bison in Nuevo León; De León reports only that Gaspar Castaño de Sosa saw bison in West Texas on his 1590–1591 journey from modern-day Coahuila to New Mexico. Although De León does not mention bison, Chapa and other Spanish diarists repeatedly report seeing and hunting bison south of the Rio Grande in the more open prairies of northern Coahuila.

De León also identifies the fish found in the streams (which concur with the fish named by later historians and diarists): the *robalo* (bass), *bagre* (catfish), *mojarra*, *trucha* (trout), and *besugo* (bream).

The author continues his *Second Discourse* with the early political history and initial settlement of the province. He commences with the entry of Captain Luis de Carvajal y de la Cueva in 1576.[16] De León writes about Governor Carvajal's royal grant establishing the province or kingdom of Nuevo León in 1579, his mining and slaving operations at León (or present-day Cerralvo), about forty miles south of the Rio Grande, and finally Carvajal's imprisonment by the Inquisition and the death of this early Jewish Portuguese colonizer. As mentioned, Carvajal's realm extended northward into South-Central Texas, and thus, the exploration and colonization of northeastern Mexico and parts of South Texas were under way decades before the Puritans reached the shores of New England.

De León also notes the story of Carvajal's lieutenant, Gaspar Castaño de Sosa, including his early settlement of the modern city of Monclova (then called Almadén) and his daring (but perhaps unauthorized) trek by cart with 160 settlers and soldiers across the Texas Pecos region to resettle along the upper Rio Grande in modern New Mexico.[17] Castaño's 1590 expedition occurred after the earlier explorations of New Mexico by the relatively small Chamuscado-Rodríguez expedition (commenced in 1581) and the similarly sized Antonio de Espejo expedition (1582).[18]

Carvajal's initial trek into the area later known as Nuevo León began in the 1570s as an effort to find an overland route to the Gulf Coast from the newly developed silver mining area of Mazapil (located approximately twenty leagues, or about fifty-two miles, south-southwest of modern-day Saltillo). The mines around Mazapil were opened in 1569, and Carvajal received a grant to settle Nuevo León ten years later. It would be another nineteen years (1598) before Juan de Oñate would set out in the west from Santa Bárbara, Nueva Vizcaya, with 129 men and their families to settle New Mexico.[19]

After recounting Carvajal's activities in northeastern New Spain in the 1580s, Captain De León writes that this was the area that Cabeza de Vaca crossed in 1536; he states that Cabeza de Vaca crossed the Rio Grande and entered Nuevo León near, possibly a few leagues north of, Cerralvo. De León's early account of Cabeza de Vaca's route into present-day Mexico from Texas is consistent with that projected in recent scholarly works that demonstrate to my satisfaction that Cabeza de Vaca's Rio Grande crossing in fact did occur in the vicinity of Falcon Lake, Zapata County,[20] about forty miles north of present-day Cerralvo, as De León reported.

De León's comment on Cabeza de Vaca's route is also consistent with the number of leagues recorded in Oviedo's *Joint Report* detailing the Spaniards' escape route from the Mariame Indians in South Texas into northern Mexico.[21] Accounting for each day, the *Joint Report* records that Cabeza de Vaca's party departed their Indian hosts, probably from a village in the vicinity of Jim Wells County, headed for Pánuco on the Gulf Coast on or about August 1, 1536, and crossed the chest-deep river, "as wide as the one in Seville," on or about September 30. Recent studies have demonstrated that seventeenth- and eighteenth-century Spanish travel accounts with a continuous itinerary that provides information on the direction taken and the number of leagues traveled daily are reliable sources for accurately projecting expedition routes.[22] During this thirty-day period, Cabeza de Vaca's party traveled seven days (stopping and resting twenty-three days), for a total distance of approximately thirty-nine leagues,[23] or about ninety-eight miles. According to the U.S. Geological Survey maps *Laredo*, NG14-2 and *McAllen*, NG14-5, a movement southwestward of approximately ninety-eight miles from central Jim Wells County (a location about forty miles west of Corpus Christi) would cross the Rio Grande near Falcon Lake. A. D. Kreiger, Thomas N. Campbell, Donald E. Chipman, and other scholars have suggested that this projected description of the route is accurate.[24]

By the 1580s the Spaniards were engaged in silver mining and slaving operations near modern-day Cerralvo, in the area that Cabeza de Vaca apparently crossed about fifty years earlier. Cabeza de Vaca's account of meeting Indians with bags of silver two days after crossing the large river was first published in his 1542 edition of *La Relación*. His report might have sparked the early (1580s) search for and discovery of silver near Cerralvo, although Oviedo attempted to dampen such mercenary interest.[25]

Captain De León describes the bustling little community of León, or Cerralvo, where slaving ventures rounded up local Indians and marched some of the captives, often chained, south to work in the mines of Zacatecas. The demise of the community of León in the 1590s, he writes, resulted in part from the king's order halting the forced enslavement of natives. During this period of exploration and development along the lower Rio Grande (in the 1580s), the Spaniards likely established slaving and mining outposts and camps at other locations in the area. It was perhaps the remnants of one of these outlying posts that René-Robert Cavelier, Sieur de La Salle, visited with his brother, the Abbé Jean Cavelier, and a small French exploration party from Matagorda Bay in the summer of 1685.[26]

Captain De León's *Third Discourse* begins with a review of the administration of Don Martín de Zavala, which began in 1626.[27] The captain details several significant trade expeditions conducted from Monterrey southeastward to points along the Gulf Coast and enumerates several catastrophic events that occurred in the province during the period, including floods and a very severe smallpox epidemic that killed over five hundred Indians and Spaniards in the Monterrey area in 1647. Finally, De León covers the founding of the city of Cadereyta, where he, his son Alonso, and their companion Chapa lived and served.

The captain does not offer any general comments on the African American presence in Nuevo León during the early seventeenth century, but the *Discourses* are filled with numerous accounts in which *negros* or mulattoes are mentioned. A mulatto named Francisco de Sosa, who had arrived in Nuevo León with Carvajal and Gaspar Castaño de Sosa in the 1580s, was the head of the last family to leave Cerralvo when it was abandoned in 1612. Juan, a *negro*, was among the residents killed in 1626 by an Indian attack reported along the road between Monterrey and Boca de Leones. In 1632 an unnamed mulatto was part of a squad of seven soldiers from Cerralvo who rescued several comrades after the Tepehuan Indians attacked them. In 1637 the Alasapa Indians killed a number of shepherds, including a *negro*, near Monterrey. In the early 1640s a *negra* working in the kitchen of Governor Zavala warned him of the Indians' plan to strike Cerralvo.

References to African Americans in Nuevo León are also found in Chapa's account. According to Peter Gerhard, African slaves were brought into neighboring Mazapil in the 1580s to work the mines. The 1779 census of the mining district of Mazapil (which bordered Nuevo León) records that the number of *negros* and mulattoes slightly exceeded the combined population of Spaniards and Indians.[28]

One of the principal subjects covered in the *Discourses* is a description of the numerous Indian tribes and their uprisings in the province.[29] As early as 1624, Indians mounted on stolen Spanish horses raided Monterrey. In reprisal, Spanish troops captured and punished members of the Huachichil tribe. In 1632 and 1633 the Tepehuan revolted near Cerralvo and killed several Spaniards, mulattos, and friendly Cataara Indians. During the same year, the Aguata, Sucuyama, Icaura, and Iquaracata attacked a village and killed fifty-six Cataara Indians who were friendly and loyal to the Spaniards.

De León also describes encounters with the Camalucano, Carana, Amapuala, and Cataara tribes in 1638, when an expedition was sent from Cerralvo east to investigate an Indian report that red-headed Dutch soldiers had landed and occupied part of the nearby Gulf Coast.

De León did not always write about Indian misdeeds; on several occasions the captain was very critical of the Spaniards' excesses in enslaving the Indian population. In some instances he offered tolerant comments and demonstrated a distinct sympathy for the native population, many of whom were held by Spanish *encomenderos*.

Under the *encomienda* system,[30] a grant was made under contract with an *encomendero* (such as De León), who was given jurisdiction over the Indian population brought into his designated area of occupation and use. When his Indian population fled or died, the *encomendero* often was permitted to search out and round up other Indians in the general area as replacements, an activity that may have appeared to the Indian captives as an operation very similar to slaving.

The Indians were parceled out to the *encomenderos* to work and, in limited instances, to be educated in the ways of the church. In 1912 Bolton noted that one of De León's and Chapa's principal contributions was their description of how the *encomienda* system operated in northeastern New Spain in the seventeenth century.

Captain De León was well qualified to write in detail about the lifeways of the Indians in northern Nuevo León in the mid-1600s. He not only lived near the natives but also had daily dealings with them both in his capacity as *encomendero* and in his duty as a military officer, both of which positions dictated that he restrain and punish Indians when necessary. He observed first-hand how the Indians lived, how they hunted, fished, cooked, related to each other, and survived; he witnessed them resist Spanish occupation, succumb to European diseases, and bury their dead.

De León says that tribes living only a few leagues apart spoke different languages and often could not understand one another; consequently, he devotes a chapter to the diverse Indian languages spoken in Nuevo León. Some authorities have noted that during the period between Cabeza de Vaca's visit to Nuevo León (1535) and the time of De León's description (1640s), the local native population was decimated by Spanish occupation and disease and was probably replaced in part by natives from outside the immediate region.[31] This may partially explain the profusion of native languages.

The tribes (called nations by the Spaniards and French) were so numerous that they could not be counted. The native Indians of Nuevo León, De León says, lived without any god or system of government. He says, after Aristotle, that there are basically three recognized forms of government: "monarchy, aristocracy, and democracy. In a monarchy, one rules, like the king. In an aristocracy, a few rule, like a senate. In a democracy, all the people are in common. Of these three, the best one has the fewest heads, the monarchy." He then assesses the native population and concludes that "none of the three types of government is found in this realm. From our experience we know the natives live in a bestial state, without political organization, assuming a fourth type of government . . . namely, anarchy."[32]

De León writes that the Indians moved about and lived in small communities (called *rancherías* by the Spaniards). They were housed in fifteen or more bell-shaped grass or reed huts, which were arranged in a semicircle with guardhouses located on each end of the crescent. The huts were sufficiently large to permit a fire to be maintained in the middle. The Indians slept on the ground and used grass or a deer hide as a pillow, and the residential area was usually filthy, as were the Indians themselves; they bathed only to cool off.

The men were usually naked (but occasionally wore buckskin sandals) and wore their hair long, down to their buttocks and sometimes tied in the back; some men, however, were bald, having deliberately pulled out their hair. Members of each tribe painted their faces and bodies differently. The women were more fully dressed, sometimes wearing a deerskin, or a spun or twisted grass material like flax as an apron that hung from their waist in back and front. To this garment they attached beads, shells, or animal teeth. De León adds that the women enjoyed hearing themselves stroll about. Some men and women pierced their ears and nostrils and hung feathers or bones from them. Occasionally the women wore capes made by weaving together rabbit fur yarn and yarn made from other pelts.

In both hunting and warfare, the Indians used the bow and arrow as their principal weapon. The author describes in more than customary detail how bows and arrows were constructed in Nuevo León. Its intended use determined the size of the bow, but most arrows were half a man's full reach, "thumb to thumb." They used different woods, but mesquite roots made the best and strongest bows. The bowstring was made of lechuguilla fibers twisted together "to a thickness of six harp strings." The arrow shafts were made of slender, fire-dried cane: one end of the cane shaft was notched and two or three feathers, some about four fingers wide across the shaft, were tied to the end with deer sinew. At the other end of the cane, a fire-dried hard stick was placed up the hollow cane about four inches, until it hit a joint, and then was tightly tied, also with deer sinew, to the arrow shaft. A flint arrowhead was then secured with sinew from the two barbs at its base to the tip of the shaft and was fashioned with harpoons on the side to ensure that the arrow would securely lodge in a target.[33] When the Indians used bow and arrow, they tied a piece of coyote hide to the left forearm to protect it from the whip of the bowstring.

The men were accomplished hunters, and deer were their preferred game. (As mentioned, De León makes no reference to bison in the area.) The successful hunter customarily kept the deer hide and shared the meat. Snakes and rats were also acceptable food, but toads and lizards were not.

Both the men and the women fished, utilizing various techniques, including using a spear with an arrow point and employing torches to frighten fish into nets at night. They prepared their food with salt or sometimes used an herb similar to rosemary. To carry drinking water on long trips, the women used hollowed-out prickly pears that were placed in nets (called *cacaxtles*) and fitted on two small bows that they placed over their shoulders.

De León also describes the Indians' custom of eating human flesh, but he offers a tolerant comment that cannibalism was an ancient practice reported in the Bible and followed by the "Tartars" (a probable reference to people of Mongolian origin). In Nuevo León, he says, the natives ate parts of their deceased friends as well as captured enemies. Dead friends or relatives were eaten after the flesh was cooked on an open fire; their bones were ground into a powder and ingested in a drink at feasts and dances. The Indians cremated or buried the relatives who were not eaten, and the graves were protected from wild animals by planting a thick hedge of cacti around the burial site. Enemies were eaten as an act of vengeance, and the top of their skulls was used as a cup or bowl.

De León describes the natives as having good stature, attractive features, general good health, and the ability to run like a horse. The local natives did not, however, apply their energy to cultivating the land or to planting, although tribes living near the coast, fewer than one hundred leagues to the south, were agricultural at the time. In the winter, they ate the heart and fleshy leaves of the lechuguilla and the roots of other unidentified plants. In the spring they ate wild fruit and cooked the green tunas of the prickly pear, which they also dried for future use.

The natives made a fire very quickly, reports De León, by rubbing two sticks together (as did the East Texas Caddoan tribes and other Indians), but De León does not describe in detail the selection of wood for the fire sticks or their use. Ethnologist John R. Swanton, however, cites reports that Caddoan tribes and other Indians rubbed together a cedar stick and a hard mulberry to start a fire that arose from the cedar to ignite some dry moss into a quick, continuous flame.[34]

According to the captain, the mesquite bean ripened soon after the tunas dropped (a sequence that continues during the autumn). Mesquite beans were a part of the diet from the time the beans started to ripen until they dried, at which time they were ground with wooden mortars into a coarse meal or a finely ground flour and stored in reed bags.

The Indians are described as a dancing and festive people who used peyote as a stimulant. De León renders the word *peyote* as an Indian word and says that the Indians would trade goods such as skins or arrows for peyote if it was not locally available. The Indians ground up the peyote and mixed it with water to create a potent drink.[35]

Music was provided for tribal occasions by shaking gourds containing small rocks (like the *maraca*) and rhythmically rubbing a grooved ebony stick with a rounded one. De León does not mention flutes (which Chapa later describes). The males and females, feet close together, elbows out, shoulders lowered, danced together in circles around the bonfire. The dancers hopped forward, almost dragging their feet, and stayed close together so they were almost touching and kept their stomach close to the next person's buttocks. The dance continued for four to six hours. In the dance ring of one hundred or more Indians, the participants sang as a chorus, using meaningless sounds, but maintaining a uniform harmony as in one voice.

De León claims that with such unbridled liberty, no young girl remained a virgin after ten years of age. One bitter result of their openly sexual behavior is described vividly in the deadly effects of venereal disease.

With respect to the Indians' reaction to violent natural phenomena, the historian records that they were not afraid of lightning or thunderstorms. The men chased away the thunder by running toward the cloud, yelling, making faces, and angrily throwing rocks and sticks at the menacing cloud until it drifted away. The men then proudly returned home to a joyful reception.

The men and women married, but the relationship lasted only as long as the two remained interested in each other. This informal marriage relationship differs from that found among the Caoque (Coaque, Capoque), the Indian tribe with whom Cabeza de Vaca lived when he first arrived on the central coast of Texas. Cabeza de Vaca wrote that the Caoque (identified by Thomas N. Campbell as probably associated with the Akokisa Indians)[36] had comparatively strict rules allowing most tribesmen (except for shamans) to have only one wife and even specifying the formal relationship between the husband and the wife's parents. In contrast, in a village in Nuevo León, a woman might have five or six children, each with a different father, and no jealousy existed among the women. The captain also noted an Indian custom that he thought curious (but that would not appear strange today): Indian parents carried their children on the back of their necks or shoulders and the child's feet dangled on the parent's chest.

Although he describes clearly the incestuous life of the local Indians, De León does not know the origin of the native custom of having intimate relationships with family members. Surprisingly, he suggests that the practice of incest perhaps came from Asia, "where the Indians originated." The captain does not give the reason for his opinion that Native Americans were descendants of Asian people. The undisclosed source of his statement is probably Joseph de Acosta, a Jesuit priest who in 1590 wrote *The Natural and Moral History of the Indies*, in which this human migration by land from Asia to the Americas was postulated. A learned man like De León would have known of Acosta's works, and Chapa refers to Father Acosta's writings in his *Historia*. The theory, accepted by De León in 1648, that North America was populated first by the overland migration from Asia is today the dominant scientific explanation of the origin of Native Americans. Although a major area of uncertainty is when that migration occurred into Texas and northeastern Mexico, recent studies conducted under the direction of Thomas R. Hester, Thomas N. Campbell, and Dee Ann Story confirm human occupation in the area about 10,000 B.C. and note one site near Matehuala (located about four leagues west of Nuevo León, in San Luis Potosí) where a scraper and fire hearth were excavated and radiocarbon dated between 32,000 and 33,000 years ago.[37]

De León writes that it was common to find Indian men who served and dressed as women and did the work of women. However, he dismisses the

matter as not being particularly significant because the same relationship between men is reported in the Bible. He adds that in Spain young boys who
were sent to elite schools to learn to read and write often learned the same
behavior. The presence of homosexuals (also called *berdaches*) in American
Indian tribes has been widely reported,[38] and Cabeza de Vaca's account of
Texas coastal Indians records seeing men serving as women.[39]

There are further similarities between the customs of the Nuevo León
Indians in the 1640s, as described by De León, and the customs of the
Caoque Indians with whom Cabeza de Vaca lived for about a year after he
and his companions landed near Galveston Island in 1528. Both tribes used
the bow and arrow as the principal weapon in hunting and war, had domesticated dogs, and believed in healers, or shamans. Both loved dances and
parties, used strong hallucinogens, and neither tribe cultivated crops. Finally,
Indians from both areas, as a ritual, drank a mixture that included the ground
bones of deceased relatives.

The tribes of these two areas also differed in many respects. The Nuevo
León tribes or bands as described by De León were small (although there
were numerous bands), each having about one hundred members. The
Caoque may have had a population of up to one thousand, as suggested by
the report that two hundred bowmen from the tribe arrived to confront the
small Spanish party when Cabeza de Vaca first landed. It should be noted
again that the tribes in Nuevo León in the 1650s may have been more
intensely subjected to the highly contagious and deadly European diseases
than had the natives along the Central Texas coast in the 1530s. Cabeza de
Vaca reports that the Caoque communicated immediately with the Spaniards
with signs and that members of his party continued to use signs to communicate with the tribes in northern New Spain. He observed earthen pots during his first visit to a native residence on the Central Texas coast, but De
León does not mention the use of earthenware by the local Indians in Nuevo
León.[40] Cabeza de Vaca's party shocked some of the Central Texas coastal
Indians by eating their deceased Spanish companions, while De León
speaks at length about cannibalism among the Indians of Nuevo León, who
ate both deceased relatives and the enemy. For stimulants, the Caoque drank
a tea apparently prepared with yaupon berries and leaves; the natives below
the Rio Grande drank pulverized peyote tea.

The relationships between husband and wife and between parents and
children differed widely in the two native groups. In Nuevo León a father
would sell or trade his daughter for a deer hide, newlyweds would remain

together as long as the interest lasted, men had several wives, and fathers engaged in open incest. Among the Caoque, marriage was a more lasting arrangement: each man had only one wife (except for the shaman, who could have up to three), and children were protected and loved by their parents. The Indians in Nuevo León seldom helped each other and ignored the needs of family members, the ill, and the aged; in contrast, the Caoque were very cooperative and helpful and provided gifts of food for months to bereaved neighbors.

In closing his account on the Indians of Nuevo León, De León observes that, despite the church's efforts to save the natives, no Indian had ever been truly converted to the Catholic faith, and that the wrath of God and the Spanish military ensured the eradication of the Indian population. In his *Historia*, Juan Bautista Chapa reiterates the view that the natives in all of New Spain would soon be exterminated. The history of Nuevo León and Texas from 1630 to 1690 can be understood (I believe) only with a full awareness that the Indians were suffering a disastrous depopulation. Peter Gerhard projects that the native population in Nuevo León decreased from over 100,000 to approximately 1,000 during the two hundred–year period 1540 to 1740.[41]

CHAPA'S *HISTORIA*

Chapa's *Historia* picks up where Captain De León's *Third Discourse* ends and reviews events that occurred in the early 1650s. Chapa continues to detail the serious local Indian uprisings, but he concentrates on a new threat— invasions by Texas tribes from north of the Rio Grande, the "Indians of the North." These Indians from present-day Texas raided the region around Cerralvo and as far south as Monterrey in search of goods and animals, particularly horses. Chapa's accounts of Indian theft of Spanish horse herds in the 1650s and 1660s suggest that at least some tribes who lived or ranged in South Texas during that period were mounted and had horses to trade, just like the Jumano and associated tribes who lived near Spanish settlements in modern Chihuahua and New Mexico. In his discourses, De León tells of Indians capturing horse herds and of mounted Indian captains leading attacks on Spanish communities. For example, as early as 1624, mounted Indian leaders and their followers attacked Monterrey, and in 1648 and 1649, hostile Indians, some on horseback, appeared on the Pesquería River and valley. As

Thomas N. Campbell suggests, more study is needed of Indian acquisition and use of horses along the lower Rio Grande and in South Texas in the seventeenth century.[42]

It is nevertheless clear that by the middle of the seventeenth century, the wealth of the province below the lower Rio Grande was attracting Texas Indians, particularly the Cacaxtles, who lived or roamed north of the big river. Chapa's is the only known account of two large Spanish military expeditions from Monterrey in the 1660s that were directed against the Cacaxtle Indians in the north. The first was a sizable and extended operation in which 125 Cacaxtle men, women, and children, were captured; this exercise required the troops to remain in the field from October 1663 to March 1664. The second raid involved perhaps the first military expedition into South Texas from northern Mexico; it culminated in a battle fought by a combined force of approximately 400 Spanish soldiers and friendly Indians against the Cacaxtles south of the Nueces River, probably in the Webb-Duval County area.

The two battles against the Cacaxtles demonstrate the ability of the Spanish local militia, supported by volunteer settlers and friendly Boboles, to organize and execute relatively sizable and sustained military operations during this period. The size of the combined force of Spanish troops and friendly Indians employed in the 1665 expedition into South Texas exceeded the number of troops sent to rout the French at Matagorda Bay in 1689, and the 1663 expedition remained in the field longer than De León's 1690 expedition, which established the first Spanish presence in East Texas. Readers will enjoy Chapa's narrative of the second engagement; he adds to the historical account by including the personal story of an elderly female Cacaxtle captive stubbornly playing her flute in the middle of the battle in order to encourage and sustain her tribe in their nearby encircled barricade. In retaliation, the Boboles that night ate a young relative of the defiant flutist.

Chapa develops, through the presentation of correspondence and legal documents, the Spaniards' theological and political justification for crushing the Indians. He cites an extensive record compiled in the 1630s that detailed numerous Indian raids and other justifications for Governor Zavala's actions to punish the rebellious native population. The record recites instances in the early 1600s in which Indian raiding parties desecrated church property, including the cross, and humiliated the clergy by forcing captured priests to bow their heads and kiss the cross before being executed. In retribution, the Spanish military was authorized to hang Indian raiders who were captured, although other offenders were often given a trial.[43] Chapa vividly describes the bitterness and suffering of both sides.

Drawing from his many years of senior government service, Chapa assesses the administrations of Governor Martín de Zavala (whom he first served), Domingo de Pruneda, Domingo de Vidagaray, Juan de Echeverría, Alonso de León (the younger), and the first Marqués de San Miguel de Aguayo. He does not hesitate to write of his admiration and respect for each of these officials. In reviewing developments in Nuevo León, Chapa occasionally comments on events that occurred in present-day Coahuila, but he does not mention the missionary activities of the priests and other Spanish explorers in Coahuila, such as Fernando del Bosque in the 1670s.[44]

One of Chapa's contributions to the understanding of the native population of northeastern Mexico and the lower Rio Grande is his lists of the names and principal areas of residence of over 250 Indian tribes. These tribal names were probably available to Chapa in the provincial records that identified by name the Indian groups formally assigned to *encomenderos*. As previously mentioned, his comments about the depopulation of the Indians are consistent with De León's earlier observation; both men recognized that the Indians in northeastern New Spain were then being exterminated by war and disease in the same manner as the Indians had earlier been depopulated on the island of Hispaniola (modern Haiti and Dominican Republic).

Appendix B includes an alphabetical list of 86 Indian tribes that are referenced in Captain De León's *Discourses*, Chapa's *Historia*, and Governor De León's revised 1690 expedition diary (this Appendix does not include the 250 tribes listed by name in Chapters 27 and 28 of the *Historia*). The listing indicates that many tribes encountered in Nuevo León were originally from areas outside the region—from modern Texas, Durango, Chihuahua, and the New Mexico area.

Chapa's *Historia* includes the only known copy of Governor De León's 1686 expedition diary and his own informative accounts of the 1687, 1688, 1689, and 1690 military expeditions into Texas in search of La Salle and his party, who had landed on the Central Texas coast in early 1685. The first account, written in 1686, covers the expedition of Governor De León, Chapa, and troops from Monterrey and Cadereyta to the mouth of the Rio Grande searching for La Salle's settlement. Because Governor De León's diary includes accurate information on the distance and direction traveled and the terrain, the expedition route can be projected with a high degree of confidence. The route projections for this expedition and those that accompany this study have been prepared by plotting route information on large-scale topographic maps of Texas and northeastern Mexico.[45] To identify as precisely as possible the line of march, I employed the methodology used in projecting the detailed expedition routes in *Spanish Expeditions into Texas*.

The 1686 expedition party left Cadereyta with Indian guides on June 27 and traveled along the left bank of the San Juan River. They continued moving eastward for three days (about fourteen leagues) to the ford where, as Governor De León accurately notes, the river turns northward. On June 30 the troops marched to the northeast and continued in that general direction for three days (about nineteen leagues), to camp a few leagues south of the Rio Grande, between the present-day Mexican cities of Camargo and Reynosa. During the next ten days (July 3–13) De León slowly moved about thirty-five leagues through heavy brush and swampy floodplains downstream to the Gulf. After investigating the area on the south side of the mouth of the Rio Grande, he led a detachment of troops south eight leagues to reconnoiter the coastline. Although he initially sought a shortcut to rejoin his main camp, De León had to retrace his route up the coast and along the river route because of the difficult inland coastal terrain.

The second trip is covered in Chapa's short account of Governor De León's early 1687 expedition from Monterrey into Texas, which apparently ended on the bank of a large salty river (perhaps Baffin Bay) without finding La Salle's settlement. No diary has been found of this journey—which apparently Chapa did not join—and only a brief reference to the trip is found in Fray Damián Massanet's accounts. By the time the 1687 expedition reached the Gulf coastal area below modern Corpus Christi on March 20, the man whom De León sought was dead. La Salle had been assassinated by his own men the day before (on March 19) near the Brazos River, as reported accurately by Pierre Meunier, who was at the assassins' camp, and as subsequently confirmed by Herbert E. Bolton.[46]

Chapa's narrative continues the following year (1688), when Governor De León again crossed the Rio Grande, this time marching from Monclova to an area east-northeast of present-day Eagle Pass to capture Jean Géry, a Frenchman living as a leader among several Indian tribes in South Texas. Chapa's description supplements De León's own diary account of the expedition.[47] De León's capture of Géry from the Indians' tightly guarded encampment required more than military skill; it needed a forceful diplomatic presence. Later the old Frenchman would befriend De León, helping guide him to the French settlement and surrounding bay area and serving as his interpreter with the Central Texas tribes, who held him in high respect.

Chapa concludes his narrative with detailed comments on Governor De León's last two expeditions into Texas—in 1689 and 1690. Chapa's narrative of the 1689 trip enlivens the rather staid military account in De León's diaries. For example, the narrator lists the names on the military roll call made on March 28 after the companies from Nuevo León joined forces on the Sabinas River. In addition to General De León, Chapa, and Géry, there were two priests, eighty-four soldiers, and twenty-five mule drivers and servants. Chapa's respect for detail is found in a note omitted by De León, that 490 Indians were counted near the Rio Grande (which did not include those on a bison hunt and some who had hidden nearby). Chapa also gives latitude readings, some of which duplicate those reported by De León, but others apparently correct De León's mistakes or are readings not reported by the governor. Chapa makes clear that, when any dispute arose, the expedition party always followed the Quem guide's direction. It is significant that Chapa's journal supports De León's diary, which clearly states that the Spanish leaders in 1689 were following Indian guides who knew the Indian trail out of Mexico and across southern Texas—a trail that was an ancient route, marked with Indian petroglyphs and cairns.

Chapa also adds two sketches made at Matagorda Bay during the 1689 trip. The first is a drawing of the carving found above the doorway of the fort. The second is particularly interesting because it helps identify the creek on which the settlement was located by indicating that the "arroio," or creek, flowed from the west-northwest into the bay. Had the stream been the Lavaca River, as some historians have argued, the sketch would have shown a much larger stream flowing from the north. (See Figure 5.)

Although Chapa did not participate in the 1690 expedition, his observations on the trip enhance Governor De León's diary account. De León and Chapa describe the same Colorado River (called the Maligne by the French) crossing area in modern-day Fayette County that La Salle used in 1686 and 1687 and the same Indian trade route that La Salle's party followed east to the junction of the Brazos and the Navasota, where La Salle was killed.

Chapa names the three priests who were left to work among the Tejas— Father Miguel de Fontcuberta, Father Antonio Bordey, and Father Francisco de Jesús María. He also mentions an Indian, Tomás, who said he had come from Parral to live with the Tejas two years earlier; as Tomás spoke both the native Mexican or Aztec language and Tejas, he functioned as an interpreter. Chapa's account regarding the Tejas Indians, although brief, strikingly illustrates the Tejas's far-flung trade and communication, including with Parral, a Spanish mining community located over seven hundred miles to the southwest in modern southern Chihuahua.

The author also tells a story of French intrigue that Governor De León omits. Chapa says that the Tejas governor told De León that Frenchmen had requested permission to settle among his people, but the Tejas governor had refused, saying that he was friendly with the Christian Spaniards and was awaiting them. This report is consistent with other accounts indicating that La Salle's associate Henri de Tonti had visited the Tejas, probably in search of La Salle's survivors.[48] It is clear from Henri Joutel's detailed journal account of La Salle's party that the Frenchmen in 1687 and De León in 1690 were following the same route from the Colorado crossing in modern-day Fayette County to the Tejas village concentration along San Pedro Creek in eastern Houston County.

Appendix A is an annotated translation of Governor De León's revised 1690 expedition diary, which has not been published previously in Spanish or English. The publication of this revision is significant because it cannot fairly be characterized as simply another rendition of the diary that De León forwarded to the viceroy from the Rio Grande on July 12, 1690. With very few exceptions, each daily entry made on the trip—from March 26 to July 15—differs from the corresponding entries in the first edition. De León rewrote whole segments of the diary, added entries about the closing days of the expedition, named the Spanish officials on the trip, described the movement of the supply party, fine-tuned distances and directions with minor (but occasionally significant) clarifications, and included the names of Indian tribes he encountered. It is believed that no other seventeenth-century diary of a Spanish expedition into Texas was subsequently revised and extended by the author in the manner and to the extent that De León altered his 1690 diary.

De León's 1690 expedition is significant for many reasons, but for us its significance may rest in part on the fact that it clearly confirms the location of the northern leg of the ancient trade route out of Mexico, across Texas to the Caddoan Indian villages on the Red River. The Tejas and other Indians along the way guided La Salle's men eastward to the Mississippi.[49] The identification of an ancient trade route from northern Mexico across Texas to the Mississippi is new to some scholars. Although numerous studies suggest that the development of the early (2000 B.C. to A.D. 1000) American civilization of mound builders along the Mississippi was heavily influenced by the importation of agricultural products and practices from Mexico, most experts, being unfamiliar with any more direct overland route across Texas, have assumed the trade route used to introduce the new products proceeded up the Rio Grande to New Mexico, across the Great Plains, and down the Mississippi.[50] Readers will find the annotated translation of this too-long-ignored manuscript an interesting and informative complement to Chapa's *Historia*.

Historia del Nuevo Reino de León
by Juan Bautista Chapa

Translated by Ned F. Brierley

To the Devout Reader

THIS history is written so that the important journeys made by Captain Alonso de León (may he rest in glory) will not remain buried in the tomb of oblivion. The captain was a settler who lived in the town of Cadereyta in Nuevo León. Because of his clear understanding of the period, he wanted to leave to posterity a record of his explorations; the reasons for the journeys; the customs, rites, and nature of the Indians; and the events that occurred from the time of his reconnaissances to the year 1649. His chronicle required an extensive effort to secure information from the older residents of the area and from old documents, which, as a careful person, he collected. Captain De León prepared a volume that included three discourses, each divided into chapters.

This very careful manuscript was dedicated to Dr. Don Juan de Mañosca, Mexico City's inquisitor, so that it might be printed. This did not take place, however. Although I do not know the reason the work was not published, I attribute it to the fact that soon after the manuscript was completed, the author left Mexico to visit Spain on business for Governor Don Martín de Zavala. That may have been why the publication of the work was frustrated. I have continued these discourses from the year 1650 to the present year of 1689 because of the deep affection I had for the deceased, who wrote, as he did, an account of the services, wars, and other things that have occurred in Nuevo León.

I well recognize how difficult and dangerous it is to write histories in these times, because of the disbelief of some and the censorship of others who boast of censuring others' vigilance. But even if those who read these poor scribblings, censure them, as other malicious critics do, they shall not be able to point a finger at me, because I am an anonymous author. Since they do not know who I am, they will not have a target at which to fire shots, as the fortunate Zoilus did when he criticized the writings of the Prince of Poets, Homer. I quote from Carlos Esteban's *Historical and Geographical Vocabulary*,[1] from which, omitting the superfluous, I record only these words: "quod Homerum poetarum omnium Principem libris ad versum cum scriptis ausus sed reprehendere." Here is where the custom originates of calling those who criticize others' works "*zoilos.*" Ovid confirms it in these words: "enxenio magni lucor detrectur Homeri quisquis es exsilo Zoile nomen habes."

I would like, then, to give thanks to him whom I owe so much (for death does not extinguish the obligation that was contracted in life). In the last analysis, payment is partly an acknowledgment of the debt, even when it is not possible to pay it.

Most of those who write histories first identify the subject with which they will deal, the drive that moves them to write about it, and the arguments they will use to prove what they are to conclude. The first two I have already advanced; the arguments I do not need to state further, because the title I give to the work (*Historia del Nuevo Reino de León*) is sufficient.

The style will not be lofty because of my personal inadequacy. Moreover, the concepts will be crude, because those who live in remote areas tend to forget the polite language of the court, even if they once learned it.

It will be necessary to give in this *History* an account of some subjects who have distinguished themselves in historical actions, but the account, although clothed in truth, will be stripped of adulation. The truth shines on all occasions and is pleasing to all, because *veritas est ad quatior ei ad intelectum.* I hope the reader will have the good grace to pardon all shortcomings.

Chapter 1 / The History of Nuevo León from 1650

THE history that Captain Alonso de León wrote of the Nuevo León's discovery is so full of erudition, ideas, and the other attributes that any history requires that I, in my inadequacy, recognize my presumption in pursuing them. I am completely lacking in the mastery of the basic skills necessary in matters of such importance. Nevertheless, I have taken courage with only the information available to me of the occurrences that have transpired since the end of 1650.

Although Captain De León lived until 1661, he did not continue his history beyond 1649—for reasons that must have been sufficient for him, or for those that I explained in the Introduction. I have very little or nothing to say about 1650 because I came to this province at the end of that year,[1] and nothing offered itself that was worthy of remembering. However, this was not the situation in 1651, when the Indians who lived in the Papagayos Mountains became restless and continued their customary thefts of horses. This action required Governor Don Martín de Zavala,[2] through a Tacuanama[3] Indian named Francisco, to determine where the Indians were camped and who was their leader in these offenses.

Francisco, because he was faithful and loyal, and because the enemy did not suspect him, went to the mountains and remained with the Indians for some time, applauding their plans. The Indians were to convene a large meeting and dance, according to their custom, where they would discuss their evil plans against the Spaniards. After learning of these, Francisco left to give the news to the governor. The governor maintained his office in Cerralvo, from which he dispatched an order to Captain Alonso de León (the chief justice and military captain of Cadereyta). The captain was directed to take soldiers to reconnoiter the meeting and put the Indians to flight; the governor dispatched the Indian, Francisco, as a guide.

The captain collected eighteen soldiers and some friendly Indians and set out about the middle of August. The party marched all night toward the Papagayos Mountains, which are seven leagues [toward the south] from Cadereyta. Because the party had mistaken the route, it was necessary to cross a heavily wooded area from which all the soldiers emerged with their clothing torn to pieces. I, who went along on this campaign, lost a very good bronze pistol (it fell from my belt without my noticing it). At dawn, we reached the foothills. Earlier in the evening, we had sent out the guide so that he could return to find us after he spied on the council. Then he was to take us where the council of Indians was meeting. However, he missed us.

At daylight, a small dog appeared and began to bark. As the dog retreated, we followed him down a little path that led to a group of huts where the Indian called Cabrito, the leader of the band, lived. Following the path, we spotted this village near a ravine at the foot of the mountains.

The Indians sensed our presence and abandoned the camp, escaping into the mountains. Although we besieged them, all the men escaped, and we captured only six Indian women who were trying to escape into the rocks. A soldier, Luis de Zúñiga, saw another Indian woman trying to hide at the foot of a small boulder. As she was within harquebus range, he fired at her, but the bullet struck the boulder with so much force that it ricocheted to where I was, a short distance away, and almost hit me in the forehead. The Indians, who apparently numbered no more than seven or eight, by that time had climbed halfway up the mountain, where our bullets could not reach them. From there they called down a thousand insults upon us.

With the Indian women gathered, we used one of the captain's tricks. The huts were separated from where the [male] Indians were, and we wanted to capture some of them when they came down after we had gone. The plan was to put four armed men inside four of the huts. We then had four friendly Indians from among those who had come along ride off on the armed men's horses, since leading them by the halter might mean that the enemy Indians would notice the friendly ones. Thus the company left, and the ambush was set.

As the enemy had seen our departure and we were a half-league distant and were entering a thicket, they descended the mountain to the huts. But before entering the huts, the Indians, suspecting our ambush, began shooting arrows at them. The soldiers came out, pulling the triggers of the harquebuses at the same time, but none fired. One of the Indians wounded the alferez, Andrés de Charles, in the hand with an arrow. The alferez cocked the trigger again, fired, and killed the Indian as the others fled.

After the four soldiers were reunited with the company, the Indian guide appeared and said that on the previous day he had not understood what he had been ordered to do. For this reason, he had missed the encounter. He said that during the first part of the night he had been with the Indians. They had told him that the Indians whom Cabrito had summoned had not gathered because an old Indian woman had died. Cabrito's wife was one of the prisoners, and this created substantially more trouble that year than we anticipated.

❧

Chapter 2 / Indians Attack Alonso de León's House

A S was mentioned in the previous chapter, one of the Indian prisoners captured was the wife of the tribal captain, Cabrito. She was held as a prisoner in the home of the chief justice, Alonso de León, who had gone to the city of Zacatecas on business. In his absence the captive escaped. Doubtless, she told her husband, Cabrito, of the condition of the house—that it was located about half a league from the town [Cadereyta], of the few people who were available to defend the place, and of everything else she had seen. So Cabrito, as an offended party (and knowing that the chief justice was absent), with his followers called together ten villages of Indians to exact revenge and attack the house. If they were successful, as he anticipated, the Indians would advance to the town and destroy it. Cabrito would have been able to achieve this without risk to himself because of the limited defenses of the place at that time.

But God—who with His infinite mercy prevents barbarians' depraved efforts from being fulfilled—ordained that two days before the planned attack, Chief Justice Alonso de León would return from the city of Zacatecas. He arrived on Saint Catherine's Day. It was customary each year to celebrate that day by having both the settlers and the soldiers who were stationed in the town display their offensive and defensive arms. The customary review was held in the afternoon; everyone then went to his post or his home.

One thing in this occurrence is to be pondered, namely, that some warning had always preceded all previous [Indian raids] in this province. But this one was like a bolt from the blue, whose effects occur immediately with no chance to foresee the danger.

At midnight, while we were in deepest sleep, God disposed that one good woman of the house would be awake and would hear a noise in the Indian settlement nearby. The Indians lived next to the river, a distance shorter than the range of a harquebus from the house. She realized that the Indians were slipping along secretly, and that on the other side of the river there seemed to be movement in the trees and some noise, although the situation was confused. Therefore, she called at the window of the room where Alonso de León was sleeping. Responding to her knocks, the captain asked who she was. She told him to get up because a large number of Indians were nearby and were coming to attack the house.

Although the chief justice generally questioned any news that was given him, he was so animated by this report that he immediately got up and opened the door. At the same time, the good woman called me. I was living in a small house that was the dwelling of Joseph de León and his wife and children; he was the crippled brother of Alonso, the chief justice. I immediately got up in my white undergarments and grabbed my firearms. By then the enemy Indians, shouting loudly, were slowly approaching the house.

Alonso de León was already on horseback when a neighbor, Antonio Cortinas, arrived at the house looking for some Indian women who had fled from him. Everyone gathered in the fortress house that was made of stone, and the two who were on horseback began firing their harquebuses when the Indians began their attack.

Alonso de León wanted to send his eldest son, Juan de León, to the town for help. He ordered his son to mount a horse, bareback (because the attack did not give him time to saddle the horse). Juan's mother opposed this, fearing the Indians would kill him, which could have happened. For this reason, and because this was no time to display cowardice, I mounted the horse. I was recovering from a *deadly* three-day fever that had left me extremely weak. By that time the Indians were shooting numerous arrows at the riders and at the windows and doors. They were aided by the light afforded them by the flames of a shack that they had set afire.

So that I could leave without risk, riding bareback, the chief justice fired a harquebus shot at the Indians who were near the route that I was to take. While the Indians were fleeing in terror, I was able to get away. I reached a little hill and the horse threw me, but I went on foot to notify the town. By this time Luis de Zúñiga and Juan López had come to our aid, and the incident ended.

Because of the assault of the Indians with their arrows, it was necessary for Alonso de León and Antonio Cortinas to turn their horses loose and withdraw to the house to defend themselves from inside the door, which they kept ajar so as to be able to shoot. Alonso's wife, an illustrious lady, was giving them powder and bullets so that they had a sufficient supply. With the door open, an Indian was able to shoot an arrow at her. If it had not first struck the door with the edge of the arrowhead, doubtless it would have gone through her. And despite the fact that the arrow was somewhat splintered, it hit her in the throat and wounded her, although not seriously.

The siege lasted half an hour. When Luis de Zúñiga and Juan López arrived, one of them by each of the two paths to the house, they attacked the enemy Indians with such force that they ended the siege and killed an Indian who appeared unexpectedly near the house.

When Juan López reached Cabrito at the river, the Indian was covering himself with a quilted sleeping pad. Juan removed the bedding and stabbed the Indian in the back with a broadsword, which went through him. On pulling the sword out, Juan opened a large hole in the Indian's stomach, so that his entrails came out. With them in hand, Cabrito fell to the earth. According to what was discovered later, Cabrito died three days after that. In his oral testament Cabrito charged his companions to steal all the Spaniards' livestock if they wanted to conquer them, because once these were taken away, they could grab the Spaniards like chickens. Some repentance for a person who had committed robberies and had caused others to commit them!

Thanks be to God that, in spite of there having been so many enemy Indians, the only loss to the house was the burning of some nearby shacks and some clothing of little value that the Indians carried off. At dawn, the trail by which the enemy had come was detected. It was on the other side of the river, along a wide path. More than a thousand arrows, from those the

Indians had shot that night, were picked up from the patio and from around the house.

It was learned later that, when the Indians had crossed the river, an Icaura captain[1] had breathed on the heart of each to instill them with power. This was a ceremony from which he drew no advantage, because it was verified that he was the one who died that night. His Divine Majesty permitted him to be punished for his crime.

When Luis de Zúñiga was passing by, the group of enemy Indians by the path that I mentioned shot an arrow at him that, had it not hit a rib, would have gone through him. He was in great pain all night because of the blood he lost, but he healed quickly. He and Juan López were acclaimed because of the daring with which they had attacked the six hundred Indians.

When Alonso de León informed the governor of this occurrence, the governor verified that there had been ten nations of Indians in this fray and mentioned each one by name, as I saw from his letter. It was also verified that some Indians who were in a mining camp that General Juan de Zavala had in the vicinity of Monterrey (seven leagues from Cadereyta) had been seen during the first part of the night in the mining camp, but were found taking part in the attack, and at dawn they had returned to the mining camp. This was proof of the agility of these barbarians!

Another occurrence that night gave the chief justice a great deal to think about. When Juan López and Luis de Zúñiga came to our aid, an Indian named Jusepillo appeared to them on the way. He was from Alonso de León's *encomienda*. Jusepillo had been exiled to the Zacatecas mining camp more than two years before for his many crimes. He told them that he had just arrived, having fled from Zacatecas, and he went with them to Alonso de León's house to help them. Once the siege was lifted, Jusepillo presented himself to his lord, the chief justice, who suspected that Jusepillo might have been among the enemies. But Jusepillo answered every question he was asked—and in obvious matters—so that finally the truth of what he said was known, namely, that he had arrived that night simply by coincidence.

Chapter 3 / Governor Zavala Requests the Establishment of Two Presidios

THE movements of the Indians of this province did not cease with the death of Cabrito, the head of the tribe. Their depravity caused them to continue their insurrection the next year, 1652. They stole from shepherds and killed sheep and livestock, both in the Pilón River Valley and in other places. The governor had depleted his estate by maintaining salaried soldiers at his expense in Cerralvo. The troops were employed to go out to the field whenever necessary and also to guard four hundred warhorses that the governor maintained at Cerralvo. (I attest—without being a notary—that I saw the horses at the post called Cañada Honda, in the vicinity of the town, and the animals were of such good quality that they appeared to have been chosen individually.) This [loss of resources] motivated the governor to report Indian uprisings and his financial condition.

The governor sent a dispatch to the Count of Alba,[1] who at that time was governing New Spain, in which he proposed the establishment of two royal presidios in the province. The first, with a complement of twelve soldiers and a captain, would be for Cerralvo; the other, of eight men with its captain, for Cadereyta—as these were the two frontier settlements. The troops' salary would be paid from the royal pay office at Zacatecas. The governor's reports were presented to His Excellency, with the other information proposed to him, and a treasury council was called. Although there were objections, His Excellency finally granted the presidios (which remain to this day) with the charge that the governor should obtain approval from His Majesty within a given period of time.

With this condition and the Viceroy's dispatches, including orders for the royal officials at Zacatecas, General Juan de Zavala raised personnel in the city. The salary outlay was 725 pesos for each captain and 450 for each soldier, which has continued to the present. This action has greatly hindered the Indians near our frontiers. Although (as I have said) the governor was granted a period of time to obtain approval from His Majesty, a fleet of vessels

was lacking on that occasion. He therefore appealed to the Duke of Alburquerque,[2] the Count of Alba's successor, to request a two-year extension.
His Excellency ordered the treasurer to investigate, and the latter responded
that one year should be conceded to him, as is evident from his order.

In 1653, it was resolved—having been previously deliberated upon—
that there should be an expedition from Nuevo León to explore the Palmas
River,[3] which enters the Northern Sea [Gulf of Mexico]. This was not to
benefit His Majesty, or the province, but to discover lands and to learn directions, for whatever purpose this might serve in the future. In furtherance of
this, the governor commissioned Captain Alonso de León to make this exploration with thirty men. The captain made the trip in just a few days' travel
from Cadereyta, since, if one moves quickly, it is a journey of only four days.
From the mouth of the [Palmas] river to Tampico takes six days.

It was proposed that in the same year a journey should be made to
Tampico. This one did not take place. The purpose was to explore certain
treasures of *reales* that the Indians say are on the coast from a galleon that
was lost in the time of the Emperor Charles V. As will be told later in this history, there is no question about the shipwreck.

Based on what Captain Alonso de León reported, the land they crossed
between Cadereyta and the [Palmas] river, along the coast, is very fertile.
The river has a bountiful supply of fish, and on it live many nations of very
peaceful natives. Doubtless, they did not inherit the evil ways of their ancestors, who killed many Spaniards who tried to settle those lands.

Since I have reached this point, the reader should know what Dr. Francisco López de Gómara[4] says in his *Historia General de las Indias*, in Chapter 47 (which I have translated from Italian to Castilian). It says this:

> After the death of Juan Ponce de León, who discovered Florida,
> Francisco de Garay outfitted three caravels in Jamaica in the year
> 1518. He sailed to Florida; considering it to be an island, he went
> ashore. The Indians discovered him and killed many of his troops.
> Then he went on to reach Pánuco, but the Indians, who were very
> aggressive, did not allow him to settle there. In Chila they killed
> some of his troops and ate them, so he went back to Jamaica. He re-
> supplied his ships and returned in 1519. This venture was more dis-
> astrous for him than the first. Finally he sailed to Spain and negoti-
> ated a royal contract for the conquest of that area and the title of

adelantado.[5] He sailed from Spain in 1523 with eleven ships, more than seven hundred Spaniards, and 154 horses. He also had many pieces of artillery. He was lost in Pánuco with his whole party. The Indians killed four hundred of his troops. Pánfilo de Narváez, with the title of governor, sailed from San Lúcar in 1527. He came to settle the Palmas River with nine ships, six hundred Spaniards, 100 horses, many provisions, and arms. They did not learn the route, nor come to know the land. Narváez went ashore with three hundred troops, almost all the horses, and a few provisions. He sent them to look for the Palmas River; but while looking for it, they lost almost all the men and horses. (Gómara ends here.)

From such a true history, one can gather how much natural audacity the Indians of the Palmas River coast had and, by comparison, how domestic they are today. Doubtless, all should be attributed to Divine will; perhaps the time of their reduction[6] will soon arrive. May His Divine Majesty wish it, for the greater glory of His evangelical law.

Based on what Captain Alonso de León reported, the mouth of the Palmas River is at 24°30′ north latitude. This reading differs very little from that of this city [Monterrey], which is at 24°, as we have noted, although not with the exactitude that is required, because of the lack of a good astrolabe or quadrant.[7]

❧

Chapter 4 / The Events after 1653

THERE was nothing worth noting in the year 1654. But events in 1655 are noteworthy because of the disturbances caused by some Indians from the *encomiendas* of this province, who lived in the Pilón Valley and its vicinity.

There is abundant material to treat the subject at great length in this chapter. In addition to the damage that these Indians (with scant fear of God) began to cause by stealing horses and killing livestock, one night they came upon Captain Alonso de León's cattle in the Pilón Valley. With a great outcry, they attacked the small residence of Miguel Angel, the estate manager and a brave man. He came with his harquebus to save his wife and children.

He had scarcely appeared at the door when the Indians shot an arrow and killed him. They sacked the house and captured his wife and children; and because a small child was crying, they smashed him against a boulder. The Indians departed through El Pilón Chico Pass with the captives and a few valuables. After traveling about four or five leagues, they climbed into the mountains on the right, so as to be secure.

When Governor Don Martín de Zavala was told this bad news, he ordered a company formed to punish the aggressors. He placed the troops under the command of Captain Gregorio Fernández, chief justice of the Salinas Valley, who was an experienced settler. Unfortunately, however, he was the cause of a sad development.

Captain Fernández camped in the Pilón Valley and asked for information about the aggressors. Hearing that the Indians had camped in the mountains, he attempted to climb them, but they were impassable. This unexpected situation led to a tragic end. However, it is also true that the captain never understood that the enemy occupied such a well-fortified site.

Leaving the encampment in the Pilón, the captain set out with most of the soldiers. Marching at night, the troops arrived at the foot of the range. Leaving the horses to be guarded by members of the company, the other soldiers began to climb on foot in search of the aggressors. The Indians saw the Spaniards and established defensive positions. The palisade and fortification they built prevented the troops from hurting them, and the Indians began rolling so many stones down the mountain that it was a miracle they did not kill all our men. Three were killed: Nicolás de Solís, Esteban de Lerma, and Alonso de Charles—valiant and well-known soldiers who in this case were not able to demonstrate their courage, because the big stones and rocks that the Indians were hurling overtook them. This development obliged the others to withdraw to where the horses had been left.

This occurred on the eve of Saint James's Day, which was not favorable for this company—but which was favorable to one of the soldiers, Santiago de Treviño. In dodging a stone that came rolling toward him, Santiago sheltered behind a relatively small boulder. God was pleased to spare his life, and although the Indians passed quite near him, they did not see him. I heard him say that, when he knew that he was hidden but in great danger, he invoked the name of the apostle Saint James many times and promised to celebrate his feast day every year if he would deliver him from that danger. So our patron (as he gives such favor to his devotees) was pleased to deliver him from such a dangerous situation.

Santiago carried out his promise as long as he lived and celebrated the feast day as he had promised, because it is a Christian act to commit oneself to the saints when one is afflicted, so that they may intercede with His Divine Majesty and attain His grace. Santiago de Treviño waited until dark and came down from the mountains and took the path that led toward the encampment. The next day at eight o'clock, he arrived—to the great joy of the surviving troops, although there was also sadness for the three men who were killed.

The next year, 1656, these Indians and others persisted in their evil ways. After the Labradores post was settled,[1] some ten leagues from the mouth of the Pilón Chico River, a settler named Nicolás Vásquez (a man of great valor) located there with his wife and children. He had some Indians attached to the land he cultivated, among whom were some of those who took part in killing the soldiers.

When Nicolás, in all tranquillity, was helping the Indians with farming and harvesting corn, they saw that he was alone and attacked and killed him. The Indians then captured his wife and children. There was, however, no response to the attack because aid was not locally available. Assistance that could have come from the Pilón Valley was ten leagues away, and from Pablillo, five leagues away. After this evil band of Indians safely committed these and similar crimes—carrying out the attacks with the security of knowing that no one could resist them—they climbed into the mountains with the deceased's wife to join the Indians who had killed Miguel Angel and who still held his wife and children. There was some consolation for the two women because, assuming there can be consolation while under the control of such a barbarous band, at least they could communicate and grieve together over their mutual hardships.

Chapter 5 / Punishment of Indians
Who Committed the Murders

BECAUSE of His hidden justice, His Divine Majesty is accustomed to delaying punishment of the wicked, as He did with those in Babylonia, by allowing their crimes and sins for many years. Finally He sent them their due and corresponding punishment in the form of hunger, war, oppression, and death, as divine and human histories attest. Thus His Divine Majesty permitted the time to arrive when these perverse Indians would pay for their insults. When Governor Zavala recognized the impossibility of conquering the Indians because of the inaccessibility of the areas in which they lived, he dispatched orders to Captain Antonio Orpinel. The captain lived in an area called Matehuala,[1] located about fifty leagues south of Monterrey on the road to Mexico City, and here, fourteen leagues from the Las Charcas camp. Matehuala separates the jurisdictions of this province and that camp.

Captain Orpinel was one of Governor Zavala's lieutenants and a man of very good understanding who would know if there was any way (using wiliness and astuteness) of capturing the aggressors on his property. His approach was to let some of the aggressors, who were already among the Indians living near there, know that, if their companions wished to attach themselves to his land, he would receive them very willingly. With this speech, the Indians went to look for their companions and brought them to his property.

After allowing the Indians the opportunity to reassure themselves for several days, entertaining them, and giving them supplies (having already forewarned a company of ten or twelve chosen men), Captain Orpinel one day told the Indians that he had clothing to distribute to them because he wanted them to remain on his land. When the day arrived for this distribution—with the alerted company having been ordered to hide in the large shed, which had divisions where they with all their arms could hide—Orpinel opened the shed and had all the Indians enter to take the clothing he wanted to distribute to them.

A house servant, who entered with him, was already warned that, after all the Indians had entered, he should shut the door—which was done.

When those who were hidden came out with their harquebuses, the Indians, who had not brought arms, gave themselves up. The Indians then were tied up and marched to the Pilón Valley, on the frontier, where Major Jacinto García de Sepúlveda and his company were. The prisoners were turned over to him, and he dealt justice to them, hanging twenty-two. These Indians were the ones who died on that occasion, and this punishment pacified the land for some time.

These Indians were of the Hualahuis nation.[2] It was necessary, however, to pardon some of the Indians; those who paid the penalty on that occasion were the guiltiest ones. Martín, the captain of that nation, was brought to Monterrey. The governor pardoned his crimes, dressed him in very fine clothing, and presented him with a gilded sword. Thereby, he has remained at peace; he is now old. Of that nation there remain fewer than ten Indians, who now have been congregated for more than fifteen years in a mission called San Cristóbal,[3] located thirty leagues from the city, with a minister who attends to them. The mission, which is very pleasant, is next to a river of the same name. For six months each year, the area is visited by shepherds who come from New Spain to pasture their flocks.

The Indians gave up the women and their children whom they had carried off in that uprising. This action comforted everyone, but they had no consolation for the loss of their husbands.

❧

Chapter 6 / Captain Alonso de León Represents Governor Zavala before the Royal Council

AS has been mentioned, Captain Alonso de León went to Spain on business for Governor Don Martín de Zavala because Don Martín wished to give an account of having complied with the agreement and contract that he had made with His Majesty in 1625, which authorized him to settle two towns, one with forty settlers and one with twenty. For this he carried a special *cédula*[1] empowering him to apportion lands and water to the settlers and to commit area Indians as laborers to both the settlers who would enter the two new settlements and the older settlers whom he found on the land. Since the governor had fulfilled the contract and taken testimony in support of his effort, everything was to be reviewed by the Royal Council of the Indies. The text of the memorial that the governor presented to the Royal Council is as follows:

Memorial

Sir:

Don Martín de Zavala, governor and captain of Nuevo León, states: Since Your Majesty has been pleased to order a contract and agreement to be entered into with him concerning the settlement and pacification of the province, he, Don Martín de Zavala, has not only carried out that which was offered—as has been declared by a decree of the Royal Council of the Indies—but, besides this, has gone further in the service of Your Majesty. He has placed in Monterrey and within its jurisdiction more than one hundred settlers and assisted them at the time they entered the province. He has assisted in the construction of their houses and has given them plowshares, oxen, and seed. With this help they have cultivated more than sixteen farming properties in the province and have set up two silver smelters in the city. He has founded and settled the San Nicolás de las Salinas camp and mines, where there are six silver smelters, many mines, some grain fields, and large herds of livestock.

The governor has founded the settlement of San Gregorio, near Cerralvo, where there are four silver smelters and large herds of livestock. In all of these settlements he has placed government-service horses, arms, harquebuses, and munitions for their defense and preservation. As a result, Your Majesty's treasuries have received from the province many *marcos*[2] of silver from taxes levied on its mines. In addition, great quantities of lead and clay have been removed and carried in carts and by teams of pack animals to Zacatecas, Parral, Sombrerete, and other mining districts. This amounts to more than three million *marcos* of silver.

He has explored the route to the Province of Huaxteca and the port of Tampico and has established trade with them and pacified the Indians who live in the region. Likewise, he has explored the Palmas River, its mouth, and the coastline for more than twenty leagues to the north and has given gifts to the region's Indians, thereby reducing them to obedience to Your Majesty and instilling in them the desire to receive holy baptism.

He has commenced the exploration of the northern area, in which he has reconnoitered more than fifty leagues,[3] so as to continue until a connection with the Spaniards of Florida has been attained. He has obtained almost certain information about the Plata Mountains,[4] so that we may be able to visit the area. This is a goal that has been attempted many times by the governors of Nueva Vizcaya and Nuevo León, but that was abandoned because of the Indians' restlessness.

The governor has built roads and has leveled them so that the sheep herds of New Spain may enter the province. Mountain ranges, thickets, and wildernesses along the routes formerly blocked this traffic. This has been accomplished at his expense and by his efforts.

At the time of his entry, the governor relieved Your Majesty of the expense of 20,000 pesos per year, which the Royal Treasury paid for the presidio and warehouse of the city of Monterrey. In the twenty-eighth year of their existence, the cost had reached 570,000 pesos—such a great treasure being consumed uselessly. It was redeemed with the same number of pesos, which he has spent out of his father's great wealth and out of his own limited means. From these contributions have followed many additions to the royal possessions of Your Majesty, as is clear from the evidence presented.

In the last paragraph of the agreement, Your Majesty was pleased to offer the governor, when he had fulfilled the stipulations, payment for his services and agreed to favor him by pledging your royal faith and word to have him invested with the insignia of the Order of Santiago[5] and two thousand pesos in Indians; to this point this has not been done. In light of this, he prays Your Majesty to order a *cédula* to be dispatched so that at one of the pay offices of Zacatecas or San Luis Potosí, the royal officials will pay him, as quickly as possible, the salary that has been owed him since he first entered the province in Your Majesty's service so that he may continue in his duties. In addition, the salary that is still owed him should be paid as punctually as the royal officials would have paid it to one who lives so far from them and is so occupied in the service of Your Majesty. He prays that you also give him the title of *adelantado* in perpetuity for him and for his heirs, with the income that Your Majesty may be pleased to concede to him as a perpetuity of estate.

It is requested that the staff of lord mayor, with which you favored him for two lifetimes, be made hereditary, with the income that Your Majesty may be pleased to grant him, with there being paid at the royal pay office, after the two lifetimes, whatever may be just for as long as it is not renounced. He also prays that you concede him the privilege of adding in one quadrant of his coat of arms a golden lion, rampant, in a field of green to signify his having pacified and settled that fertile province called León.

Because it is a land of war and it is necessary to go from one settlement to another, may he also be granted the favor of four soldiers, as the other governors have them as a personal guard and company. Let these be paid, with his bills of exchange, at the pay offices, where it shall be ordered that their salaries be paid.

Because some of his relatives and other persons worthy of his obligation have aided in the pacification and settlement of the province, may Your Majesty grant the governor lifetime appointments for the captains he may name to the presidios founded in the province, and others that may later be founded.

May he be given a *cédula* so that every five years the viceroy of New Spain, or whoever may be charged with the government of New Spain, should dispatch an examiner from the Royal Audiencia[6] to review the governor and his ministers; and may the *cédula*, closed and sealed, be carried to Mexico City so that the viceroy may remit it to the Royal Council.[7] There it should be seen and adjudicated. This should be observed and executed inviolably in order to avoid the inconveniences that habitually result from doing it in some other way. Thereby, the governor shall obtain the action that he expects and that is promised from the royal hand of Your Majesty.

This memorial was well received in the Royal Council, according to what I saw in the decrees that resulted. So as not to prolong the history, these decrees will not be repeated here.

A royal *cédula* was dispatched to Governor Don Martín de Zavala ordering that his salary be paid. With regard to the Order of Santiago, the proceedings were to be executed in the Council of [Knightly] Orders. As to all the other matters, it was resolved that they would be remitted to the Viceroy: as someone who had the matter at hand, he was to execute it insofar as there was no inconvenience. Insofar as there might be such, it was to be remitted to the Council.

The collection of the governor's salary was effected. The amount totaled one hundred and some thousands of pesos, which was withdrawn from the royal pay office at San Luis Potosí by order of the Count of Baños,[8] viceroy of New Spain.

As to the other efforts, the governor declined to pursue them, considering himself already old and full of years.

All these negotiations were conducted in the Royal Council by Captain Alonso de León. The captain had arrived at Cádiz from Madrid to embark with the fleet, but at that point eighty English ships arrived within sight of the city. It was therefore necessary to postpone the fleet's departure from the bay. Instead, the fleet was unloaded, and an armada was formed to pursue that of England. General Alonso de León (who today is governor of the Province of Coahuila and had gone with his father to Spain), having received his navigator's commission, embarked on the ships to serve His Majesty as an unpaid adventurer. He thus began his service to His Majesty at the age of sixteen, a fact that is recorded in the certifications [Governor] Alonso de León has in his possession.

General Alonso de León's father, having been at the court on Governor Don Martín de Zavala's business and having performed many services in this province, did not solicit for himself nor for his children anything at all. He was content simply with a royal *cédula* commending him and his sons to the viceroys; and he was commended in the same way to the governors of this kingdom by another *cédula*.

Chapter 7 / Other Military Action in Nuevo León

F E W events that warrant recording took place during the next three or four years in this province except for ordinary losses such as thefts of horses and livestock on the sheep farms. As these thefts were a daily occurrence, reporting them would carry the narration on infinitely. But in 1661, some nations of Indians who lived at lower elevations in the Papagayos Mountains gathered and began to commit offenses in the jurisdiction of Cadereyta, such as stealing herds of mares. This obliged the governor to form a company of soldiers under the command of Captain Diego de Ayala. In his company was Captain Diego Rodríguez who, although crippled, was a man of judgment and astuteness in matters of war. The company camped near Cadereyta, and from there the troops went to spy on the nearby Indian encampments. The Indians must have detected the spies, because when the Spaniards tried to attack, they found no one. The troops simply reconnoitered the many fires—which the enemy had set as a ruse: there were not as many Indians as had been thought.

When the company returned to camp, Captain Diego de Ayala notified the governor of the evasion, of how the Indians retreated down the Pesquería Grande River, and of the route they had followed. The captain stated that he needed many more very experienced soldiers to follow the Indians. The governor received the report on the eve of Palm Sunday and sent orders to different posts. All the captains, officials, and other people who lived far away were summoned to gather at eight o'clock in the morning on Holy Monday, at the post called El Tule Redondo. There the troops would find their orders.

On the appointed day and hour, the troops were all at the designated post, and Captain Alonso de León appeared shortly thereafter. After dismounting, the captain took out the order that the governor had secretly sent him to come to that post and assume command of the company that was to be formed. This action seemed strange to those who were already in the field, especially to their captain, who felt he had been demoted. However, many of the new troops were pleased by the action. It was inaccurately said among the troops that the reason Captain Diego de Ayala asked for this help was to have both the old and the new captains under his command. As I have noted, this was not the case. This opinion as to the motive remains open to doubt because it is impossible to judge mental acts.

The soldiers set out with the high commander to Punta de Papagayos. Finding no trace of the enemy, the troops marched east and found a sizable trail, which they followed. On Holy Wednesday they came upon the enemy in the middle of a woods and captured some Indians, including several boys. Because they were convinced of the enemy's crimes, the soldiers hanged six Indians on that same Holy Wednesday. Thereby it seemed that the land was pacified for a time.

That same year, because of a shortage of salt in the province, Captain Alonso de León requested leave to go to the San Lorenzo salt flats. He collected a company of more than twenty men for this journey and, having completed the trip to the flats, the captain commenced the return. On Encadenado Creek he again was struck with the illness that had crippled him in one foot and one hand and half of his body; he was now left wholly crippled and mute. It was therefore necessary to carry him on a litter to his house in the Pilón Valley. He died there within two months, to the great sorrow of the whole province and the governor, who had always held him in high esteem.

That year seemingly was more fateful than others, because at the beginning of January General Juan de Zavala, a relative of the governor, also died. The general, having come from Mexico City to Monterrey, was attacked by four-day fevers, which affected him so much that he was overpowered. He became so despondent that no entertainment could revive him. However, his illness passed without his having to retire to his bed. Instead, he was strolling about the city, and the illness was not thought to be grave. Therefore, he was not advised that anyone should help him to prepare his soul and his belongings. When a good woman who was taking care of him went to see him quite early in the morning at the governor's house, she found him dead. The incident caused much sorrow to all, including his relative, the governor. The general left no children, although he had been married in this province to a sister of the governor's mother.

Chapter 8 / Indian Nations of the North

BECAUSE the Indians' natural unreliability and malice is so well known and so extensively described in all the histories of New Spain, it will not be necessary to ponder the matter on the occasion of the uprising of some nations that live toward the northern part of this province. These Indians were beginning to attack along the routes from the province to Zacatecas, Sombrerete, and other places. No small effort was required to quell the revolt.

The trouble began when a group of Indians attacked a pack team traveling from Zacatecas. This occurred at Ojo Caliente, eight or nine leagues from Monterrey. The Indians killed a boy, Joseph Páez, a mule driver, and carried off the team, which belonged to a lady named Doña Clara de Rentería, the widow of Major Jacinto García.[1] They took the team up through a little pass that leads to Las Mesillas, in the jurisdiction of Saltillo. At the same time, they wounded two other boys with the same pack team; one died of his wounds shortly afterward. However, he had the good luck to escape on horseback and reach Monterrey, where they could administer the sacraments.

This new uprising began to cause concern in the province. It was feared that the enemy Indians would enter the province, which finally happened, with savage massacres and offenses, as will be told later.

The next year [1662] at the post called Portezuelo (which is located about eight leagues beyond Saltillo), a settler named Don Vicente de Saldívar was coming from Zacatecas to this province with a nephew of that city's treasurer. The Indians attacked and killed them both and carried away the mules they were bringing.

These murders and others, along with the thefts of horses, led the governor to convene a council of war, to which he called the men of Nuevo León who were most experienced in this matter. From this call, companies were formed to enter the enemy Indians' land to punish them.

Because its residents had an interest in the Indian attacks, notice was also given in Saltillo in case it might wish to offer aid. Once the time was specified, Saltillo sent a very good company, together with a company of Tlaxcaltecos,[2] with their provisions of supplies and arms. They joined forces with the men of this province, and together all were under the command of Major Juan de la Garza, a man of great experience.

More than one hundred men, eight hundred horses, eighty loads of meal, a good quantity of hardtack, and other necessary supplies were carried on the journey. After they reached the enemy's land, which was more than sixty leagues from this city,[3] the troops attacked the Cacaxtle encampment[4] and killed up to one hundred Indians in the battle. Not a single Spaniard was killed, although some were wounded. One hundred and twenty-five natives of all ages and both sexes were captured. When those captured were brought to Monterrey, the governor ordered them taken to Zacatecas. This was done. This expedition lasted five long months,[5] during which time many pesos were spent, both by the governor and by our settlers and the residents of Saltillo. It seems that the land was somewhat pacified by means of this entry.

Governor Don Martín de Zavala decided to report this fortunate occurrence to the Count of Baños, who was governing New Spain at that time. Thus, a dispatch was sent. His Excellency was pleased to answer the governor, to whom he expressed his great esteem. He thanked him for the information and told him that he would give His Majesty an account of the service rendered, because to him redounded the tranquillity of the roads that led to the mining districts of Zacatecas, Sombrerete, and México. As I have stated, this expedition lasted more than five months; the companies departed in early October 1663 and did not return to this city until March of the following year.

❧

Chapter 9 / The Death of Governor Don Martín de Zavala

SO as not to prolong this history I should like to reduce this chapter to a brief eulogy on the many abilities and qualities that Governor Don Martín de Zavala possessed both internally and externally. But I must extend myself somewhat so as not to pass over his many attributes.

As stated in the discourses of Captain Alonso de León, Zavala was an illegitimate son of General Agustín de Zavala,[1] who owned mines near the city of Zacatecas. The general was so wealthy that, as truthfully said, the 20 percent tax he paid to His Majesty from the silver that came from his smelters alone amounted to 400,000 pesos.

The general reared Don Martín in the manner expected for anyone with such immense wealth. When he was old enough, Don Martín was sent to Spain to study in Salamanca. I adjudge that he had advanced studies. His manner of conversation and discourse and his elegant style of writing letters reflected an extensive education. His conversation was very agreeable, and he spoke to all (it is said) in their own language. He spoke Latin as elegantly as he did his mother tongue. He spoke Tuscan so naturally that he seemed to have been reared in the city of Florence. He possessed more than eighty books in Italian, on history and other subjects. Of this I am a witness, as he lent me some of them. He also spoke Basque and Flemish.

In addition, he was a special man in all other respects, worthy of greater offices than those of this minor government. One might very justly apply to him the verse on Pompey the Great's tomb as it is stated by its author, who composed *The Internal and External Wars of Rome.* This verse reads that, as an Athenian boy was walking along the banks of the Nile, he saw that the floods had uncovered a white stone that seemed to be marble. He dug down to better see what it might be and dug up an urn (the tomb of the ancients). As was later discovered, this was the tomb of Pompey, the one who had King Ptolemy killed when he went to help him. The help that he found was to take his life for doing no more than applauding Julius Caesar, from whom he was fleeing after being defeated in battle with him on the fields of Pharsala. With the urn uncovered, then, he found on it this epitaph: *Templi pondus erat modica qui clauditor urna.* This epitaph seems to have even more meaning than the one deduced from its literal sense, which I have seen expressed in the Tuscan language in this form: "He who is interred in this small monument was worthy of a more sumptuous temple." One might well say this of our governor, Don Martín de Zavala, and he might well be counted with the heroes of antiquity for his special actions.

The governor, spending much of his father's wealth while it remained with him, extended this province in every way that his strength could achieve. Afterward, he also used the little that he had in war and in sustaining settlers in Cerralvo. This is so well known in this province that there is no one who is ignorant of it. Up to the year 1648, he constructed at his own expense all the houses that are still standing in Cerralvo (and those that have fallen down because of the residents' carelessness). He did it as alms for the priests who attended to Cerralvo and Cadereyta. After that, he arranged that His Majesty should pay them out of the royal pay office at Zacatecas, as continues to be done. Finally, he was the father of his country (he called the Province of León his country; he went there during the best years of his life and governed it thirty-eight years) because he favored it so greatly.

I heard him mention on several occasions that he was born in the year 1597 in Pánuco, near Zacatecas. He suffered an infirmity in one leg, which caused him so much pain on one occasion when he was in Zacatecas that the surgeons tried to amputate it. It was becoming infected, and it seemed to one surgeon that it was hanging limp. In 1664, the illness began to progress more rapidly and the leg developed a cancerous growth. He died on August 8, which caused much sadness and grief throughout the province and outside it.

The governor stipulated in his testament that, contingent on the viceroy's being notified so as to provide as he might please, the municipal council of Monterrey should govern. The viceroy was then notified and approved the choice. The council governed until February 4 of the following year, 1665, when the interim governor took office. This will be told in the following chapter, along with other events.

❧

Chapter 10 / The Government after Governor Zavala's Death

THE government of the Province of León became orphaned after the death of Governor Zavala. Although the municipal council (all of whose members were local landholders) handled public affairs and matters of war as necessary, the lack of leadership was recognized. Moreover, life was difficult for many shamefully poor widows to whom Governor Zavala had secretly and publicly given considerable alms.

Eight days after Governor Zavala's death, the municipal council dispatched the public prosecutor to Mexico City with a copy of the municipal council's nomination and a clause from the governor's will. After His Excellency the Marquis of Mancera,[1] who was then governing in New Spain (with his power of nominating interim officials), saw this clause, he was mindful of the merits and services of General León de Alza, knight of the Order of Santiago, and named him governor and captain general of this province. Moreover, using the same *cédula* that the deceased had brought from His Majesty, he broadened his title to include the power of giving and apportioning everything that Don Martín de Zavala had given and apportioned.

Because news was received of his good conduct in the offices he had held in New Spain, the new governor was received in this province with great enthusiasm. Alza took office on February 4, 1665. To a noteworthy extent, his method of governing followed the example set by the deceased governor. When he was uncertain, he asked how the former governor had responded in similar situations. He loudly proclaimed that he would follow in his predecessor's footsteps, because such a great man could not have erred in politics or military matters.

It seems, however, that this poor gentleman entered into this government with the wrong foot first, as they say. Soon after his arrival, the Indians of the north began to make trouble everywhere. They carried away horses from areas near the city, from the farms, and even from the city itself. This moved the new governor to station six mounted presidial soldiers near the city. He also ordered the settlers to keep their horses nearby so that, if events should require, the horses would be more quickly able to engage in the necessary pursuit and to escort the pack teams that left Monterrey for Saltillo.

This year, as a convoy of shepherds was coming from Pablillo along the route called Pilón Chico (which river mouth comes out at the plains of Pilón), a band of Indians from the north came upon them on a plain and killed two mule drivers and all the mules. One mule driver who escaped reported the attack in the valley. Immediately, Alonso de León—who at present is the governor of the Province of Coahuila—arrived with a company of nine soldiers. The other men in the company were shepherds, because at that time the valley was not settled. The next day, almost at sunset, the captain reached the band of Indians near the post called Labradores. His troops fought with them, wounding a Hualahuis Indian. In turn, the Indians, shooting arrows, wounded and disabled one of the horses.

Because most of the company were shepherds and not experienced in war, the company could not resist the attack of the enemy, who numbered more than seventy. Only Alonso de León and his brother-in-law Juan Cantú resisted them. After the two killed the leader of the Indian band and others, the remaining Indians withdrew. The horses had been very badly treated; the one belonging to Alonso de León later died.

What happened on that occasion was actually a great stroke of luck and aid from Heaven. That only two men could resist so many Indians should be considered a miracle. Especially notable in this case was that it occurred at an unknown location, one not traversed except by shepherds, and that bands of northern Indians had gathered there although their encampments were so far away. It was concluded that someone who knew the land very well must have come with them.

❧

Chapter 11 / Developments in 1665

IN the year 1665 there were many military actions and a continuation of the uprising of the Indians from the north. The Indians appeared in several bands and advanced not only to the roads but even to the Spanish settlements, including Saltillo (which is eighteen leagues from Monterrey) and other settlements in this province. The Indians would rob and do as much damage as they could. Therefore the governor, in his foresight, named four captains to travel to the passes of the Valley of Salinas, Nacatás, Muertos, and others. The four captains were Antonio de Palacio, Francisco Botello, Pedro de la Garza, and Alonso de León [the elder]. These captains made excursions alternately with twenty-five to thirty men. The fact that these troops were being seen by the enemy (as they were) seemed to serve as something of a deterrent. Nevertheless, the Indians continued to gather near Saltillo. This obliged the lord mayor of Saltillo, Don Fernando de Azcué y Armendáriz, to form a company and to ask the governor of Nuevo León for another company. The companies were organized to enter the enemy's land and to eradicate, in one fell swoop, the base of the encampments that were causing so much damage.

A war council was convened in Monterrey and, as a result, assistance was given to Saltillo. Thirty soldiers were enlisted, with Juan Cavazos as captain. The Monterrey troops joined Saltillo's Don Fernando, who came to Nuevo León with 103 soldiers, 800 horses, and 70 loads of supplies.

FIGURE 1. *Fernando de Azcué leads 1665 expedition from Saltillo*

into South Texas against the Cacaxtle Indians.

The companies marched out in very good order, and in six days they arrived twenty-four leagues beyond the Río Bravo [Rio Grande] in search of the warlike Cacaxtle nation. It had been announced that an Indian (named Don Nicolás el Carretero) who was peacefully settled in Saltillo would gather Indians loyal to him to support the Spaniards. He collected more than three hundred Indian troops; the majority were of the Bobole nation.[1] Ambrosio de Cepeda—who knew most of the languages of the northern nations—was named as their leader. Although the Bobole were suspect, they behaved very loyally on this occasion and assisted bravely.

The enemy was hidden in some woods, but they were surrounded at dawn and could not escape. The Indians resisted valiantly. Because the woods were very thick and the Spaniards could not penetrate them, the troops shot the Indians they could see. An enemy Indian (very conversant in Spanish) named Juan, a brother of Don Benito, a very ruthless man, urged the Spaniards to cease the struggle because the Indians wanted to make peace. But the Spaniards recognized this as a ruse to allow the Indians a chance to regroup, which they did, to build a protective enclosure of tree limbs, prickly pears, and branches. When the diversion and feigned peace were recognized, our men continued their attack, and the fight lasted until the hour of prayer. One hundred Indians were killed and seventy small and large weapons were taken.

During the engagement, an old Indian woman played a flute to give the Cacaxtle courage.[2] She, however, was at the time a Spanish captive, and the friendly Indians asked if they could eat her. The Spaniards would not allow this, nor any similar cruelty that would serve as vengeance against her. However, the Indians knew that a boy among the prisoners was a relative of hers. That night the Indians secretly managed to secure *him*, and they ate *him*, for which there was no remedy.

In this great battle, twenty-two Spaniards were wounded, although none were killed. Two friendly Indians died, and others were wounded. When the enemy had no more arrows, they fought the Spanish troops and the friendly Indians with clubs.

During the siege General Don Fernando went hunting with his harquebus. In a wooded area he ran into a tree branch; this caused the harquebus to fire and strike a horse, which later died. This expedition was very successful because many of the enemy were killed and their settlement destroyed.

Chapter 12 / Other Developments in 1665

IT is necessary to interject into this history some particular cases that occurred at this time. Although they are not of critical importance, they at least serve as an example for correction, so that we should not continue in our mistakes and vices.

Two Borrado Indians, one called Don Juanico and the other, as a nickname, El Becerro, continued for some years to steal animals and livestock and to rob shepherds. Finally they were taken prisoner. Their pending cases were tried along with the new crime against them (they were heard by an *alcalde ordinario*).[1] After their many crimes were proved, using their own testimony, the *alcalde* condemned them to death.

This decision moved many people to pity, particularly some priests, who advised the defense to appeal the sentence to the governor, whom the priests had notified and had asked to moderate the sentence. Convinced by these supplications, the governor commuted their sentence to four years of personal service, in shackles, in a mill. After being at the mill for scarcely four months, the Indians escaped and resumed their criminal ways. They then were pursued by several squads of troops, but they could not be captured. Later, realizing that at last they were to be caught once again and punished, the natives captured a friendly Indian boy from a Spanish ranch one night and took him up the Pilón Chico River. After traveling very far inland, the Indians were unexpectedly attacked by a group of northern Indians, who hanged the Borrado and freed the boy.

Thus the boy escaped and told his story. The report gave everyone a great deal to talk about because of the mode and type of death (a hanging) that those two Indians suffered, since hanging was not customary among the Indians. There was no report of Indians ever having hanged any of their enemies; they usually killed them with arrows. The hanging of the Indians was taken as a divine mandate that it was a death warranted by their guilt, particularly as the hanging had been prevented here because of supplications to the judge. Divine justice had ordered the sentence to be executed as their guilt warranted.

I remember that when I was in Genoa,[2] an uncle told me that he had been living for many years in the city of Lisbon, where he had married. There, an Indian, a native of East India, was condemned to the gallows for his many crimes, and when he was on the scaffold someone interceded. The Indian was pardoned and returned to jail. Since there was a galleon in port that was leaving for India, local officials put him aboard it, under pain of death if he should return to Lisbon. He went to India, but not being able to contain his natural evil instincts, he began to steal where he had disembarked. Because he was not a prisoner, he later embarked on a galleon that was returning to Lisbon. There he was taken prisoner once again and was sentenced to the gallows—with particular note (as was told me by my uncle, who was present when the sentence was carried out) that the hanging take place exactly a year later than when they were going to carry it out previously, and at the same hour.

To whom are these two cases not striking? They certainly have given me much food for thought about the death that God has preordained for each person. Some may attribute the strange events to celestial influence, with which I have never agreed, because, although the stars may incline one toward a thing, they do not force it. This is why God gave man free will, so that he might conquer any evil intentions, because *sapiens domanibitur astris.*

No less notable was a development that occurred in this same year in Saltillo to a married man who was a native of Spain and was called something-or-other Vozmediano. He was very intelligent; I communicated with him many times. Although he lived for some time in this province, neither his wife nor his daughter (a maiden) ever mentioned their names or where they were from.

I shall not explain the motive for the cruel act that the mother and daughter committed. However, one night when the poor man was dining, they attacked him, striking him repeatedly in the head with an ax and killing him. In the silence of the night, the two carried him away. They left him in an irrigation ditch that was quite distant from the house but near a neighbor's house, so as to make it appear that he had been killed there.

Later the next morning, the lord mayor of Saltillo found out about the death and investigated. He took into custody the neighbors nearest the spot where the deceased was found. However, they could not verify anything. Some people gave careful attention to this case and examined the body before the authorities ordered it buried. They found drops of blood near the body and followed the track of blood, which led straight to the house where the deceased had lived. With this information, the woman and her daughter were taken into custody. Although they denied it at first, the two confessed when pressed and excused themselves with frivolous pretexts of the bad treatment that they had received from the deceased. The case was being prosecuted by written communication from the royal court of justice, and in this situation there was no shortage of people to assist the ones being held. Finally they escaped from the jail, so this enormous crime remained unpunished.

❧

Chapter 13 / Two Other Strange Occurrences

PRODIGIES and portents that merit the greatest wonder occur not only in very populous and rich provinces, but also in small provinces and settlements. The first occurred in the Pilón Valley Province to Captain Lorenzo de León, a person who is completely trustworthy. I have heard him recount the story many times. It took place before five witnesses, and is as follows: One Friday morning, when an Indian whom he had sent fishing brought him catfish ready to cook, they ordered that the table be set at the usual hour. At the table were seated five guests—one was Tomás de León, his uncle; another was Santiago Vela; and I do not know the names of the other three. They were brought the cooked fish on plates (for they were small). A small fish among those included in Captain Lorenzo de León's portion began moving about on the plate, making a valiant effort to swim and spilling the soup out of the plate and onto the table with a motion that frightened everyone. The captain refused to eat the fish, so his uncle, Tomás de León, ate it.

This event gave much food for thought because of the time between when the fish was taken out of the river and when it was put on to cook. If so much time had not passed, one might have thought that the fish still had some life in it. For we see, by experience, that a fish commonly stays alive a half hour after it is removed from water; although in the case mentioned, the fish could hardly maintain any spirit after it had been boiling for a good while. These are secret matters, reserved only for His Divine Majesty. Our understanding cannot grasp them, and thus my limited intellect precludes discoursing upon them.

So as not to separate into another chapter another portent that occurred in this province, I shall include it in this chapter. It was this: Because of the continuing war that the Indians of the north waged upon the province—attacking on all sides and carrying away as many horses as they could—a company of soldiers was formed to go out via El Alamo (which was a town of natives founded by Governor Don Martín de Zavala and located twelve leagues from Cerralvo). They were to destroy or capture the enemy. The company was under the command of Captain Alonso de León.

The expedition made camp for the night, and the soldiers kept vigil over the horses according to their watch. A soldier named Felipe de la Fuente, a mestizo, took the first watch. The blade of his sword (which was un-sheathed) began burning and changing color from the point to about a third of the way up the blade, as when blacksmiths take iron from the forge to hammer it on the anvil. Although the soldier and others succeeded in extinguishing the hot blade with their cloaks by taking hold of it between folds of their wet cloaks (it was drizzling), the blade did not lose the color of fire even after it cooled.

This continued for nearly an hour, as was certified by fourteen witnesses who saw it. Although many men of good judgment discussed this case, no one could think of any certain foundation from which such a portent could arise. I commented—not with fundamental reason—that it was because that sword had belonged to Governor Don Martín de Zavala, which I verified, and because the lowest-ranked soldier of the company was carrying it in his belt and had not held the sword in high regard. All this was by divine permission, if it may be said thus, because nothing happens by chance: as the philosopher says, *nihil fecit natura frustra*. As the sword had belonged to a famous man, Don Martín de Zavala, the soldier should have held it in higher regard.

The event, however, could also be interpreted as a prediction of the many wars that would occur in the province. His Divine Majesty commonly permits signs that indicate future events. Saint Augustine—in Book 10 of *The City of God*, Chapter 16—says that at some intervals He allows monsters, determined by His providence, that on most occasions signify some ill that is to come, and other prodigies and portents that always announce calamity. Saint Isidor[1] is of the same opinion in his *Etymologies*, Chapter 3.

Chapter 15 / Developments in the Province in 1667

THE administration of Governor León de Alza was not a period of great disturbances, because it seems that some relief was enjoyed, which was effected by the patrols of the four companies I have mentioned. But there was no relief for the spirits of those who were fond of Governor Don Martín de Zavala. In early 1667 a royal *cédula* was sent to this province from the queen, our lady,[1] that there should be repaid into the royal treasury offices at Zacatecas and San Luis the quantity of pesos Zavala received as his salary during the thirty-eight years of his government service. This amount had been paid to him at these same pay offices in conformity with an earlier *cédula*. Moreover, Zavala's property was to be confiscated and any amounts lacking were to be made up out of the property of the Count of Baños, who had ordered Zavala's salaries paid.

Andrés de Mendoza appeared at the confiscation. He attached all that was recognized to have belonged to Governor Zavala, which was very little. Great harm was done to the town of El Alamo as a result because the governor had left numerous sheep for the sustenance of its inhabitants. In Zacatecas, some large houses that had belonged to Governor Zavala's father, General Don Agustín de Zavala, were auctioned off for seven thousand pesos. They had cost forty-five thousand. And so it went with the deceased's other possessions. Had it happened to him while he was alive, doubtless it would have given him great sorrow, because he would have experienced the ill recompense for the great service that he had rendered to His Majesty in this province. As he had no descendant either in Spain or in the Indies, he had no defender in the case.

The cause was said to be the ease with which he had taken out all at once more than 100,000 pesos from the royal pay offices, that being the amount of salaries in this province. It could scarcely be repaid to the pay offices, because there remained no property other than a mining venture in Cerralvo and a number of sheep. The whole estate scarcely amounted to 3 or 4,000 pesos. What was taken out of the royal pay offices was more than 100,000, as may be gathered from the length of time he governed (which was thirty-eight years) and the rate of 2,000 pesos from the mines per year. This matter, as there was no legitimate party to defend it, went unmentioned. If it had been brought up and pleaded before His Majesty, and if the court of justice had declared that it would assist the deceased, I do not doubt that it would have defended his actions.

This year there was a change of government; the Royal Council named as governor of this province Don Nicolás de Azcárraga, knight of the Order of Santiago. He was a person of very great understanding. He took office on July 12. At the end of September General León de Alza, his predecessor, returned to Mexico City, accredited by his good work in the government.

~

Chapter 16 / The Indians of the North Continue Their Incursions

THE natural intrepidness of the Indians of the north precluded any end to their depredations. They did not content themselves solely with carrying away horses from the estates farthest from the city; in November an Indian party appeared about one league from Monterrey in the foothills of the Mitras range. After they were seen by nearby Indians, a squad of soldiers set out in search of them. The troops were able to capture one of the enemy; it is said that they killed one or two. The rest escaped into the mountains. According to the captured Indian, the party was of the Tetecuara nation,[1] and they did not appear again.

After he was notified of Captain Alonso de León's [the elder's] successes, Governor Don Nicolás de Azcárraga selected him as captain of the presidio of Cadereyta and lord mayor of that jurisdiction. The governor entrusted the peace of that area to him and hoped that De León would ensure peace in the north. Although many others sought the office of captain of the presidio, and some oaths of duty were taken, the governor did not admit them because they lacked petitions and intercessions from persons of authority.

At this time the Pelon[2] from the Papagayos Mountains and the Borrado from the Tamaulipas Mountains had also begun to commit offenses such as carrying away horses and attacking shepherds in the field. They stole live-stock from them as well. This impelled Captain Alonso de León to initiate two or three expeditions to the mountains, first with twenty-five, and then with thirty, soldiers. He paid their expenses and punished the guilty Indians. So for a time, those parts of the province remained peaceful.

The northern Indians, however, continued their actions. The next year, 1668, a band of Indians approached Monterrey and at less than a half-league from the city they carried away about eighty pack mules from two traders, Joseph Canales and Francisco García. On Monday morning, September 17, it was realized that the mules were missing, and the governor ordered Captain Alonso de León to present himself with as many soldiers as he could marshal. Despite the fact that it is seven leagues from Monterrey to Cadereyta, he arrived on Monday afternoon and began to track the Indians. On Wednesday, September 19, he reached the Indians before sundown, at a distance of more than sixty leagues. The captain's troops killed one and captured another, whom he hanged. He was unable to capture or kill any of the others because they had detected the troops and gone into the mountains by the time the Spaniards arrived. The mules were brought to the city and turned over to their owners. It was a great stroke of luck to have recovered the animals from so great a distance. Only one mule, which the Indians had eaten, was missing.

The enemy attacks did not stop because of this action. The same year [1668], two Las Salinas settlers—Alonso Rodríguez and Joseph de las Casas—went to settle the mines of Camaján, and a band of Indians attacked them and killed them with utter inhumanity in El Pozo Pass. It was not possible to verify who the aggressors were. If people who were at the mines had not come down to get provisions four days after this occurrence, the attack would not have become public because of the distance between the victims' home and the mines.

Captain Alonso de León went out again with another company in search of the Indians who had committed these killings, but he could not find any tracks. When the Indians of Punta de Papagayos again became restless, the captain returned to that post and pacified them.

Chapter 17 / Tetecoara Indian Attack

THE year 1669 seems to have been the one in which the most disturbance occurred in this province. A band of fifty Indians, from those who had risen up in the north, had entered the region; they wandered for many days from one mountain range to another searching for a target.

At the mouth of the San Juan River they killed an Indian shepherd and then they fled into the mountains. When the governor heard of the death, he formed a company in Monterrey, and another company went out with Captain Alonso de León [the elder], seeking the aggressors' trail. The Indians had reached the mountain called La Silla, which is very rugged and inaccessible. The company could accomplish nothing at all there because of the rugged terrain. When one of the friendly Indians with the captain approached, the enemy Indians killed him. Although the soldiers went out to save him, they were not able to make a move.

After several days, information was received that the Indians were again trying to enter this province by way of El Alamo[1]—which is twelve leagues from Cerralvo—in order to attack that town. To meet this threat the governor ordered that two companies be formed, one under the command of Captain Lázaro de la Garza and the other under Captain Alonso de León, who was also to serve as the commander of both units. The troops set out by way of El Alamo and went through the entire Iguana range, but they did not find a single one of the enemy. They searched for many days, because their patrol to ward off the evil intentions of the Indians was very important. (The event that was referred to earlier, namely, that the sword carried by one of the soldiers caught fire, occurred on this excursion. I set it down at that point so that it would accompany the other strange things that happened.)

At the end of that year, some of Captain Gregorio Fernández's attendants, who were coming down from the mines of Cerro de las Mitras, were attacked by the enemy Indians and wounded. Although the wounded were questioned about whether they had recognized any of the Indians, they said they had not recognized anyone. The governor asked Captain Alonso de León to form a company to follow the enemy trail. When camp was made in the vicinity of Mitras, an Indian boy came by who apparently was coming from outside the area. When the captain called to him and asked where he had come from, the Indian answered, "From Saltillo." When the boy was asked if he had seen any Indians or had any news of the enemy Indians, he said that in the spot called Agua Escondida (about five leagues from Monterrey) he had run into Miguelillo, who was an Indian from an *encomienda* of the heirs of Captain Diego de Villarreal, and ten other Indians. This Indian was also called "El Generalillo" [the Little General]. They had pressed the boy to go with them, but he had refused.

For this reason the governor wanted to go on to Las Salinas camp, where El Generalillo was from, so that Captain Alonso de León could travel to the other posts. But the governor decided not to go himself; instead he sent the captain with an order that all should be under *his* command. When he reached the camp, the captain found that the Indian called Juanillo, who was captain of the Cuauguijo[2] (a very warlike nation), had just arrived. He asked Juanillo if he knew where El Generalillo was (the latter was already suspected, although he was at peace in Las Salinas). Juanillo responded that El Generalillo had left Saltillo ten days before. The captain asked the camp's lieutenant to give him this Cuauguijo Indian and three or four other Indians to follow the trail. This was done, and when Juanillo was talking that night with Captain Alonso de León, he recited many fantastic stories. He said that in his country the Most Holy Virgin and Our Lord had appeared to them and had told them that the Spaniards should come three-by-three to see them; and that they would bring the captain to see God and he would sit down at His side—fictions that the astute and evil Indian had made up.

That night El Generalillo arrived with the ten Indians in his company. So he and the Cuauguijo and others were employed to follow the trail of those who had wounded Captain Fernández's attendants. They were warned that, if the friendly Indians who were in Las Salinas should be needed (these were the greatest enemies that there were—secretly), he was to send them to him.

Having gone about three leagues with the expedition, the captain decided to take the Cuauguijo and his two companions captive. Once their confessions were taken, the Indians told of a conspiracy that they had planned with Juan Carretero. Carretero, who was living in Saltillo, had a good reputation and was considered a friend of the Spaniards, El Generalillo, and others. However, he [Carretero] had advised his conspirators that within ten days all were to leave and carry away as many horses as they could and kill as many Spaniards as they could lay their hands on. The captives also confessed that, in various locations, more than ten thousand Indians had been called together to lay waste to this province and to Saltillo.

Captain Alonso de León secretly warned the governor and had the governor send him thirty men and a formal demand to leave for Saltillo to capture Juan Carretero and all the other members of this group. At the same time the captain was to go out to La Caldera, as it is called (twenty-five leagues from Monterrey), to face the Indians. These Indians were together on the mesa called Los Catujanes, the name of a very warlike Indian nation.[3]

Incidentally, I shall say that this mesa is a long hill, four or five leagues in length, which is on a plain. It is shaped like a flat table with a circumference of fourteen leagues, and it is little more than a quarter-league high.[4] Its physical nature makes it so unassailable that the very might of Artaxerxes[5] could not have conquered it. It is protected all around the top by boulders in the form of a rampart—a thing of wonder. It has only one entrance, on the northwest side, and the Indians affirm that above this everything is flat land and that there are water holes so as to be able to raise livestock.

Continuing with the attempt to capture the enemies, the first thing done was to charge everyone with the secret of the confession and to protect the Indians who had made it by separating them from the company. The captain sent to call the Indians of Las Salinas in secret, with two soldiers (because these Indians were friends, even though they were secretly enemies) to come out with them to the battle, the result of which will be told in the next chapter.

❧

Chapter 18 / Success in Capturing the Indians

CLEVERNESS and guile are very important in achieving success. Roman histories are full of successes that were achieved for this reason and because their captains were prudent. Julius Caesar, in the battle against Pompey, took the risk of crossing the Rubicon River in a boat and, disguised, inspected his opponent's whole army. In light of this, he did battle in the so-called Fields of Pharsala and vanquished him. Although it may seem a frivolous matter to bring up these considerations in all their detail, nevertheless, it seemed fitting to me to note it here.

Now, to continue our history. Once the Indians of Las Salinas had been brought to him, he [Captain Alonso de León, the elder] imprisoned them all and stationed a sufficient guard. At the same time, I went to Los Catujanes mesa, and a squad of soldiers went to Saltillo with the requisite letter for the lord mayor, Juan Antonio de Sarria, of Navarra. He was a lieutenant captain general who, perceptively, took care of the matter in such a way that, although the Indians under El Carretero's control were in different locations and estates, they were all taken prisoner with Carretero. This all occurred in one afternoon so that no one remained who could give notice inland. In the meantime, the captain went with all speed to Los Catujanes mesa. There he found a way to set an ambush at a convenient location. Thus the enemy was defeated, and he brought them to a place near Monterrey.

Camp was made a short league from Monterrey, where the governor was waiting. The arrival of the troops from Saltillo, with the prisoners, was also awaited; this took very little time. Thus in eleven days this operation, so much desired by all, was completed. When it was learned that General Juan Antonio [de Sarria] was approaching with the prisoners, a solemn reception was arranged, with one hundred soldiers from this province, accompanied by the governor, going out to meet him with all-white horses. There was a great round of applause and other festivities, but I shall not recount the details so as not to extend this history.

To completely verify the plot the Indians had planned, a formal case was brought against the aggressors. They were found guilty and confessed. However, Governor Don Nicolás de Azcárraga was of a benign and merciful nature and had pity on them. Although he could have sentenced the fifty prisoners to death, he had them draw lots and hanged only six. The others were exiled to Zacatecas. They were condemned to personal service, in shackles; this was carried out.

The lord mayor took Carretero, with others, to Saltillo to be tried, so that he might serve as an example to the Indians of that town. When those who had been condemned to personal service in the mills of Zacatecas—they were being escorted by the soldiers of this province—were passing through the jurisdiction of Mazapil,[1] the lord mayor of that station ordered them freed, I do not know on what pretext. So they were released with no punishment at all. Their action resulted both in difficulties concerning this case and in a more forceful prosecution of the war, because these murderers, highway robbers, and thieves of livestock and horses had been given their liberty.

I remember that, while all the guilty Indians were prisoners in the camp, a Carmelite monk who taught theology in his order came there. He had entered this province to beg for alms and already was well informed of the guilt of the Indians. Seeing the Indians tied in a chain gang, he said publicly (and most heard him) that it was a pity not to hang all of them. A Franciscan monk, who also taught theology and was retired from this province of our Lady of Zacatecas, was present and replied to his observations. He (the Carmelite friar) responded that he would propound in the schools that which he had pronounced. Finally, after some discussion concerning the matter, all was quiet.

I shall not pass over (because I recall that which I have heard old settlers of this province tell) what took place in the year 1632. The Province of Zacatecas had chosen a monk named Fray Francisco de Ribera, a theology instructor, as guardian of Cerralvo. As he was coming to his guardianship he found on the road a chain gang of Indians who were being marched to the city of Zacatecas to serve time for their offenses. It seemed to him that the Indians were innocent, and he had pity on them. He even said that it was a known injury that was being done to them and that the matter was to be laid on the conscience of the governor. Finally, before he came to this province, the governor received the news of what this padre had stated.

Ribera arrived at Monterrey and, in order to go to Cerralvo, awaited the opportunity to have an escort, because the twenty-league route led through a completely unpopulated area. So he joined soldiers and other individuals who were taking five hundred rams and ewes to Cerralvo. When they reached a post called Urquiza, a force of more than six hundred Indians came out and killed two soldiers before their eyes and began taking away the livestock and all that they were carrying. Although the padre cried out to them and urged them not to continue taking the livestock, the Indians did not stop. The padre, very surprised by the occurrence and sorry to have had compassion on such evil scoundrels, reached Cerralvo with those who were still alive. The cruelties that the Indians committed upon the dead bodies horrified and frightened him.

Since on this occasion the municipal council of Monterrey was sending a request to the governor to stiffen the penalties of the captured Indians, the governor ordered a review of all the writs, reports, and other papers touching upon the offenses, murders, and thefts those Indians committed. By way of deliberation, the governor passed the papers on to Padre Ribera, the instructor, with the request of the municipal council. Since this request was well founded and since the crimes that many nations of Indians had committed were mentioned, it seemed fitting to include the request in this history, with the opinion that Padre Ribera, the instructor, expressed concerning everything.

❧

Chapter 19 / The Request from the Municipal Council of Monterrey to the Governor

MY intent is not to prolong the history by including things that seem not to be worthwhile. But so that the history may be understood with the justifications that existed from the beginning, and the basis that has existed for the punishments carried out on various occasions against these blind natives, I did not want to omit this. Thus the [1632] request of the municipal council follows:

Request

In the city of our Lady of Monterrey, of the New Province of León, on the twenty-first day of the month of May of 1632, the justice, municipal council, and government agree as follows: Captain Rodrigo Ruiz, lord mayor and military captain in it and in its jurisdiction, by the king, our lord; Captain Alonso de Treviño and Diego de Montemayor, district magistrates; Gregorio Fernández and Antonio Durán, councilmen; being in the chambers where they customarily hold their councils, and having gathered and congregated to confer on things relating to the service of His Majesty, the welfare and utility of the land, said:

During the past thirty years, the Chichimeco natives of the Aguata nation, the Tepehuan, Cucuyama, Matolagua, Quibonoa, Tacuanama, Icabia, Cayaguagua, Quien, Guinaimo, and the Borrado of the Valley of San Juan,[1] and many other nations in the confines of this province, have been accustomed to rising up and denying the recognition and obedience that they have pledged His Majesty. In these uprisings, the natives have caused notable and growing damages. Yet they have never approached the impudence that in the space of four uninterrupted months they showed this location. This was notorious and very sufficiently verified and proved by the confessions of some who were captured, to whom justice has been done. Without any fear (and since they are so crafty, they were even used to coming to the borders of the town of Saltillo), the enemy fell upon the pack team and Pedro Camacho's people,[2] who were camped for the night. If a black and Indian mixed-blood who was driving the team had not escaped and left the mules in a secure location, the enemy Indians would have killed and robbed the people.

They carried off all the meal and corn that the pack train was bringing to this province, and what the enemy could not load and take away, they dumped and scattered. The Indians decided among themselves to hide in the Vivanco Pass, near Encinillas; this was a strong pass and one disposed to their convenience. From there they would intercept the carts,[3] wagons, and pack teams that might enter. If their plan had been put into execution, this whole province, including the nearby towns, would have been totally ruined. The enemy did not do it because two of the most warlike captains who were involved in it, namely, El Malacui and El Calabazo, were captured and brought to justice.

The enemy then gathered again in the Salinas Valley and killed two Indian laborers. A few days later—running through the whole land, premeditatedly, to steal and kill—the enemy Indians found the Indians who were friendly to Captain Joseph de Treviño and shot two of them with arrows. Going on to Santa Catalina Pass, two leagues from Monterrey, they struck the camp of Captain Colmillo's Indians who, out of devotion to His Majesty, were peacefully sowing seed. The enemy killed an Indian called Tomás and his wife and killed two others by shooting them with arrows. They carried away three Indian women, whom they killed on the road on the way back to their land. They put a Christian Indian girl in a shack and set it on fire and she died. Also, in a raid against the Indian sheepherders belonging to the owners of the San Francisco ranch, they captured an Indian and, casting ignominy upon the form with which the law sentences evildoers to their just deserts, they hanged him.

Going on to greater offenses, the Indians convened a very large gathering and raided the people and soldiers who were transporting more than nine hundred head of livestock, and at the post called Papagayos Chicos these Indians killed them. The enemy shot three friendly Indians with arrows and left them for dead and stripped naked the Spaniards they killed, namely, Juan Durán and Lázaro Ruiz. There at Papagayos Chicos the Indians distributed among themselves the livestock as well as the clothing, animals, coats of arms, harquebuses, and everything else they captured. Various Indians then left for their own camps. All this was seen by the Indians who were left for dead and who, once out of danger, went to give the news to Sr. Don Martín de Zavala, governor and captain general of this province.

A little more than a month later, gathering again, the enemy Indians raided the carts. Confronting sixteen soldiers who formed an escort to accompany the carts, they killed Agustín de Urquiza and Juan Baptista de Aldape, brother of Martín de Aldape, and a friendly Indian boy. They also carried away more than four hundred head of sheep, with no other violations than those that they had perpetrated a few days before.

All of this has been caused by the situation of the Indians who, in conformity with the act of war declared against the Indian nations because of their uprisings and crimes, have escaped and returned from the cities of Zacatecas, San Luis, Fresnillo, Cuencamé, and other more distant provinces. In addition, the Indians have become so clever and astute, and with the courage and valor of Spaniards, that they have learned about the Spaniards' plans. So today the other Indians, taking these returnees to heart, use them and do what they never had done before, even when they numbered twice as many as now and had among them—as they did—braver captains and leaders.

Concerning all of this, and so that the most important part may be remedied, the suitable manner is to present this information to the governor: that the Indians commit more crimes and do not serve the time for which they have been sentenced, but instead break out of the prisons in which they had been held. They return and cause irremediable offenses by their murders, and they impede commerce that Cerralvo (where Your Lordship is posted) should have with this one [Monterrey].

It is not expected that there is any remedy other than executing the punishment of the Indian nations with all rigor, carrying it out without mercy. For in natural defense there should be, by all rights, a strengthening of the penalties of the act of war. It should be declared with a new writ that the Indians who are of age should die for their guilt, or at least that their right hand should be cut off and their feet crippled. The women and young Indians from five to twenty-five should be forced to leave this province for the time that Your Lordship may determine and judge. As these latter Indians are more docile, one can root in them the Spanish customs and they can lose the natural evil of their fathers. Outside of this province, they might attain the usefulness of being reared in complete politeness and instructed in the matters of our holy Catholic faith, and they will come to be Christians. This cannot be achieved in this city of Monterrey or in Cerralvo. No matter how strong a guard is put on them, the Indians will return, because they are so near their homeland. Then they will tell everything they have seen and heard from the Spaniards.

These offenses will be averted if Your Lordship executes what this writ requests of him, because thereby a very fixed peace will come to be effected. Moreover, this province will be made secure, and there will not be unceasing protests of the harm to this republic. At all times in formulating the foregoing, what was appropriate for the province was requested by those charged with its protection. Therefore let this writ be turned over to one of the councilmen of this city, so that it may be made well known to Your Lordship. Thus they provided and signed it—*Rodrigo Ruiz. Alonso de Treviño. Diego de Montemayor. Gregorio Fernández. Antonio Durán.* Before me, *Francisco Sánchez de Barrera*, scribe of the municipal council.

When the councilman had carried this writ to Cerralvo and the governor had seen it, in conformity with what I have mentioned, he gathered all the papers and reports dealing with the war and turned them over to Francisco de Ribera, who drew up a writ in the following form:

In the town of Cerralvo, of the government of the New Kingdom of León, on the twenty-sixth day of May of 1632, before Señor Don Martín de Zavala, governor and captain general of the aforesaid kingdom and its provinces, by the king, our lord: Antonio Durán, councilman of the city of Monterrey, presented the writ that the court and council of Monterrey ordered. The writ was turned over to him so that, as a councilman, he should present it before Your Lordship and should request that, because it is suitable for peace, security, and the punishment of the offenses and murders that are referred to in it, Your Lordship should judge what is contained in the writ. Concerning it, he asked for justice in the name of the city of Monterrey, because of the offenses carried out in his district.

Without ignoring the justification with which he has declared the punishment that is presently made to the Indian nations named in the writ, the governor said that for what is newly presented, with the means that are requested in it, there should be set down once and for all the punishment of these barbarians, and that the minors should receive the advantages that are proposed in the writ. He ordered the disclosure of the writ and reports made, the provisions and other proceedings, opinions, and arrangements that have been made so many times to the Indian nations to Prior Fray Francisco de Ribera, instructor in holy theology; and that once His Paternity sees it, he should give his opinion in regard to what is requested in the writ, and he should order that which may be just. Thus he provided and signed it—*Don Martín de Zavala*. Before me, *Juan de Abrego*, secretary of government, justice, and war.

Chapter 20 / The Opinion of
Fray Francisco de Ribera

JESUS, Mary. It is with difficulty, if at all, that one can make war at present against certain rebel Indians in a manner consistent with the request that the municipal council of the city of Monterrey has made to the governor of this Province of León: a manner of waging war by which, they assure us, the land will remain at peace.

If I were asked, I should say what in God and in good conscience I felt concerning the justice that could and should be done concerning many Indians of diverse nations who for some time now have been in rebellion, committing notable offenses (and at present greater than ever). They are murderers of Spaniards and of peaceful Indians; they have stolen great numbers of livestock, mules, mares, and horses, as is told more lengthily and distinctly in the reports this writ contains. So now this whole province suffers grave oppression. Commerce with the people who bring provisions is impeded; livestock and horses are decimated; defense is impeded; the population is decreased; and one lives in great hardship, anxiety, fright, and continuous danger. This has caused an impediment to the service of God and to the benefit of the souls of the peaceful Indians, who are numberless, by instructing them in the holy Catholic faith. It has caused the loss of the royal 20 percent taxes from four mines that are in Cerralvo and others in Las Salinas. All due to the anxiety and danger that continually, night and day, the population experiences from these perverse and blind natives. As it is, the work in the mines and in the charcoal kilns has ceased because, at various times, assaults have been made there. Many Spaniards and friendly servant Indians have been killed; the livestock that was there has been stolen; and the shacks have been set afire, with everything lost and ruined.

Therefore, in conformity with this and with the reports that have been made, all for my examination, I say that Señor Don Martín de Zavala, governor and captain general of Nuevo León, not only can but should, in good conscience, proclaim the writ, according to and in conformity with what the municipal council of the city of Monterrey requests. In the first place, they are individuals of good judgment and of long experience in this province. Second, this province has been notably harmed, both in general and in particular, and should be compensated for its injury.

Having received the holy Catholic faith and given obedience to the kings of Castile, the Indians are not only public highway robbers but also declared enemies both of the Spaniards and of the Divine Majesty. They trample underfoot the holy faith that they have received and professed. They uproot the crosses in many locations where the Spaniards have placed them and they treacherously kill people. In other places, they have dragged the crosses away and broken them in bits and pieces. At many and diverse times for the last thirty years they have never maintained peace for even six months. Instead, they violated it as soon as an occasion arose for committing their customary robberies, and then they committed greater ones.

We have lived incautiously with the Indians. We have pardoned them many times and have tried to go on by gentle means (in case they might get tired and settle down). This was one reason that the settlements did not expand in this province, and that the province [did not] show great growth, either in ranches of tilled land and livestock or in mining camps. (It is a very opportune land for all this.) Another reason was the omission and laxity that there has been in punishing the Indians. Therefore, they became worse and committed many atrocious crimes and outrages, which they continue to commit. This menaces the Spaniards so that, until the Indians stop, the Spaniard will have no rest. One Indian says to other Indians, to encourage them, "There is nothing to fear from the Spaniards. If they kill us, we'll kill them as well; we will swallow up their properties. No one should be afraid, because at most they'll take us away and place us in Zacatecas for a few years." So they become restless and attract to their company many other Indian nations and make *tlatole*[1] for them so that they will follow.

Because they see that no other form of punishment or harshness is used to stop their daily crimes, the Indians decide at every step to commit greater ones, as occurred about three months ago.

More than six hundred Indians gathered in the Papagayos Mountains, on the road from Santa Lucía to Cerralvo. There they killed two Spaniards, shot with arrows other friendly Indians who were coming with them, and stole more than nine hundred head of sheep, goats, and rams.

Then within a month, near the same post, when about eleven Spaniards were coming along (and I with them) with three carts and up to five hundred head of livestock, a great number of Indians emerged from an ambush that they had set next to the road. They killed two Spaniards and a friendly Indian and carried away all the livestock. The Spaniards were crying out to me, in this tight spot, to hear their confession. Not content with that, but rather with acts of greater impudence, Indians went away one night, not fifteen days later, to Las Carboneras, a league from Cerralvo. There they stole more than two hundred head of sheep, killed some friendly Indians, and shot others with arrows. The Spaniards escaped with great risk—although they had harquebuses and other arms—because the number of the Indians was so great. The Indians set fire to the shacks. They also visited the mines at this same time, to steal whatever they might find there, as they had done at other times. Some Indians who were captured on this occasion confessed to such a motive.

Then immediately thereafter, the Indians decided to steal the sheep from San Francisco. This amounted to more than eight thousand head of livestock. If the defenders had not come out—of whom one died and another was shot with arrows—they would doubtless have stolen them. Then the town would have perished there and this whole province would have suffered notable harm.

The natives were not content with all this, but in less than a month's time, Captain Guapale, a baptized Indian, who was conversant with Spanish and was their leader, convened a gathering of more than eight hundred Indians to ruin and destroy this town of Cerralvo. He desisted from the attack because another Indian was of a different opinion. It was at a time that we had a weakened defense. Here it seems that divine mercy worked for all of us to deliver us from their arrows.

All this I have experienced here within the space of three

months. In accordance with this, let there come to live here for
a time whoever may be of a different opinion than mine. First, so
that in time he may not be of a different opinion, he will see that his
own opinion will change, as I changed my own opinion after I considered all these matters. And second, if he does not change his
mind, that will in effect give the Indians all liberty and power over
the lives and properties of the Spaniards. That will tie the hands
of the Spaniards, impeding their defense and putting an end to
everything.

These Indians, full of ingratitude, do not cease doing evil except when they are unable to do it. As for carrying out treacheries,
there are no soldiers of Flanders more adept. Justice has not been
served in such a long time; there have been so many diverse occasions in which rigorous punishment should have been used against
them. Instead, care was given to them. For example, the governor
spent on various occasions a great number of pesos to give them
clothing and food, just to pacify them. In response, they never tried
to maintain the peace. Instead, they always took the kindness as a
justification to steal more and wage greater war. So the governor not
only can but should in good conscience act, not only as the municipal council of the city of Monterrey proposes and requests, but
with much greater rigor. The lack of punishment, in so many and
diverse ways, and the superfluous and imprudent laxity that has
been practiced with them have caused many and notable damages
in Nuevo León.

I test this conclusion, first, with the most erudite Medina, Dzip.
(*sic.*) 39, where he says the following words: *Mortifere peccat prin-*
cips Cibelum rei publice falentem ad fidem conservandam at enim eo
nom espirituale bonum necesarium non gerat precipue; etta. This
very grave doctor could not be speaking more apropos of this war if
he were at this point looking at all the things he points out. So he
obliges the prince to wage war, because without this war the republic will end as the enemies are taking lives and seizing the ranches,
and with it the faith; for once the Spaniards are exterminated, there
will be no one to preach good to the enemy Indians in the mountains. Although some Indians may be killed in the war, it is more advantageous for the other Indians even to be made slaves for a few

years than to spend their whole life in the mountains and woods, with their insults and thievery, as public enemies of their neighbors and of the Divine Majesty. When these areas are finally pacified, there will be innumerable souls in this large and rich province to communicate spiritual well-being to them. At present, because of the Indians and the danger present in traveling about the land, the faith has ceased to be communicated. Therefore, the governor should make war on the Indians to subjugate and pacify them.

Further, as long experience has taught, there has not been found, nor is there now found, a more convenient and effective way to subdue and pacify the Indians. Not only should war and punishment be used, but also, in good conscience, the preceding recommendation [concerning minors] should be used and put into effect, for what it is worth. The recommendation is well known, and with it there will be achieved, without doubt, the effect of what is attempted.

I examine the consequence. Does this land belong to the kings of Spain or not? The second alternative no one dares to suggest, because it means being thrown out of the land and exiled from the kingdom. Also, it will oppose the power that the supreme pontiff has to give them. As they were able to conquer the other lands of the Indies as theirs—because His Holiness Alexander VI had given it to them—they may also conquer this one. That the pope could give it to them is proved very learnedly and extensively by Fray Bartolomé de las Casas at the beginning of the book that he wrote against the conquests of the Indies.[2] So, they may conquer it as theirs and throw their rebellious and treacherous enemies out of it.

If it is answered that in conformity with the papal brief of Alexander VI in which the empire of the Indies is conceded to the kings of Castile and León, the Indians should be conquered by gentle and charitable means, cultivating the souls with the divine word, I respond, interpreting the brief, that the intention of Alexander VI was that the kings of Castile and León should conquer the Indies in the described ways, if they can conquer in that manner. However, since there is no possibility of that, the Spaniards should conquer the Indians using the ways and means necessary for conquering them.

It is evident that this is the intent of the pontiff. Of all the conquests in the Indies, none were carried out according to the letter of the brief. This is evident from Fray Bartolomé de las Casas, who mentions all of them. Nevertheless, the supreme pontiffs have let all these pass, and continue to let them pass, as justified. The kings of Castile, for this reason, have these lands as their own, in whatever way they may have been conquered. So they were taken in conformity with the intention and will of the pope.

This truth is still more evident, because in them the Spaniards were favored with help and assistance from heaven and with supernatural means when in the greatest danger. This is evident from Father Joseph de Acosta,[3] in the *Moral History of the Indies*, Book 7, Chapters 26 and 27. In New Mexico at the present time—according to what is recorded in the record that Father Manso,[4] *procurador* of New Mexico, printed in Mexico City in the year 1631—there have also been some miracles in favor of the Spaniards. So with just title and clear conscience, the kings of Castile hold the Indies, although they may not have been conquered in accordance with the letter of the brief. God favors and assists them in the conquests even if they may have been as cruel and bloody as the cited author, Fray Bartolomé de las Casas, states. His vicar gave the lands to the Spaniards in divine power and virtue.

Therefore, with the same security of conscience, the Spaniards may conquer this province of León with the means necessary to achieve the goal of the conquest. If this land cannot be conquered with the necessary means by which the others were conquered, His Majesty will have it if he conquers it not in good conscience, and, consequently, all the other lands. This, according to Donadillo, is not to be said. So neither shall I say the first, unless he should say that there is another new concession and another new brief for the conquest of this province. For that, he should show it. This he will not do, because there are not, nor have there been, more than two briefs, in which the supreme pontiffs generally concede the empire of the Indies to the kings of Castile and León—without making a difference of conquest in this or in the other. Therefore, His Majesty may conquer it with the necessary means and hold it with as much good conscience as the others are held. For this purpose, it is necessary to put into effect the means that the municipal council of Monterrey proposes. Therefore, the governor should use them, in order to subdue and pacify the land, and do with diligence and care what the municipal council directs, and what His Majesty so much charges.

This is the more evident because almost all the lands of the Indies that have been conquered in this way were already settled with towns, villas, and cities. They were living under a government and in a polite manner, following natural law. Nevertheless, the ways and means by which they were conquered have been allowed to pass. So with still more reason the Indians that are at war in the Province of León may be conquered. Although the majority are baptized, the Indians induce the others to rise up and lose their obedience to the kings of Castile, which they gave many times. The Indians do not, all and sundry, follow any law, because after being baptized they abandoned the gospel that they received, as is clear from the contempt that they show the crosses. Moreover, there is not found nor has there been found another law among all the Indians of this kingdom. The Indians use neither rite nor ceremonies with idols and false gods. They live like animals, without a nationality or a permanent dwelling, or goods or clothing other than bow and arrow. Like savages they sustain themselves on roots and herbs from the mountains and fields, and on the horses and livestock they steal from the Spaniards. The Indians are very hostile to working, inclined to rob and steal what they can, and capable of great cleverness in carrying out treachery, as is clear from their deeds.

With this justification the governor may, and should, conquer and subject the Indians by the stated means. If necessary, still more rigorous ones should be employed than those proposed by the municipal council of Monterrey, and than those with which the other lands of the Indies have been conquered, because the other areas were populated with a government and followed natural law. Otherwise, the war and conquest would be superfluous and of no advantage. Instead, notable damages would be incurred at great expense, as has been the case until now. Over forty years His Majesty and Señor Agustín de Zavala, with the governor and the other conquerors, have spent more than three hundred thousand pesos.

All this has served for nothing more than to have many Spaniards die far from their homeland at the hands of these Indians for whom they have worked. In the past, when the land was much more peaceful (although we were always at war), there was a great abundance of livestock and horses. This was so much the case that there is a man in the land from whom it is said they stole, over time, nine thousand head of cattle—to name but one example. Therefore, if justice had been done regarding all these thefts, this province would be so rich and abundant that Spaniards could draw out of it, as they did then, a great quantity of livestock and horses for many other lands. For on this occasion, and many others, great numbers of Indians went to the houses of the settlers of the city of Monterrey and of this town of Cerralvo to take away all the livestock and horses and whatever else they could from the houses and burned the houses. The owners were wounded and driven away from their houses and from their estates. Therefore, who can doubt that those who do these deeds should be conquered and punished, as public robbers and as traitors to His Majesty for having violated the oaths of obedience that they gave him?

I examine this question in the stated manner because, for the war to be legitimate and to be waged with a clear conscience, four things are required, according to what the theologians say: legitimate authority, sufficient cause, good intentions, and convenient means.

The legitimate authority lies in the prince or whoever has equivalent status. Such is evident from Saint Augustine, Book 22, "Against Ostentation," Chapter 75, where it says: *ordo naturalis et acomodatus ac exposit; etta.* I have not set down all the Latin, because it was so badly written that it could not be understood.

The sufficient cause, and that which justifies the war, is to be known injury. See the same saint on question 10, concerning Joshua, where he says: *Justa vella definire solent quod; etta.*

The worthy intention will be the intention based on the preceding. The prince should attempt only to execute justice and restore peace, thereby punishing the offense that disturbed it.

The fourth condition, which is the convenient means, consists in waging the war with the least damage possible, without harming the innocent, except in case one stumbles by chance and it cannot be otherwise; as the same Saint Augustine says, Book 22, "Against Ostentation," Chapter 74: *nocendi Cupiditas, etta.*

That which should be censured with good reason in war, says Augustine, is the desire to do harm; the cruelty of vengeance; the belligerent and implacable spirit; the ferocity of rebellion; the greed for dominion; and other things similar to these, which justice prohibits. All of these immediately cease in the prince who at present is waging the war, as is clear to this whole province. It is clearly advisable to leave off the neglect and pardoning of the crimes of the enemies against whom it was reasonable to use war with the means that now are set down. Therefore, not only can he do it with justice, but he should do it in good conscience. For that reason His Majesty has put him here.

This is still more evident from the conditions indicated by the theologians, because all of them find themselves in this authority. If the first be considered, no one can say that it is lacking to the governor, because one of those to which he agreed before His Majesty was that it was necessary to pacify and subdue the land. To achieve this, he was not limited in the necessary means nor could he be limited in them, because that would make necessary an implied contradiction. The second, which is sufficient cause, also is notable in this whole province, because these Indians have given so many reasons. That the Indians should be punished with great rigor as a penalty for themselves and an example to the others is evident from reports made.

Good intentions, which is the third, are no less notable, because for many years, when the Indians made peace many times, and when the governor had accepted it, nevertheless, they never maintained it. Instead of punishing them, as was reasonable, he, in order to pacify the land—and not trusting them—did not do it with the just punishment that their crimes called for. Instead, to persuade them to remove themselves, His Lordship spent a great sum of pesos on several occasions to give them clothing and food liberally, without pressing them to work. With all these false peaces, and gifts they received, he never waged war against them with the penalty of death, but with the exile of some years outside of this province for those eighteen years old and older, and inside the province for those younger, so that in that time they should be instructed, both in the holy Catholic faith and in politeness.

Chapter 21 / Fray Ribera's Opinion Continues

CONTINUING with his opinion, Instructor Fray Francisco de Ribera says this:

Convenient means, which is the fourth condition, has been used by many and various governors for forty years to attract the Indians to peace and tranquillity, to subdue their land, and to be better able to communicate to them the light of the holy gospel. This has availed nothing. Since the municipal council of the city of Monterrey has examined it [the question of convenient means] with healthy and mature agreement, the council has signed its name to the effect that there is no means that is convenient other than the one that the council proposes to the governor, with the request that His Lordship execute this means. Therefore, he may execute it without stinting. However, a very serious problem would arise if the governor were to be remiss in observing the council's request. Necessity requires the action and the goal of what is attempted by it, and the action is expected with assurance. Hereby, says Saint Augustine, letter 207, one seeks and attempts peace: *pacem habere dabet; etta.*

So the just war that is occasioned brings with it peace. The peace imprudently conceded—as is the one that has been conceded so many times to the Indians, since they never honored it, and only requested it so as to be better able to carry out their thefts—results in there always being war. The lengthy experience in this province has shown many times (and continually shows) more bloody war: killing as many as they can, robbing the estates of Spaniards, and setting fire to their houses. So the governor should carry out the aforesaid means to cleanse and deliver this province from so much oppression, fatigue, and labor as this perverse and blind people cause, or he should leave office. Being lax in punishing such crimes will mean that the Spaniards will continue to be extinguished, and that the province will be left without succor and deserted.

I support this with the writings of Father Remesal,[1] who wrote in the *History of Chiapa* [*sic*] and *Guatemala*, Book 10, Chapter 63, that it was just for the king, our lord, to make war on the Pustecas and other Indians, not because they are infidels, or because they eat human flesh, but because they burned many churches in the neighboring towns; broke the holy images; sacrificed children who were the offspring of Christians to their idols on the holy altars and on the cross itself; and committed many other evils. To this responded the very pious and merciful fathers that they greatly loved the Indians, yet that not only was it just for the king, our lord, to make war on them, but that in good conscience he was obliged to do so; and that in order to defend his subjects totally, the king was obliged to destroy the Lacandones and Pactlas.

No fewer dangers are shown by the determination and manner with which these Indians continue to accomplish their thefts and insults. This is clear from the reports made of so many murders of Spaniards and peaceful Indians. Because they are friends of the Spaniards, the friendly Indians are killed by the warlike Indians, although the two may be of the same nation, camp, and kin. The warlike Indians steal large herds of livestock and horses, burn whatever houses they can, show contempt for the holy crosses, and say to the Spaniards whom they kill at the point that they wish to put them to death (out of mockery and derision and contempt for the holy cross) that they should say "Jesus." The Indians then hit them on the neck to make them bow their heads and violently and irreverently give the cross to them to kiss—even though the Indians are baptized and speak Spanish.

So with a clear conscience, the governor is obliged to punish and conquer these Indians and to subject them by any necessary means, even if it means to destroy and exterminate them; because they, as declared enemies, are trying to destroy and exterminate the Spaniards. This they continue showing by their deeds. In addition, some Indians who were captured have legally confessed and declared it. Therefore, in conformity with all this, His Lordship should provide and pronounce an act of war to be waged against the Indians, at least in conformity with and in the spirit of the request that is made him by the municipal council of the city of Monterrey.

This is what in God and in good conscience I feel and answer, under the declaration that I make, with all the requirements that in case of danger of death the priests should fulfill. In this it is not my intent to advise or influence the proclaiming of an act, nor the execution thereof, in which death or the cutting off of a part of the body should result, without responding to the proposed difficulty.

In this Town of Cerralvo, where there are few books, on the fourth day of the month of June of 1632.—Fray Francisco de Ribera, instructor in theology.

❧

Chapter 22 / The Governor Submits This Opinion to the City of San Luis Potosí

THE reader will know well, even though he may be of mediocre reasoning power, that Father Ribera's opinion is well founded. The father seems to have exercised his understanding well, citing Saint Augustine and other authors to support the just war being waged against these Indians. Strong foundations are given with which the father supports his proposals and he employs firm arguments. Using his clear understanding, he soundly defended his position with Governor Don Martín de Zavala, which is publicly recognized. It is also publicly known that besides the studies that Governor Zavala completed in Salamanca, he could speak many languages and had traveled in Italy, Flanders, and other places. So, he was educated in all matters. Nevertheless, he [Zavala] did not resolve to execute the act of the municipal council. He sent the opinion to the city of San Luis Potosí, so that others of the Order of Saint Francis would see it and would say at the end of it what they felt, in order to further assure his conscience. In response to this, they gave their [opinions] at the end of it as follows:

Approval

The authors who deal at length with just war and its qualities and conditions are Saint Thomas, 2–2 question, 44; *Caeitanus ed sequas Valina*, disp. 3-9-16 asor, Volume 3, Book 2, Chapter 7; Covarrubias, part. 2, & 9, n. 1 *et sequentibus*; *Bict. de Veri beli*, Chapter 15, no. 15, *et sumonistoe, Verbo belum*. These rationales and arguments were touched on briefly by Father Instructor Francisco de Ribera in his opinion and verdict. Therefore, without verbosely giving more reasons than the ones previously advanced or wearying with infinite authorities on the two bodies of law and with masters in all faculties, one may judge and consider the war against the Indians as just and punishing them in conformity with the occasions in which they may give reason therefore.

There is only left to be feared—and in no small measure—the insolences, cruelties, and atrocious acts into which the soldiers, having the license of public authority against the enemies, thrust themselves. These acts are well proved and experienced in all the conquests of the Indies. Perhaps it is for these sins that all these provinces today suffer the calamities and punishments that God has sent us. For although in the public battles of opposed armies there appeared persons and saints—and the Saint among Saints, holiest Mary—to favor and assist them, nevertheless, this did not occur in the private actions of the soldiers, who did them without fear of God and without the aim and goal of serving Him. Whereby the governor should give great forethought and reflection to this harm, with salutary means that would occasion him glory and honor, as a Christian captain. He should execute the procedures and means appropriate to peace and security and safe passage of the innocent. Because, at the least, women, maidens, and children are innocents; they are those who do the least harm and suffer the most on these occasions. In addition, many adult male Indians will be on our side, and it is necessary to support and defend them.

As to the rest, let there be noted the not-insubstantial distinction between the enemy's coming to look for me in my house and my going to kill him in his. In the first case, all laws defend me, and in the second they tie my hands so that I do not accomplish all that I might. Finally, the proposed war is just, and since the governor has sufficient mandate for it, without recognizing another superior, he can proclaim and make changes in it. Wherewith may the Lord give him, over and above bodily victory, that best and most praiseworthy one, which is the true knowledge of our faith and its reception in those barbarous and rebellious souls. In this case let there be understood the same declaration as that made by the father instructor, in virtue and condition of which all those present sign.—*Fray Alonso Rebollo. Lic. Don Juan de Herrera Sandoval.*[1] *Fray Alonso de la Mota. Fray Pedro Rubio. Fray Pedro Venegas. Fray Pedro de Cabrera. Fray Antonio Mondragón. Fray Andrés del Campo. Fray Cosme Martínez. Fray Pedro de Prado. Fray Nicolás de Salazar.*

When the opinion with the foregoing approval had been returned to the hands of Governor Don Martín de Zavala, he passed it on to the father instructor Fray Francisco de Ribera, so that he might see it. Having seen it, he added the following:

Esteeming the grace that the very reverend fathers have done me in signing this opinion, attending jointly with me to the service of the two Majesties, advantage of the souls, and common good of that extensive kingdom; with all this, in case someone may be pleased to read it and be free of all doubt, I shall respond with all brevity to what they seem to show as giving appearances of reservation, so that I may remain free of all negligence in this matter. As to the authors they cite who deal with war, I say that I would have cited them if I had had the books here. Because of this lack, I say in the last paragraph, next-to-last phrase of this opinion, that there are few books in this post. The books are so few that there are none that expressly deal with war.

Regarding the comment that I touched briefly on the reasons they bring forth, I answer first that, as I did not get them from books, but from the reasons that my understanding dictated, it is a small matter that they did not go to such length; and additionally, I am a friend of brevity when it is sufficient. In addition, the reasons are not touched on so briefly that after having read or heard them once, one would not remain satisfied—as the fathers remained, because they did not add any new ones, there being paper left over here to be able to add them.

The comment that they [my opinions] allow fear of the atrocious cruelties that the soldiers commit on public authority does not bear on the subject for two reasons. First, because this is *per accidens* and is not to be placed before that of *per se* nor to cause one to refrain from waging war when necessity requires it. Besides these, there are things and occurrences that those in charge cannot remedy—especially in this province, because the war is in rugged and extensive mountain ranges where one cannot find at hand the prince who governs so as to succor and defend the town, and there must not be killings while he goes to other places. The other reason is because of the third condition placed in this opinion. Here he points out that for the war to be just, it should be waged with the least harm that can be done. The governor always attempts that, as much as it falls to him, if it is not a matter that His Lordship cannot remedy. Besides, Father Mariana says that the harm that was done in the conquests of the Indies was all recompensed by the spiritual goods and fruits that the natives received and are receiving. He says that all that evil did not exceed this benefit.

As to differentiating between battles and private attacks—and that in the former the saints appeared and in the latter they do not—I do not find any differences. For if the armies and public battles were to remove the provinces from their natural lords (and for that reason the Spaniards made war without mercy, as cruel as the histories recount it), the private attacks were not ordained for any other goal but to capture the whole dominion, which in fact they did capture. The damage could not be so much in these private engagements as in the public battle, because private engagements are not fought with so many soldiers. Even if they had been, all was a military stratagem. If the war in the public battle was just, it would also be so in the private one. If the Most Holy Virgin and the saints did not appear in the private one, it would be because there was no need, for the Spaniards would participate in this type of engagement with the necessary sureness. So if the war is just when an army of Spaniards fights an army of Indians in this Province of León, it also will be so in the private engagements and stratagems that may be used against the guilty ones.

I would approve the distinction that they make between the enemy's coming to look for me in my house and my going to look for him in his, if the enemy were in populated land, where he could not come out safely to the roads to steal as much as is carried on them and kill as many as carry it. Besides, as I say in this opinion, they *have* come to the populated area various times, killing as many Spaniards and friendly Indians as they found and stealing the livestock and everything else that they found. Since they do not fight hand to hand with the Spaniard, but always by stratagems and wiles, who doubts that to be delivered from them it is necessary to go look for them, not in their houses (since they do not have any), but in the mountains, where the troops may find them? It is from there that they impede settlement by killing the Spaniards and robbing their properties. Otherwise, it would be impossible to wage war on them, or for the Spaniards to defend themselves from them.

As to the comments on the governor's jurisdiction, faculty, and authority for declaring the war that may be necessary against the Indians in order to quiet and pacify the land, let there be noted Ordinance 137, of the royal *cédula* of the new settlements. Therein His Majesty says with all his council that, if they were asked various times to make peace and let the Spaniards settle, and after all this they wanted only to upset and perturb the settlement, let there be waged against them all the war that may be necessary so that settlement may go forward. Let there be noted one of the orders that His Majesty makes to the governor, by which he may bring one hundred harquebuses to this Province of León for the conquest and pacification thereof. So if (there being the necessity) His Majesty orders him by his royal *cédula* to make war on them and gives him license to bring arms therefore, it very well follows that he has authority to declare it in the manner that he sees convenient—as he did declare it, setting aside from the punishment of the others the innocents who are presumed not to be guilty.

This seems to me to respond, in order to leave everything very clear, under the said declaration. In this Town of Cerralvo, on the thirteenth of November, 1632.—Fray Francisco de Ribera, instructor of theology.

Chapter 23 / Other Skirmishes That Took Place in Nuevo León

THE Indians of the north kept the settlers of Nuevo León oppressed not only by entering the province but also by forming raiding parties and venturing distances of forty-five leagues inside the province to reach an estate called Matehuala, near the Charcas camp, and the posts of Sandi, El Grande, and Chico. At the beginning of the year 1671, there was news from Captain Fernando Sánchez de Zamora that at the mines of the Blanco River, a party of Tetecora had attacked a pack train that was entering Nuevo León. The pack train belonged to Antonio Méndez, who was accompanied by Licenciado Diego Alvarez, a resident priest of the town of Huichapan, New Spain. Méndez was traveling to this province, where he had a sheep ranch.

As the pack train was moving along, traveling with some merchandise, the Indians attacked the mules that were trailing behind. Antonio Méndez and the cleric were up ahead, at a distance of about the range of three harquebus shots. The Indians killed a Spanish boy and an Indian, which obliged those who were ahead of the pack train to abandon it and try to reach the Blanco River post. From the post Captain Zamora came out with some soldiers to see if he could engage the enemy. However, as soon as the Indians had committed the murders, they began to destroy the cargo and to take away all they could carry. The Indians left the cleric's breviary, which one of the deceased may have been carrying in some saddlebags, on a tree branch. When assistance arrived, both the merchandise and the bodies had been destroyed. The troops buried the deceased and gathered the remaining goods.

This same year another attack occurred involving Captain Miguel de Escamilla's pack train, which was carrying corn from the valley of San Antonio. Some Indians from the Tamaulipas Mountains attacked the pack train, and it was fortunate that those involved escaped unharmed. It was therefore necessary for Captain Alonso de León [the elder], with a company, to come out to address these damages. In all such similar circumstances, those who suffered loss used his help.

During that same year, many other military excursions were necessary, and the Indians who were captured were punished. But on these people such examples and persuasions make no impression; the Indians simply continued their evil deeds. The only one corrected is the one who dies.

❧

Chapter 24 / A Great Uprising in the San Antonio Valley

A S mentioned at the close of the previous chapter, these Chichimeca people are not impressed or corrected by examples from others. They must receive the penalty themselves. An Indian well conversant with Spanish, reared among Christian Spaniards—called, as a nickname, Cualiteguache—had moved from this jurisdiction. He took refuge in the Tamaulipas Mountains. By way of pacifying himself, he became associated with the Mission of San Antonio, forty leagues from Monterrey. Franciscan priests there ministered both to the natives and to Spanish settlers. The settlers had a way of getting by, farming and raising livestock. Since some ranch operations from New Spain were beginning to use the area for pasturage, the valley was developing.

Then without warning, more than six hundred Indians rebelled under the leadership of the previously mentioned Cualiteguache. One night they killed Diego de Hinojosa, a lieutenant in the valley. When the Indians came to his door and said in Spanish, "Praised be Christ!" they seemed to the lieutenant, by their voices, to be Spaniards. He therefore came out with that confidence, and with the first arrow they shot he died. They shot more arrows, wounding his wife, though not seriously.

The Indians immediately continued their evil. In the same valley there were two sheep ranches, one belonging to Don Martín Pérez Romo, a settler from Querétaro, in the charge of Gabriel Candelas, and the other in the charge of Rodrigo de Adame. The Indians killed 38 shepherds and carried off at least fifty thousand head of livestock, including sheep and rams and four hundred horses and mules. All were driven toward the Tamaulipas Mountains. His Divine Majesty willed that the Indians not find and attack the two associated camps, where at least 250 persons (the majority women and children) could have been easily destroyed.

Gabriel Candelas then informed Captain De León [the elder], who came out with the soldiers that he had available. The captain requested a briefing of the situation to advise Governor Don Nicolás de Azcárraga of the occurrence. After the captain had followed the Indians, he was able to recover thirteen thousand sheep and twenty horses; he could not make any greater move, because they had already reached the mountain range.

The same night that the captain recovered the livestock, the Indians returned (or perhaps there were others) and attacked the nearby settlements. If the captain had not had the settlers collected and congregated near the camp, doubtless, the Indians would have killed them all. Once De León discovered the Indians, he, with only six soldiers, forced them to withdraw, after killing one of the enemy. At that time the governor reached the valley with eighty men. It was proposed that they should pursue the enemy. The troop reached the Indians at the San Marcos Pass, where the soldiers killed eight Indians and recovered four thousand sheep and twenty-two horses. In the fray the Indians wounded two soldiers. Although one of the wounds was serious, because he was hit in the cheek and it went close to the brain, the soldier was not killed.

In two days the troops returned to the camp. At nine o'clock in the morning on the following day, the Indians were so bold that without fear or thought of seeing 130 men together in the camp, besides the other people who were gathered, they approached the camp. Five men on horseback were found alone, among them Captain De León, who ran the Indians' guide through with a sword, and he then died. The others fled.

When the governor saw these audacities and impudences, it seemed to him certain that the valley would be depopulated, because it was not possible to continue the war or to defend against so many nations that had joined to harm the Spaniards. As anticipated, the settlers abandoned their houses, plots, livestock, and the many valuables that they could not carry for lack of mules. The loss in this valley was valued, counting shepherds and settlers, at more than sixty thousand pesos. It was a pity to leave the sheds full of corn and vegetables—and in such a sterile year that a *fanega*[1] was selling for five pesos. The plots of sugarcane remained, in large quantity, in the fields, so that the owners were destroyed and ruined. Abandoning their own houses, some came to El Pilón Valley and others went to the camp on the Blanco River.

Chapter 25 / Don Domingo de Pruneda Is Appointed Governor

ALTHOUGH several occurrences took place after the San Antonio uprising, I shall omit them because they were not noteworthy. However, I shall tell of the end of the administration of Don Nicolás de Azcárraga, who entered Nuevo León on July 12, 1667, and governed it until February 12, 1676. At that time Don Domingo de Pruneda, a gentleman from Santander,[1] arrived and succeeded him. Moreover, it would not be just to pass over in silence the good qualities of Don Nicolás de Azcárraga, who had been very gentle and forbearing in all his government. His ability was well known in all of New Spain.

He studied art in Mexico City and took a course of law and ecclesiastical canons. This was well recognized on due occasions because of the succinctness with which he decided business. He had a special quality: he liberally assisted whoever accepted his assistance in grave necessities, particularly those of bereavement, as was the case in supplications for burial rights and funerary cases. The same thing occurred in marriages of orphaned girls or when other persons, because of need, could not give their daughters a proper dowry. Of this I am a witness: he distributed with a liberal hand that which he had in his house, and without denying anyone their satisfaction.

Being very liberal with soldiers and also compassionate and moderate in executing justice against the Indians, whom he held to be miserable and destitute, he did not neglect to enter the battlefield when the situation required it. All these attributes of Governor Azcárraga deserve praise. He departed from the governorship of his own volition and left office known as a good and upright judge and a great servant of His Majesty.

After having finished his term of office, the former governor remained in this province for more than a year, during which time all the settlers respected and entertained him as if he were still in office. He went to live in Zacatecas, where he bought a mining property. Three years later, in 1686, he died. It is said that he left very few possessions.

Governor Don Domingo de Pruneda, who, as I have said, entered as governor of Nuevo León on February 12, 1676, was very fortunate in all respects. There was nothing worthy of note with respect to war other than a commotion among the Pelon. This required him to order the formation of four companies, which went out to punish them. With this successful action, the land was pacified.

The governor was of a very quiet and peaceable spirit. Although it was said that he was remiss in administering justice, this omission cannot be considered blameworthy because his administration was directed with a good intention that his subjects should not have disputes. Moreover, they did not under his government. He tried to put to rest all disputes that arose among settlers. During his administration he tried to maintain the custom that his predecessors had and did not innovate in any matter or ever show any ambition to acquire possessions. With this the province was very well pleased. During his administration he did not change or bestow offices, but instead retained the subjects he found in them.

Don Domingo de Vidagaray, his successor, acquitted himself well during his term of office—in which there was very little to do because of Pruneda's good works.

❧

Chapter 26 / The Administration of Don Domingo de Vidagaray

AT the end of the eighth month of the year 1681, General Don Domingo de Vidagaray entered the governorship. His Majesty gave him the office because of his merit and prior service; these are evident from his printed papers, which reflect that he served forty-four years in naval operations and in the army. He was a native of Vizcaya and somewhat rigid in disposition, as will be seen in the events that happened to him in Saltillo, before he arrived in this province.

He visited the house of Juan de Echeverría,[1] a settler in Saltillo who also was a native of Vizcaya. Echeverría entertained his fellow countryman for

eight days. All the settlers went to visit him, among them Don Pedro de Cajigal, who had been lord mayor of Saltillo and at this time was Nuevo León's
lieutenant governor and captain general. The governor did not honor him as
Cajigal expected, especially in the way he received him in his house. The
governor remained seated without coming to the door and followed the same
style when he bid Cajigal good-bye. The governor had an excuse, however,
because as was seen, he was crippled. This must have been the reason.

Don Pedro, however, was very offended. When the governor, in a large
coach and accompanied by Juan de Echeverría, went to pay him a visit, Don
Pedro did not go to the door when the coach arrived. For this reason the governor became irritated, called out to him, and reproved him. At that, the one
in question [Cajigal] came outside with sword and buckler at the same time
that the governor and Juan de Echeverría were alighting from the coach.
With their swords drawn, a horrendous fight broke out. Don Pedro dealt the
governor a strong blow, which went between him and Licenciado Don Francisco de la Calancha, who was in the coach.

Finally they were separated. The lord mayor, being warned, took Don
Pedro into his house and placed him under guard, and an action was brought
against him. While it was pending, Don Pedro took flight and placed himself
in the Church of San Francisco. The governor went to take charge of his government, sending a letter and notification to Governor Don Domingo de
Pruneda beforehand to have him send to Cerralvo and confiscate a quantity
of lead and other possessions that Don Pedro had there. This was carried
out. After reaching Nuevo León, the governor demonstrated his rancor by
showing very relentless diligence in inquiring of other possessions of Don
Pedro. He put some of them up at public auction and sold them.

Don Domingo de Vidagaray brought his wife from Spain. She was Doña
Cecilia de Heredia, a very noble and discreet lady who with all prudence
knew how to control her husband (who had been more of a soldier than a
politician). He was very liberal, fond of giving banquets and spending exor-
bitantly what he had brought. His government lasted but a very short time
because he ate too many watermelons and cantaloupes. He was struck with a
three-day fever from which he died very shortly, after having governed no
more than three months and nineteen days.

It seems that there were premonitions of his death. A son-in-law who
had come with him from Spain and whom he brought to the city of Zacatecas

(I do not know why he did not come to this province) said that his father-in-law was very fond of fruit and would get carried away with it and die shortly. This happened exactly as he said. He disposed of all his belongings.

The *alcaldes ordinarios* remained in power, and during this interval Don Pedro de Cajigal went to Mexico City to complain to the Audiencia that the governor had confiscated his possessions. He brought a royal provision that they should be turned over to him, which was done. The city notified the viceroy of the governor's death so that he should make appropriate provision.

❧

Chapter 27 / Juan de Echeverría Is Appointed Governor

THE news of Governor Don Domingo de Vidagaray's death found Juan de Echeverría in Mexico City. He was engaged in uninteresting employment, so he sought the governorship at the time that His Majesty was about to bestow it. In Spain he had favor and friends. Therefore it was bestowed on him; he entered this city in mid-December 1681.

After he left Saltillo, Juan de Echeverría suffered a debilitating disease, and although he underwent treatment in Mexico City, he could not be cured. The illness progressed, and he became worse each day. It was recognized that it occasioned choler, blood, and black bile, so that he became upset. And thus he remained during his whole term of office, during which there was nothing to recount in the matter of Indian troubles, because everything was peaceful.

The illness became more grave, and the upset that accompanied it motivated some settlers to go to Mexico City to complain. Thus, while Major Alonso de León [the younger] was in that city, he was chosen as interim governor of Nuevo León.

Juan de Echeverría, recognizing that he was very ill, resolved not to die in Nuevo León. He ordered a litter constructed, and he had himself carried to El Mazapil. On December 26, 1682, he died at the Cedros estate.

At that time news arrived of charges that had been brought against

Echeverría, and a judge was dispatched to verify them. As a result, his estate was confiscated for whatever purpose that might serve. So at the end of February 1683, the judge came with Governor Alonso de León, who, as mentioned, was chosen by His Excellency. This event was very unusual, because as the gospel says, no one is recognized as a prophet in his own country. But Governor De León, because of his record, had acquired distinction. Nuevo León owes him the pacification of the northern region. He carried out nine expeditions there on various occasions, and more than twelve expeditions to the Pelones. In addition, he led more than six other expeditions to the Tamaulipas Mountains, with famous successes, and he punished many of the evildoers. He bore the whole cost of the expeditions. During his government some quiet was enjoyed, although when he was in Cerralvo there was some disturbance there. This he calmed by having some companies dispatched.

During his predecessor, Juan de Echeverría's, time, an order came from the viceroy for forty men to go from this province to the Huaxteca Valley [1] because a priest had notified His Excellency that in a post called Taguanchín the Indians had become restless. For this expense three hundred pesos were disbursed from the San Luis pay office. When the governor had equipped the forty men, he elected Alonso de León major and had him bring the company along under his command.

The governor went with the company to the province, where he recognized that what His Excellency had been told was not a matter for concern. The governor made some efforts to find certain Indians who had disturbed the country but had since withdrawn, and then he returned to this province. In a famous gesture, the soldiers, unanimously and in conformity, donated to His Excellency the three hundred pesos he had allocated for them. During his return trip, the governor found some great salt flats. He made an arrangement to exploit them, but time did not give him the opportunity.

Chapter 28 / A List of Indian Nations That Were in Nuevo León but Have Vanished

ALTHOUGH this chapter may not seem fitting, and may appear as a break in the thread of the occurrences and history of this province, it seems to me appropriate to record the many Indian nations that surrounded Nuevo León. Most of the tribes listed in the chapter waged war against this province. In this way, the reader may understand the difficulties and fears that the few Spaniards who have lived in the province have sustained. Of these Indian nations, almost none now remain.

The tribes soon will be extinguished completely. The following tribes were near this city [Monterrey]:

Acatoyan, Aguaque, Aguata, Aguica, Alaoqui, Aleguapiame, Amanasau, Amaraguisp, Amatame, Amoguama, Apitala, Batajagua, Cabicujapa, Cagubiguama, Caguchuarca, Cajubama, Camabecuma, Camacaluria, Cami-Isubaba, Canamau, Capatuu, Catujano, Cazulpanialie, Cuatache, Estegueno, Estguama, Guacachina, Guamoayazua, Guayagua, Guinala, Hutachichil, Joqualan, Macacuy, Macapaqui, Michiaba, Miscale, Nepajan, Niacomala, Pastanquia, Pomaliqui, Popocátoque, Quiatolte, Quibobima, Siamomo, Tatoama, Tepehuan,[1] Tochequin.

The following nations were near Cadereyta:

Admitiale, Aguiniguara, Amancoa, Amiguara,[2] Añiraniguara, Baquiziziguara, Cacamegua, Caguiraniguara, Caguisniguara, Cajanibi, Camaiguara, Camatonaja, Camayapalo, Canaguiague, Canamarigui, Canayna, Capagui, Cocoaipara, Comocaura, Cotipiniguara, Cuaguijamiguara, Cuatiguara, Guaristiguara, Hualahuis, Ipajuiguara, Jiniapa, Jiniguara, Macoraena, Majanal, Manunejo, Mayajuanguara, Paciguima, Pantiguara, Parajota, Pijiniguara, Quejanaguia, Quiniguala, Soloaguas Tascuache, Tociniguara, Upaseptta, Yaquinigua, Zumitagui.

The nations within ten to twelve leagues' circumference of

Cerralvo:

Aguijagua, Alazapa, Amacuyero, Amapoala, Amito, Amituagua, Amoama, Amoguama, Caculpaluniame, Caguayoguame, Caguchuasca, Caguilipan, Cajaquepa, Calipocate, Camacuro, Camalucano, Camuchinibara, Canacabala, Canaine, Canameo, Canapeo, Capae, Capujaquin, Caraña, Cataara, Catujano, Cayaguaguin, Cayague, Cayanapuro, Coalimoje, Comite, Congue, Conicoricho, Coyote, Cuepano, Escabel, Guagui, Guajolote, Gualegua, Guamipeje, Guampexte, Guanapujamo, Guanpe, Guelamoye, Guinaima, Iliguigue, Imimule, Imipecte, Janapase, Jimiopa, Lespoama, Maciguara, Macomala, Matascuco, Moquiaguine, Noreo, Palaguine, Pestanquia, Quetapone, Quiguasguama, Quinegaayo, Quinemeguete, Sayulime, Sologuegue, Tacuanama, Tancacoama, Tatoama, Tatocuene, Teguampaxte, Yechimicuale.

All these Indian nations were written down in the records of Governor Don Martín de Zavala. If in such a limited area so many tribes were found, what will there be found in the two hundred leagues of latitude and as many of longitude that this province includes [3] that have still not been explored?

＊

Chapter 29 / Indian Nations Added by the Spaniards

A S stated at the beginning of the previous chapter, there remain few if any members of the tribes of Indian nations listed [in Chapter 28]. As a consequence, the Spaniards have had to obtain Indians from encampments forty and fifty leagues away. From information that I have acquired, and that I recall, it seems appropriate to list in this chapter tribes that have been gathered by the Spaniards. They are as follows:

Abasusiniguara, Acancuara, Aguana, Aguaranaguara, Aguijampo, Anguiniguara, Aguirtiguera, Ajuipiaijaigo, Amacuaguaramara, Ameguara, Anasgua, Anquimaniomo, Aocola, Aristeti, Asequimoa,

Ayenguara, Ayerapaguana, Ayundeguiguira, Bazaniguara, Boiguera, Boquiguera, Boquiniguera, Caguiamiguara, Caguiniguara, Caguiraniguera, Cajapanama, Camaniguara, Camisnimat, Canaitoca, Canaitoco, Cananarito, Canaranaguio, Canbroiniguera, Caramapama, Caramaperiguan, Caramunigua, Catareaguemara, Catomavo, Cayanaguanaja, Cayupina, Cocamegua, Cocojupara, Copochiniguara, Cuaquinacaniguara, Cuiminipaco, Estecuenopo, Estiajenepo, Guarastiguara, Guera, Gueyacapo, Guicopasico, Imiacolomo, Iscapana, Jaquiripamona, Jiminiguera, Locaguiniguara, Lomotugua, Maapiguara, Macatiguin, Macatue, Macuarera, Malicococa, Mapaniguara, Mapili, Maquispamacopini, Matatiquiri, Minacaguapo, Munapume, Pachizereco, Pajamara, Pantiguara, Pantipora, Patoo, Pericaguera, Piograpapaguarca, Pionicuagura, Plutuo, Pueripatama, Quiguantiguara, Quiniguio, Quinimichico, Quiniquijo, Quiriquitini, Quitaguiriaguilo, Saguimaniguara, Sainipame, Saratiguara, Tacopate, Teminaguico, Tiaquesco.

If all the nations that are mentioned in these chapters are enumerated, it will be found that they number 250; and the 88 of this chapter, who have been located and gathered during the past twenty to twenty-five years.[1] During the next twenty-five years, it will be necessary to gather other tribes, for the tribes here today will already have perished. This will occur because, when an Indian becomes ill, he dies, even if he is given special care. They are too weak a people and they make little effort to recover their health. Thus, there will come to pass in this province that which Doctor Francisco López de Gómara mentions in the history he compiled of the Indies, namely, that, of one and a half million people who were in the island of Hispaniola, all perished in fewer than fifty years.

We must attribute this depopulation to the many sins that the Indians commit and that their ancestors committed. Although these nations have not taken part in idolatries, they had (and still have) many superstitions and abuses. Therefore, His Divine Majesty punishes them and is annihilating them, so that in the course of time all the Indians of New Spain and Peru will be exterminated, as those who may live at that time will see.

Chapter 30 / The Death of Governor Juan de Echeverría and the Administration of Governor Alonso de León

WHOEVER writes of the events of this century will note how man is subject to their inconstancy and alteration. Whoever has seen Juan de Echeverría enter with so much majesty and greatness into the possession of his office as governor and has seen him leave with so little fanfare—ill, and on a badly constructed litter that seemed more like a coffin—can consider nothing else.

Let no one trust in his fortune, because when one finds one's life in a state of sublimity, he will then find it very soon in the lowest of states. We have a good example in Caiomanus from the Roman histories. He was born in a very insignificant town near Rome, but knew how to take such advantage of its fortress and empire that he obtained five terms as consul in that city. Then he came to such an end that, conquered by Sila, he went to hide by a lake. When he was found there and taken prisoner, Sila ordered that he be jailed and exiled. Thus relates Claudianus in these words: *Victus a Sila minturnis in pacu de natatuit inventus ed in carcerem. Confectus acepta que mavicula ubi debec xulabid* (*sic*).

If anyone trusts in the affairs of this world, let him look at Darius, the last king of the Persians, who with his great power scorned Alexander because of his youth. The latter conquered him three times in battle, so much so that in the last battle he obliged him to withdraw, and his own people killed him. Thus says the same author: *Darius, ultimus persam rex, qui Alexandria dole essemtiam despectui a benes velum cum aigresus* (*sic*) *est abeo que quamvis ex sixis copüs ingentibus prelüs victus eum, se fuga victori eripere conatetur a suis comprehensus set ed tuis duptus.*

With these examples of such outstanding men, we should not be surprised at the fall of our governor, Juan de Echeverría, whom reports alone removed from office. Before the charges concerning him were verified, the position of governor was bestowed (as has been said) on General Alonso de

FIGURE 2. *General Alonso de León (standing) and Juan Bautista Chapa confer on astrolabe reading near the mouth of the Rio Grande on the 1686 expedition.*

León, who entered into office at the end of February 1683—to the great plea-sure and satisfaction of all, since he was a person of the motherland.

He was chosen on December 19 in Mexico City, and Governor Juan de Echeverría died on the twenty-sixth of the same month. Alonso de León brought with him a receivership judge of the Royal Audiencia, who exam-ined the charges brought against the deceased. When the case was con-cluded, the judge carried the writs in which he touched on public claims. All was dealt with. In what otherwise concerns the government of General De León, I have already said that there is nothing else worthy of recounting. He governed only nine months. He viewed the affairs of the motherland and its settlers as a native.

·❧·

Chapter 31 / The Beginning of the Marquis of San Miguel de Aguayo's Administration as Governor of Nuevo León

THE Marquis of San Miguel de Aguayo, a knight of the Order of Santiago, disembarked from the fleet that came from Spain to the port of Veracruz in 1683. His Majesty had chosen him as governor and captain general of the Prov-ince of Nuevo León for five years. The whole province approved of the ap-pointment—because he was a settler from nearby Patos,[1] a peaceable gov-ernment would result and fate had been so adverse in not bestowing a lengthier term on his predecessor. He took office on February 4 of the fol-lowing year, 1684, with the strong support of all.

He was a very affable person, not at all selfish. He was also fortunate that during his term there was no Indian unrest. However, after the first two years of his term, the first report arrived that the French had a settlement at the Bay of Espíritu Santo. This report came from the court, accompanied by a *cédula* directing the Marquis of La Laguna,[2] viceroy and captain general of New Spain, to order the bay reconnoitered. For that reason—and because a cer-tain subject reported in Mexico City that from this province to the bay was a journey of no more than seven days—the viceroy ordered the marquis to en-list, with all precision and brevity, some companies to go on this expedition. This was done.

With the vigilance and care that the situation required, a council was convened, which concluded that such an important task could be assigned most appropriately to none other than General Alonso de León. In addition to the support of his relatives in this province, and a supply of horses, and the good luck that attended him, there was no other who had more experience.

A company from Monterrey and another from Cadereyta were enlisted to leave Cadereyta on June 25. The journal and the survey that General Alonso de León [the younger] made on the journey describes everything in detail; understand that the account was prepared by one who had a great deal of personal experience. It therefore seemed appropriate to me to quote it word for word. It is as follows:

> Daily route and description of the journey that I, General Alonso de León, lieutenant governor and captain general of this New Kingdom of León, made for the exploration of the coast of the Northern Sea [Gulf of Mexico] and the mouth of the Río Bravo [Rio Grande]; the reasons and motives that existed for the journey, with all that occurred on the trip, including the number of people, horses, supplies, etc.
>
> On June 8, 1686, the marquis of San Miguel de Aguayo, governor and captain general of the province of León, received a dispatch from the most excellent viceroy of New Spain. As a result of the news that the royal officials of Veracruz had given him—namely, that the French were settled at the Bay of Espíritu Santo and that the settlement was six or seven days' journey from this province, the viceroy charged the governor to conduct an exploration in this direction so that the truth could be determined from personal observation, and to respond in the most appropriate manner. The governor ordered that a council be convened on June 11 in Monterrey, the capital of the province, and that all the jurisdictions be notified beforehand. The governor called me for the council, which, once it was convened, decided to commence the expedition on June 25. A company of thirty soldiers, to be led by Captain Nicolás Ochoa, would set out on this day from Monterrey to march to Cadereyta. Another company to be led by Captain Antonio Leal would be enlisted in Cadereyta. His Lordship would travel from Monterrey to Cadereyta on the same day, and they would muster and submit to

the captains he would name. The two companies would be under my command. He did me a favor in this, which was due more to his greatness than to my merits.

With everything arranged in the manner described, His Lordship came down from Monterrey with the company on June 26; rain delayed him on this day longer than he had planned. On this same day, I reached Cadereyta with the company of the twenty soldiers of that jurisdiction. This one and the one from Monterrey gathered near the town so that on the next day, the twenty-seventh, they could pass muster. When they had gathered on that day in Cadereyta with complete military order, in condition to march, and when the marquis had presented the titles of the captains, alferez, and sergeants so as to turn them over from his hand to those who were chosen, he ordered that the muster be passed in his presence, which was done as follows:

The company that Captain Nicolás Ochoa led from Monterrey passed, with the soldiers from it and its jurisdiction, in the following order: first, his lordship assigned the title of captain to Carlos Cantú, which he ordered read in a loud voice, and presented the title to him. The soldiers passed in their ranks, on horseback, in this form: Captain Carlos Cantú; the alferez, Diego Rodríguez; Sergeant Nicolás Ochoa; Major Lucas Caballero; Captain Nicolás García; Sergeant Lorenzo de Ayala; Sergeant Gaspar de Lerma; Gonzalo de Treviño; Sergeant Juan de la Garza; Jacinto de la Garza; Joseph de Treviño; Francisco de la Garza; Joseph de La Garza; Alonso García de Quintanilla; Marcos Flores; Alonso de Olivares; Andrés Fernández Tijerina; Nicolás de Montalvo; Juan Pérez de la Garza; Francisco de la Garza; Juan de la Garza; Diego Martín; Joseph Pérez; Antonio Pérez; Joseph González; Francisco González; Mateo de Peña; Santiago de León; Nicolás Cantú.

In turn the Cadereyta company, led by Captain Alonso Leal, passed muster. He turned over the muster to Captain Nicolás de Medina, its captain-elect, whose title was read and presented. They passed in this order: Captain Nicolás de Medina; Alferez Tomás de la Garza; Sergeant Miguel de León; Alonso de León, Jr.; Sergeant Lorenzo de la Garza; Sergeant Juan Cantú; Sergeant Agustín García; Sergeant Tomás Cantú; Joseph Gutiérrez; Sebastián de Villegas;

Francisco Falcón; Lucas de Betancourt; Francisco de Escamilla; Luis Pérez; Nicolás de Lira; Miguel González; Matías de Herrera; Santiago de la Garza.

When the muster had been passed in this order, his lordship turned over the titles of alferez and sergeant to the persons chosen. From the company of Monterrey: Alferez Diego Rodríguez and Sergeant Nicolás Ochoa, Jr. From the company of Cadereyta: Alferez Tomás de la Garza and Sergeant Miguel de León.

Likewise the supplies of the two companies passed muster in this order: forty loads of provisions, including meal, hardtack, meat, and chocolate, plus 468 horses. The drivers, servants, and attendants of these companies were Diego Monita, Pascual de Gumendio, Mateo Esteban, Juan Rodríguez, Juan de Olivares, Juan de Villagrán, Juan Rendón, Tomás de Torres, Nicolás de Losa, Matías de Munguía, Juan Cavazos, Cristóbal de Avila, Juan de Ochoa, Bernabé de la Garza, Miguel, Juan, Joseph, Juan, Alonso, an Indian captain of the Zacatil village,[3] our Indian guide called Bernabé, and another Indian called Mateo.

After this, His Lordship ordered that my commission be read, in which he named me as head of these companies, with full authority and instruction. He named as chaplain the presiding priest of this town, Father Diego de Orozco, and His Lordship attached to me as staff Don Pedro Fermín de Echeverz, his brother; the alferez, Francisco de Benavides; and Juan Baptista Chapa.[4]

That same day, June 27, a Thursday, I set out with the company, once the muster was passed, and we made camp at the San Diego post. This is four leagues east of the town, at the edge of the [San Juan] river, on flat land.

Friday, June 28. I set out with the company to camp on this side of the San Juan River, by some ponds—on a flat road, although there were hills extending for about a league. On this day the company traveled east eight leagues.

Saturday, June 29. The company set out northeastward, keeping in view a sharp little peak that is about a half-league this side of the San Juan River; the way was wooded, but passable. We reached the river crossing, which was very good, and then traveled two more leagues beyond the crossing. On this day we marched northeast four leagues.

Sunday, June 30. When I set out with the company, it was necessary to travel southeast for about 1.5 leagues because we were not able to penetrate a large dense woods. We traveled 5 leagues, mostly east by north. We camped at some ponds near the encampment of my Indians.[5] The [San Juan] river goes due north in this area.[6]

Monday, July 1. We left the camp and traveled east by north across flat country. After traveling six leagues, we stopped at some ponds on flat land. They were of rainwater, as were the other ponds mentioned.

Tuesday, July 2 (day of the Visitation of our Lady). We set out with forty-four Indians of the Caurames nation,[7] who had joined us on the preceding day. Last night the Caurames located an encampment of their enemies. In order to see if they [the Caurames] could capture two Indians as guides, I went ahead with twenty men. But the enemy must have been warned, because they had abandoned their camp. On this day we followed a trail mostly north and northeast for eight leagues. The Indian called Alonso [a Zacatil] told us that the Rio Grande was nearby. The company, with the supplies and the horses, could not penetrate a dense woods that we reached, so we stopped at a small marsh. I proceeded through an area of stunted brush in the thick woods (which was very difficult) for a distance of more than two leagues, to the river [the Rio Grande]. In this area the river is very wide, and the water very muddy. Seemingly, it is navigable in small boats, but there was no way of sounding it. The width of the river is the range of a harquebus, and in this area it runs to the north.

Wednesday, July 3. Since a crossing was not found, it was necessary (although a lot of work) to penetrate the thicket with the company. We did not travel more than two leagues today, because I arranged for a short reconnaissance to determine the direction to proceed the next day. I set out with two members of the company. Going downriver, we unexpectedly came upon an abandoned Indian camp; they apparently had detected us and left the area. However, they left all their valuables. I ordered that nothing be disturbed. We continued to follow the river downstream and at one point watched some Indian men and women swim across the river. Although I called to them in peace, I could not get them to return. Instead, one came to the narrowest part of the river and shot arrows at us, at closer than harquebus range. We concluded that they had not seen Spaniards before, because he was not afraid of a harquebus shot. The direction followed was to the east.

Thursday, July 4. I traveled with the company toward the northeast for four leagues. We stopped at a lake and a ravine, separated from the river by about one league, because very thick woods ran along the bank. I went quickly with twelve members of the company to reconnoiter the river. Because of the thick woods it was necessary to travel three leagues to reach it. In this area the river is very broad and apparently navigable, but it has a strong current. There was no place appropriate for the horses to get down to the river and drink.

Friday, July 5. We traveled east for four leagues and crossed a half-league of small woods opened up by the Indians. We stopped next to the river and some low hills; the horses were able to drink, but with difficulty. Here the river is navigable in a small boat. I set out with ten members of the company to explore the land quickly. However, I followed a path that led into a woods so thick that we could not penetrate it.

Saturday, July 6. I set out with the company in the direction explored on the previous day and crossed some low brush with very short and thick growth on a little hill. We traveled four leagues across a plain until we came upon a dried-up marsh, which, had it contained water, would have been impassable. It was full of hollows and obstructions. We could not find a passage through a woods that we reached. We followed a ravine until it divided, and we followed the branch that went north until we reached the river—but with difficulty, because of the many thorny thickets. Here we found a watering place. The river seems less navigable and has less water than where we saw it before. I set out with some troops to look for a passage to use the next day and to see if I could locate an Indian guide. There are many paths, but none were well worn. On this day we traveled northeast.

Sunday, July 7. We set out northeastward in view of the river; there were, however, some thickets to get through. Then we came upon the river, which seems navigable. After we continued along its bank for about a league and up to some big trees on a plain, we found a little water hole that seems to have been a spring. From here I set out with twelve troops to look for a crossing for the next day. We saw some low hills, climbed the highest of them, and saw plains and the river, about two leagues away. With the intention of sleeping there that night, I remained on that hill with seven soldiers. Before the sun set, however, about forty Indians appeared. As soon as we saw them we mounted our horses, and they fled. I left them a white cloth, some hardtack, tobacco, and other things and returned to camp. We traveled six leagues today, toward the east-northeast.

Monday, July 8. We set out toward the east-northeast along the previous day's trail. I went ahead with twenty men in hopes of capturing one of the Indians seen the day before. At three leagues we passed over the hill noted the day before, where I had left the cloth and other things; we found them in the same place. Then about fifty Indians came out, near a woods. Although I made many friendly gestures to them, none wanted to approach. I put a cloth and a knife from my sheath in a little tree for them and then I withdrew. They came to take it; and in response they waved a banner of feathers for me and put up a feather crest for me to take, making signals for me to come and take it, which I did. I continued in the same direction, and they, in the shelter of the woods, followed us. On this day we traveled eight leagues in several directions, mostly to the east. As we came upon a dense thicket and did not find water, it was necessary to return three leagues to look for the river. We found the river, with a good drinking place, although it is less navigable.

Tuesday, July 9. It was necessary to camp at this location on the river. I set out with twenty-five soldiers to explore the land for the following day. It was necessary for me to travel eight leagues to reach the river, on the bank of which are many thick woods that give way to plains three and four leagues away. Without finding another water hole, I sent out six men the following day, a Wednesday, so that the company could set out following our trail.

Wednesday, July 10. The company, guided by the soldiers I had sent out, proceeded along the trail. Shortly before the pack team left, about thirty Indians on the other side of the river began to wail and signal for the troops to come there or else they would kill us all. They were playing two flutes.[8] After they had come out a little distance, another band of about sixty came out, although they never attacked. The Indians followed the company as far as a plain, where there was a wide trail and seemingly more than three hundred Indians had gathered for a dance. We camped on a plain with no water. We traveled about five leagues to the east-southeast on this day.

Thursday, July 11. The company set out along my trail and reached the river, three leagues east-northeast, where I was waiting. In this area, the river is very wide and navigable in a small boat, although it had too much current. The land was flat, and we found a good route, as far as we could make out, for the following day.

Friday, July 12. The company set out from the river and I went on ahead with fifteen men to look for a trail. We found an estuary that the river forms 6 leagues to the east-southeast. When camp was made, I again set out with twelve soldiers to look for a route for the following day. Four leagues away we found two salt lakes, although there was no [water] because it had rained so little recently. One lagoon is 1.5 leagues long and one-half league wide. The water is very salty and undrinkable.

Saturday, July 13. The company set out from the estuary, where we had slept, and I directed them, at the beginning, by the preceding day's route. We traveled in several directions on this day, a distance of four leagues, mostly toward the east-southeast. I made camp on the river and near a large trail made by Indians who had abandoned an encampment about fifteen days earlier. Here we found a barrel stave. Late in the afternoon, I went on ahead with twenty-eight men and determined that we were now very near the sea. We very cautiously traveled six leagues while continuing to look for the river. At six in the afternoon we unexpectedly came upon an Indian encampment. Because they had noticed us, they abandoned [the camp], so we captured only three Indian women. These were treated kindly and questioned using sign language. We asked where there were Spaniards and people who wore clothes. The Indians indicated that such people were in the northern area, in two locations. I concluded that they [the French] must not be at the mouth of the river we were following, since it was heading east.

The Indians many times named the two places where they [the people who wore clothes] were and said that the nearer one, to the northwest, was called Taguili, and the other, to the north, Zaguili (that was what they were called in their language, undoubtedly). The Indians did not know how to describe the distances, although we tried to find out. They did not understand us, nor we them, even as a matter of conjecture. We found at this encampment the head of a barrel, a ship's broken bolt, a link of chain, and a little piece of glass, but no other valuables. I remained that night with the troops to sleep on the riverbank, and with the calm of [the night] the roaring of the sea was heard.

Sunday, July 14 (Saint Buenaventura's Day). I sent four soldiers back to get the company to the designated location. I went on with the rest of the company to explore the Gulf, and we passed marshes, canebrakes, clumps of willows, and dense thickets along the riverbank. Two leagues away we found the sea [the Gulf] toward the northeast. The company traveled four leagues this day. There was no trace of Spaniards or of any foreigners ever having reached this river mouth. I followed the coast for one league to reach the mouth of the river. It enters the sea very turbidly. About one league outward into the Gulf, the water is vermilion colored. The mouth of the river is a little wider than the range of a musket shot. I ordered a raft constructed and soundings taken at five or six locations. The deepest was 7.5 and 8 fathoms, so that a large seagoing vessel apparently can enter about two leagues inland.

Today I followed the coastline of the Gulf for four leagues, toward the Palmas River [southward]. There were fresh Indian trails and poles set up at various locations where the Indians had camped, although for a substantial distance no stone was found along this whole shore. The coast runs from north to south (somewhat more to the northeast). The sea is very rough, even when there is not much wind. Along the shore are many cypresses, pines, palms, and giant cane as thick as a man's leg, and things that the sea has cast up. The coast is very clean, with no boulders, and the firm shore is very accessible on horseback. The tide rises and falls more than one estado.[9]

Monday, July 15. Since we were at the very mouth of the river at the stroke of noon, the height of the sun was measured with an astrolabe and we found ourselves to be at 25°45′ (discounting error,

because the astrolabe seemingly was somewhat defective).[10] Because of a shortage of pasturage, I ordered the company to set out
after noon for whatever point they might reach that day and to stop
on the next day at the estuary where they had been on Saturday.
With twenty-five soldiers I reconnoitered the coast again, toward
the Palmas River, for a distance of more than eight leagues. Along
the way we found some planking from the sides of a ship, ships'
yards, topmasts, pieces of keel and rudder, barrel staves, buoys, four
casters of an artillery piece, a barrel with willow hoops, three broken
canoes, and a little round thick glass flask stoppered with a cork—in
which I found a little spoiled wine. The glass is very comely, and,
considering its form, it seems that it was not made in the kingdoms
of Spain. Finally, there were on this shore all kinds of timber and
wreckage of ships. Doubtless, some of them foundered there, as at-
tested by the diversity of these ruins and because some of the wood
is older than the other. What I found most surprising was some
cornstalks, seemingly of this year's planting, that had been brought
by the undertow and that were beginning to put on ears and the
stalks still had their roots. I concluded that there was some settlement nearby and that corn had been brought to it by some means.[11]

Tuesday, July 16. I set out from near the shore in search of the
camp, but I was unable to cross either some lagoons or some bogs.
It was therefore necessary to return to the shore route and go out in
search of [the camp] via the trail. I did not reach the camp that day.

Wednesday, July 17. I reached the camp early, and because the
horses had been ridden hard, we did not travel that day. I found
[the camp] on the estuary where we stopped on Friday, the twelfth;
the estuary is eight leagues from the sea.[12]

Thursday, July 18. I set out for the river with the company and
traveled a distance of six long leagues.

Friday, July 19. I went with the company to the spring on the
plain, where we had stopped on Sunday, July 7. We traveled eleven
leagues on this day, having marched the same distance in three days
while on our way to the coast. There were many Indian trails leading to the river crossing where they earlier had threatened us.

Saturday, July 20. We left the above location and camped beyond the poor-quality watering place at the river, on a little hill with
no water. We traveled eight leagues.

Sunday, July 21. We left the little hill and stopped near the encampment where the Indians earlier had shot at us with arrows. Seeing more than fifty Indians, we attacked them. When Major Lucas Caballero attempted to capture one, the Indian hid in a scrub oak and shot an arrow at him. The arrow went in under his nipple, for he did not have on a coat of armor. Two Indians were killed, and two boys were captured. We traveled eight leagues.

Monday, July 22. We left this camp, traveled five leagues, and departed through the thick area of low brush, where we came upon the river. In order to reduce the length of the route, we attempted to travel another direction, but another lagoon impeded our way. We slept on a plain with ponds of water.

Tuesday, July 23. I set out with the company by different directions from the one by which I had come (because we had then descended a good deal), and came upon the Pajarito village.[13] We traveled seven long leagues and stopped at Calaveras Pond.

Wednesday, July 24. I set out from the camp with the company, passing by the encampment of the Caurames, who were waiting for us on the route. We camped at the crossing of the San Juan River after traveling twelve leagues.

Thursday, July 25. We left the camp and came to the encampment of San Simón. From there we continued, a total distance of fourteen leagues, to the encampment of San Diego.

Friday, July 26. While we were at this encampment, there arrived an order from the governor that the companies should go home to rest and should be prepared to go out again if necessary. While the horses were resting, because they had been ridden hard, we went on to the town [Cadereyta] on this day, and I then [went on] to give an account of the journey to the marquis.

Done at Cadereyta, on July 27 of the year 1686.—Alonso de León.

Chapter 32 / The Continuation of Governor Aguayo's Administration

THE Marquis of San Miguel de Aguayo always firmly believed that the French had a settlement on the Northern Sea [Gulf of Mexico], so he arranged that the journey to the coast should be repeated along the other [north] side of the Río Bravo [Rio Grande]. This route would pass through the town of Cerralvo, for it was recognized throughout this province that there was a good ford twenty leagues from the town.[1]

In early 1687, the marquis formed three companies. One was under General Martín de Mendiondo; a second was under Don Pedro Fermín de Echeverz; and the third was under Captain Nicolás de Medina. General Alonso de León [the younger] was appointed leader of them all. They set out from this city [Monterrey] at the end of February, and on March 20 they reached the seacoast. Along the way, the expedition passed through many warlike Indian nations, and the leaders had a difficult time understanding the various Indian languages. The expedition wandered along trying different directions.

The troops did not find a settlement of Frenchmen, nor anyone who could give them a report. Instead, a large salty river[2] stopped them from going farther north. So the hopes of exploration were frustrated, with ill feeling on everyone's part—especially that of the governor, who had wished that during his term the coast that had attracted so much effort would be fully explored, and now his term of office was coming to an end. He had requested permission from His Majesty to return to Spain. Once permission was granted in 1687, the Count of Monclova appointed as interim governor[3] General Don Francisco Cuervo de Valdés, a gentleman from Santander of very capable qualities. He took office in September. During his term, which lasted little more than nine months, the Indians were very well controlled. To attain this, steps had been taken to account for the fact that with these native people, fear and punishment were a very necessary means to protect property (both mines and farming plots).

Governor Cuervo's term would surely have closed very favorably if the tragedy of the next year had not taken place. In February, in the San Antonio Valley,[4] the Indians of the Tamaulipas Mountains killed several shepherds and carried away some livestock. A squadron of men set out in pursuit (I do not give them the title "soldiers," because if they had been, they would not have made such blunders) and rescued some sheep, those that they could reach. The enemy Indians hid the remaining sheep in a ravine in the Tamaulipas Mountains.

In order to follow them (not being able to enter on horseback), ten squad members ventured ahead on foot with the commander. Although there was aversion on the part of some—who warned the leader that they would be endangered because of the advantage that the Indians had in the mountains—the leader, a man of little experience, threw himself into danger. Thus the enemy attacked them by rolling stones down the mountain and killing nine of them. One man escaped, although he was badly hurt by a stone that struck him in the back. At this, the friendly Indians retreated from the mountains and returned with the wounded man to the place where two members of the company had remained with the animals. At top speed they returned to San Antonio, the post from which they had set out, and carried the unhappy news to the wives of those of the deceased who had had wives.

It seems that February of this year was disastrous in this province, because there occurred not only these unfortunate deaths in Tamaulipas, but also deaths in the city of Monterrey. Captain Nicolás de Ochoa, who was chief justice and councilman, had ascended Las Mitras peak, two leagues from the city, to look at a mine they were trying to exploit, which was at a great height. The pick wielders had already begun to work the mine. The captain took a seat on a ledge to pray, and all his companions were off guard. At this time the captain was taken with dizziness, or perhaps the ledge crumbled unexpectedly. The ledge slipped, and he fell into a ditch more than twenty estados deep and was dashed to pieces. This was something that the people could not avert. While he was falling, his companions heard him invoke the name of the Virgin, who doubtless in such a very critical moment would have favored him, as he was her devotee. The mountain is very high and it took a good deal of work to remove the body. Such a violent death caused everyone sorrow.

A report of the deaths in the Tamaulipas Mountains was given to the governor, who was in Cerralvo. He gathered out of his whole province three companies and set out in person to punish the Indians who were responsible.

Although the governor was in the field for some time and made painstaking efforts, his troops could not capture any of the aggressors. The companies therefore returned, leaving a squadron of sixteen soldiers to guard the estates.

❧

Chapter 33 / Governor Alonso de León Captures a Frenchman Living among the Indians

ON all the occasions that proved arduous to General Alonso de León in the Province of Coahuila, he never hesitated to request help from Nuevo León because it was nearest, and moreover, because of his knowledge and experience that its soldiers did not refuse to take risks. For this reason, upon finding himself excessively harassed by some Indians of that region who were carrying off livestock from the nearby settlements, he wrote Governor Don Francisco Cuervo to request the aid of twenty-five to thirty soldiers to go to the interior. The governor sent him a company under the command of General Martín de Mendiondo, which, having been gathered in Coahuila,[1] set out with the general on two expeditions that resulted in significant punishment to the enemy.

While on the third expedition, to finish smoothing out the difficulty that had arisen, De León received news that beyond the Río Bravo, which is forty-two leagues from the presidio of Coahuila, a Frenchman[2] whom the Indians held in great respect was to be found in a large encampment. With this information De León decided to go there with only eighteen soldiers, men who seemed satisfactory to him, and in six days he reached the encampment, which was twenty-five leagues north of the Río Bravo.

They made camp in a good location and, with only thirteen men, De León approached the Frenchman's habitation, which was a room of buffalo hides. Arranging for ten of the soldiers to remain on horseback, General Alonso de León with Fray Buenaventura Bonal (a friar who was going along as chaplain) and General Martín de Mendiondo dismounted and entered this habitation—although there were more than six hundred Indians in this encampment, and forty-two standing guard with their weapons in their hands.

In the most spacious part of the habitation, the Frenchman was seated on buffalo hides, as if they were a throne. Two Indians were fanning him and others were cleaning his face. When the priest approached, the Frenchman did no more than—without leaving his seat—bend his knees, kiss the sleeve of his habit, and show great courtesy to the governor and to General Martín de Mendiondo by giving them his hand and saying, "I, Frenchman." The Frenchman asked the governor carefully how many soldiers had come, to which (heeding the malice with which he must be asking him) the governor answered, "Many." Then to ingratiate himself with the Indians, the governor called for valuables he had brought for them, including blouses, skirts, knives, earrings, tobacco, etc. He turned them over to the Frenchman, so that he could distribute them to the Indians with his own hand. The Frenchman was decorated on the face in the Indian manner and knew their language very well.

The governor told the Frenchman, through an interpreter, that he was to go with him. The Frenchman resisted—and the Indians did the same—but by diligence they captured him from his encampment. They put him on a horse and went with him to the camp, with many Indians from the encampment accompanying him (although discontented that he was being taken) so that De León arrived with the Frenchman at the settlement of Coahuila [Monclova].

FIGURE 3. *General Alonso de León finds a Frenchman, Jean Géry,*

living in savage splendor among the Indian tribes in South Texas in 1688.

Chapter 34 / The French Prisoner Explains Why He Lived with the Indians

THE discovery of the Frenchman among Indians who held him in such high regard astonished the governor and those who were with him. If these people were idolatrous, it might be inferred that they adored him as their god, in accordance with pagan practice. But in none of these provinces has there been found an Indian nation that is idolatrous or superstitious.

So when Alonso de León [the younger] reached Coahuila [Monclova] with this prisoner, the Spaniards tried to interrogate him and obtain an account of why he was living with the Indian nations, and whether there was a settlement on the Bay of Espíritu Santo as reported, and where he was from, and how he had arrived. The Frenchman responded that he was a native of San Juan de Orliens [*sic*] and had come with Monsieur Felipe, governor of the settlement he had founded next to a large river. The governor had made him captain of a company. He had learned the language of the Indians and had gone to live with them some time ago.

He testified that his motive was to secure these people's allegiance to the king of France, that he had been about this task for about three years; but it was almost fifteen years ago that a settlement was begun next to the river. In this location there was a castle on the far side and a smaller one on this side, and the larger castle had twenty pieces of artillery and the smaller did not have any, but had musketry, which was of the Flemish type. He added that the settlement had four well-formed streets and six companies of soldiers, with a Capuchin monastery.[1] Ordinarily, three ships came from France to trade. The settlers harvested wheat and corn, maintained cattle and horses, and sowed tobacco and sugarcane.

When asked about the material used to build the castles, he answered that stone and lime brought from the coast were used. After he had moved away from the settlement, he had not returned, but some of the members of the settlement had visited him. Sixteen had visited a little more than a year ago; two months ago, seven others had come to see how he was getting along among these people and whether he was adding to the number [of Indians loyal to France].

He declared these and many other things. Because the statements were not of substance and had no credible basis, no attention was paid to their contents. Therefore, the governor sent the prisoner to Mexico City. Alonso de León brought him to the city of Monterrey to send him on more conveniently, and from there he sent him to the Pilón Valley to arrange the best route. In the meantime, Don Pedro Fernández de la Ventosa, a knight of the Order of Santiago, whose good qualities and talents are known in all of New Spain, took office as governor of this province. He knew the French language very well; and when the Frenchman passed through the city, he examined him in the same matters that are mentioned above, and he did not declare more than the statements recorded here.[2] The Frenchman was turned over to General Martín de Mendiondo, who had been present during the Frenchman's internment and on the journeys preceding it. The general was to convey the Frenchman, escorted by soldiers, to the Count of Monclova and was to give him an eyewitness account so that His Excellency could resolve the matter as he saw fit.

❧

Chapter 35 / His Excellency Orders an Expedition to Locate the French Settlement

AT a moderate pace, General Mendiondo proceeded to Mexico City with the Frenchman and met with His Excellency, who was particularly pleased because he thought that the location of the French settlement on the coast of the Northern Sea [Gulf of Mexico] would be discovered. News of the settlement was even arriving from Spain, as was His Majesty's charge that the location should be reconnoitered.

The presence of the Frenchman occasioned more than a little excitement in Mexico City, because it was strange to see a Christian man, who had been born in a civilized land, with his face decorated like an Indian's. But some excuse can be made for him, because he did it to please the Indians, as someone who doubtless had already dedicated himself to living with them and even to dying in their manner.

With the information that Governor De León [the younger] had given in his dispatches to His Excellency, and that which General Martín de

Mendiondo gave him in person, plus the declaration made by the French-man, His Excellency [the viceroy] resolved that another expedition would be made to discover the French settlement. This expedition would consist of one hundred men with Governor De León as its principal leader. Fifty men would be chosen from the soldiers at the five presidios of Vizcaya, and the other fifty from Nuevo León. His Majesty would pay for the journey, giving out of his royal treasury eighty loads of meal, a hundred young steers, and other things, including clothing for Indians found along the route (to earn their gratitude) and axes and cutlasses in case it was necessary to clear pas-sages in some locations. All of this came to more than six thousand pesos, which were disbursed, by order of His Excellency, from the royal pay office in the city of Zacatecas.

So the viceroy dispatched General Martín de Mendiondo, with all the necessary orders, to this province. The Frenchman returned to serve as a guide for the exploration. Although they attempted to schedule this for the end of last year, 1688, that could not be done because of the distance between the Province of Coahuila and the presidios of Nueva Vizcaya. It was neces-sary to dispatch various mailings to the captains of these posts to order each one to send his ten soldiers.

Likewise the governor of Nuevo León was ordered to enlist fifty men who had been proposed for the journey in the war council in Mexico City. In accordance with this, the governor issued an *expediente* [1] that concisely called for the formation of two companies of loyal officers and soldiers accustomed to serving His Majesty. In the middle of March the men left Monterrey by the Caldera River route, [2] and at the same time Governor Alonso de León set out from Coahuila [Monclova] to join forces on the Sabinas River with those who were being sent from El Parral. [3] All the orders De León had received from the Count of Monclova had already been confirmed by his successor, the Count of Galve, [4] who had already arrived (since His Majesty had pro-moted the Count of Monclova to the position of viceroy of Peru).

In Coahuila [Monclova], the governor made the necessary arrangements for the exploration, which will be described in the next chapter.

Chapter 36 / Governor Alonso de León Discovers the French Settlement and the Bay of Espíritu Santo

ON March 24 [1689], when all the necessary arrangements had been made in the Province of Coahuila, the governor set out by the northern route with the soldiers from El Parral and some from his presidio. After traveling four days, they reached the Sabinas River. On its bank, they saw the companies from Nuevo León, arriving and our troops rode out to meet them. Great cheers arose on both sides. Since they had gathered while it was still early, it was decided to make a general review of the troops to arrange whatever might be appropriate during the journey. As I hold the original copy of the roll call made that day, it is appropriate to set it down, to the letter, in this history. It is as follows: [1]

General list of all the men, military as well as mule drivers and servant boys, who came in the companies under the command of General Alonso de León (governor and captain of the presidio of the Province of Coahuila and principal head of companies), who are going in exploration of the settlement of the French, said to be on the Bay of Espíritu Santo. Dated today, March 27, 1689, on the Sabinas River.

General Alonso de León; Bachiller Doctor Toribio García de Sierra, priest and vicar of the province of Coahuila; Fray Damián Massanet, of the Order of Saint Francis, our chaplain; Major Nicolás de Medina; the royal alferez, Francisco Martínez; Adjutant Gerónimo Cantú; Juan Baptista Chapa. [2]

Captain Lorenzo de la Garza, Alferez Juan Cantú, Sergeant Joseph Pérez, Sergeant Miguel de León, Alferez Joseph Sánchez, Alferez Juan Ramírez, Sergeant Agustín García, Marcos de los Reyes, Juan de Benavides, Salvador de los Reyes, Nicolás de Bermeo, Lucas González, Juan Rendón, Tomás Gutiérrez, Miguel de Betancourt, Blas de Ochoa, Joseph de Urdiales, Diego Martín, Nicolás de

Salazar, Alejo de la Garza, Sergeant Gaspar de Lerma, Joseph Gutiérrez, Juan Guerra, Antonio de Escobedo, Domingo Guerra, Nicolás de Estrada, Atanasio del Corral, Captain Tomás de la Garza, Alferez Nicolás de Ayala, Sergeant Bernardo de Benavides, Captain Cristóbal de Villarreal, Alferez Francisco de Treviño, Sergeant Juan de Olivares, Sergeant Gaspar de Chapa, Joseph de las Casas, Felipe de Sosa, Alonso García, Nicolás García, Melchor de Garibay, Diego de Montalvo, Joseph de Abrego, Juan de Treviño, Juan de Charles, Antonio Prieto, Joseph de la Garza, Alonso Rodríguez, Ignacio Hernández, Sergeant Lorenzo García, Diego de Pastrana, Antonio de Espinosa, Baltasar de Sepúlveda, Jacinto de Talamante, Francisco de la Garza, Captain Alonso de León, Alferez Nicolás de Ochoa, Sergeant Antonio González, Corporal Antonio Martincho, Manuel de la Riba, Francisco de Castro, Juan Antonio Vizcarra, Gaspar de Figueroa, Diego López, Gerónimo de Tejeda, Corporal Miguel de Valenzuela, Joseph de Saucedo, Cristóbal Pérez, Marcos de Frías, Ambrosio Valtierra, Joseph de Ayala, Alferez Antonio de Adame, Antonio Saldaña, Diego de Acosta, Salvador de Treviño, Juan de Ribera, Nicolás Gómez, Francisco Javier, Juan del Canto, Joseph Hurtado, Joseph Minchaca, Gaspar López, Nicolás Hernández.

Juan Andrés [Jean Géry], who was the French prisoner; twelve mule drivers (mostly armed with offensive weapons); thirteen servants of all classes; 721 horses and mules; 82 loads of meal, hardtack, and other rations; three loads of clothing and other things to distribute to the Indians in the course of the journey.

On [March] 28 the companies set out toward the Río Bravo, which is forty-two leagues from Coahuila [Monclova]; they reached it on April 1. On the day before reaching the river, camp had been made near a large encampment of Indians who were known to the Frenchman [Jean Géry]. The Indians flattered him greatly when the companies arrived—seating him on some buffalo hides between two Indian maidens. We distributed to the Indians some gifts that had been brought, including knives, earrings, *tochomite*,[3] and two loads of meal. Five steers were slaughtered for them.

In front of the encampment where they stationed the Frenchman, a pole was planted, and hanging from it were the heads of sixteen enemy Indians whom they had killed. In this encampment were Indians of four nations, namely Ape, Mescal, Jumane, and Ijiaba. Out of curiosity the governor counted the Indians, and there were 490, not counting those who had gone to hunt bison[4] and others who had hidden in a woods near the encampment.

Chapter 37 / The Expedition Continues

WHEN camp had been made on the banks of the Río Bravo, we tried to estimate the flow and abundance of the river. It is very turbid and is about the range of a musket in width. Some think its headwaters are beyond New Mexico. The current in this location is not strong, nor is the crossing difficult,[1] and it was not necessary to put the loads over pack by pack.

Two days after the crossing, on Palm Sunday, camp was made on a creek; there, as we were carrying an astrolabe, we took the measurement of the sun although the instrument was somewhat out of order. The camp was found to be at 26°31' north, although this observation was not thought to be very exact because of the defect in the astrolabe and because the tables of the sun's declination were very old and dated before the Gregorian correction.[2] However, we tried to adjust as best we could.

Continuing the journey, they reached a large river (after having crossed three others) on April 15, which they named the River of Our Lady of Guadalupe.[3] Here, since it was thought that they were very near the French settlement, a conference was held to determine the next move.

By my natural forgetfulness I have not set down in its proper place in the description of this exploration how God guided it in a very strange way. The wife of a Quem Indian, who lived near the Río Bravo, had been abducted by enemy Indians while he was not in his camp. When the [Quem] Indian returned and learned of his loss, he began, as a good husband, to make faithful efforts to find her. He traveled alone to various locations, taking risks in remote places, in the chance of locating her. He went so far from his own land that he reached the French settlement and remained with the French for three to four days. Since he received no news of his wife, the Indian returned to his native land. From his community he traveled to the mission called Santiago,[4] located next to the Caldera River, which Fray Damián Massanet was attending. He reported his discovery, although in a confused manner, and from there he went on to Saltillo.

Since at that time not much attention was paid to the report, his information was ignored until this expedition, on which the priest [Massanet] went along. When the information was given to Governor Alonso de León, he called for the Indian when they came near the Quem encampment, and the Indian joined the expedition on the Río Bravo. He was the one who guided us on the whole expedition. He knew a great deal about the land, having traveled it with diligence. Although they had along another guide,[5] an Indian whom the French prisoner called "brother," we were always suspicious of him because we suspected that the Frenchman, moved by the natural love of his own people, would have advised him not to reveal the location of the settlement. This matter was recognized on some occasions when the two Indians argued over the route to be followed. We always accepted the Quem Indian's direction. Thereby the general fulfilled the promise he made to the Indian, namely, that they would look for his wife even though it might take a lot of work. I have made this digression because it was very necessary, and I continue as I intended.

As a result of the conference, the governor set out the next day, April 16, with sixty men to reconnoiter the settlement, because the guide [the Quem Indian] said that it was two or three days away. After hearing a mass to our Lady of Guadalupe, the company and the sixty men set out at the same time. Having traveled about three leagues, the rear guard of the sixty men captured an Indian whom they found in a motte of live oaks. When brought to the governor and questioned as competently as our guide was able, the captive said that his encampment was nearby and that four Frenchmen were there. With this information the governor decided to go to the Indian's encampment and ordered the company to stay where the Indian had been brought, because there were ponds there.

The party set out, with the Indian guiding, and within three leagues we found the encampment.[6] Seemingly, the Indians had received notice of the approaching Spaniards, because they were already scurrying into a woods of live oaks, followed by twelve to fourteen dogs laden with their buffalo hides. Using the same Indian who had guided us, we called for them to return, and most did. The Indians made it clear that the four Frenchmen were not there, but instead had gone on toward the province of the Tejas [Indians] four days earlier. Here also were two Indians from another location who said that two days' journey away, the Frenchmen would be found. The company ingratiated themselves with these Indians by giving them knives, tobacco, and other things so that they would guide us to these Frenchmen, as was done following a route toward the north until sunset.

At nightfall, in a live oak grove next to a creek, we found an encampment of more than 250 Indians.[7] Here, using the French prisoner as an interpreter, they asked about the French.[8] We were told that the Frenchmen had gone to the Tejas four days earlier. The Indians also said that the other Frenchmen who had been in the settlement on the little sea (by this "little sea" they meant the Bay of Espíritu Santo) had been killed by the coastal Indians. They added that the Frenchmen had six houses where they had lived, and that this event had occurred three months previously. The Indians also noted that before this occurrence, there had been an attack of smallpox from which most of the Frenchmen had died.

The following day we continued north in search of the Frenchmen until we reached a small encampment of Indians known to our French prisoner.[9] Here we received more news of the four Frenchmen and learned that they had gone farther on. After discussing what could be done, it was decided that, because the camp was already very far away and in an unknown country, a letter would be written to them in French by the alferez, Francisco Martínez, who was very knowledgeable in the language. The letter would be sent to them with an Indian who would be rewarded.

This was done, and the substance of the note was this: We have received news that the Indians of the coast killed their companions and that they escaped. If they wished to live among Christians, we would wait for them at the French settlement for three to four days.

This letter was signed by the governor and Fray Damián, there being added below it four lines in Latin—in case a priest were there—exhorting them to come. They enclosed a piece of white paper in case the Frenchmen wished to answer. With this completed, the mail went out and the governor, with the soldiers, set out to return to the camp. On the return trip, the governor received a note informing him that the horses at the base camp had stampeded, and although one hundred of them had escaped, some had been found. We rushed our return trip to the camp, where besides the loss of the horses it was found that four soldiers who had gone to search for the horses were themselves missing. Although three had appeared that morning, one was still missing, namely, Juan de Charles. It was therefore necessary to remain in camp two days and send out squadrons in various directions. When the soldier did not appear it was decided, on the third day, to proceed. When they were all ready to set out, the lost soldier arrived, guided by some Indians. He said that he had slept that night in an Indian encampment he had come upon, and they showed him great kindness and good lodging. On this day we observed the elevation of the Pole and found ourselves at 28°4′.[10] We slept that night by a creek of very good water.

❧

Chapter 38 / Arrival at the French Settlement

ON April 22, it pleased God that the company, directed by the Indian guide, should reach the deserted settlement where the French had been. It was composed of a little wooden fort and six small, very flimsy houses made of upright poles and mud. The roofs were made of buffalo hides, useless for any defense. The houses had all been sacked of the few belongings that their inhabitants had possessed. More than two hundred French books were torn to pieces, with their pages thrown outside; the leaves were rotted because it had rained many times there. The enemy Indians had horrendously sacked the whole settlement. Another thing worthy of consideration was noted, namely, that in the Indians' encampments that we had visited before reaching the settlement, French books were found, very well treated and meticulously bound. Other items of little value were also found. The books were recovered to send to His Excellency.

The enemy Indians wreaked havoc not only on the inhabitants but also on the arms they found. The company found more than one hundred broken harquebus butts next to the houses. Apparently, the Indians had taken the harquebuses by the barrels and had struck them against the artillery pieces, breaking the stocks, butts, and hammers. Three corpses were found scattered in the field. One seemed to have been a woman, as she still had her skirt stuck to her bones. The rest of the body had been eaten by animals. All the bones were gathered and buried, and a requiem mass was sung with the body present.

Distributed among the fort and other houses were eight pieces of new iron artillery of six- to eight-pound shot. Some were in their gun carriages

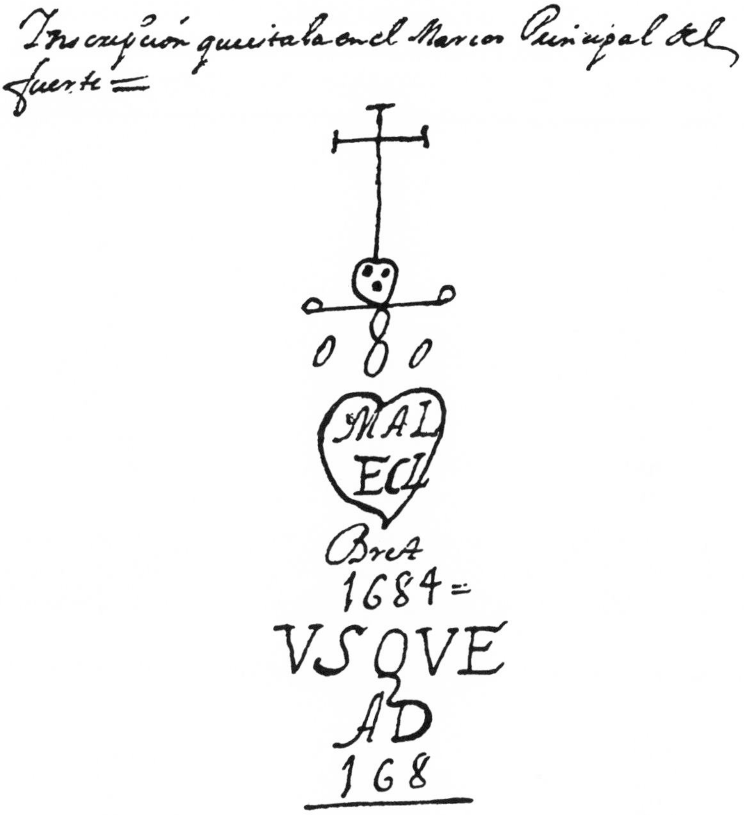

FIGURE 4. *Juan Bautista Chapa's sketch of carving on door at Fort St. Louis.*

and others on the ground. Triggers of the broken harquebuses were found near the houses; there were three stone firing pieces, although without chambers. There were some anchor-rope stays, and the whole was estimated to be a little more than twenty arrobas.[1] There were empty powder barrels without bottoms. We found only a little powder in one of the barrels. Near the houses we also found some fishing tackle, although in poor condition. It was not possible to find more of the dead than those mentioned, from which we inferred that the Indians had thrown the bodies into the creek near the settlement. This was in an excellent flat location from which to defend against any attack.

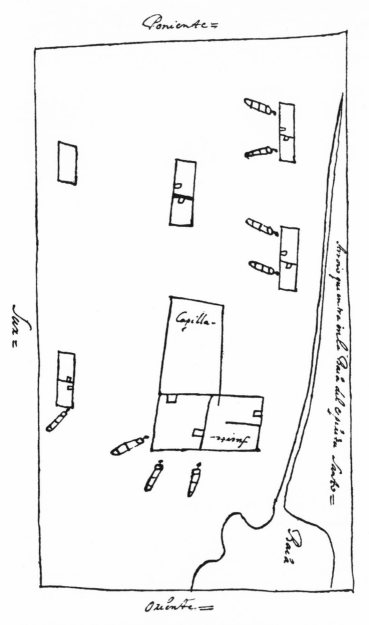

FIGURE 5. *Juan Bautista Chapa's sketch of the settlement.*

In the principal doorway of the fort there was cut with a knife the year in which they must have settled, which was 1684, with other inscriptions [see Figure 4].

And when an account was made of the leagues, day by day, from the presidio of Coahuila to the French settlement, the distance totaled 136 leagues; and from the city of Monterrey, the distance was 165 leagues.

As far as could be told, they were carving the number 168—which was fresh—on the lower part of the wooden piece when the Indians came upon them. That *usque ad* refers to the number of years listed first, [namely] 1684, which was the year in which they settled, and they tried to say "up to that of 1689" and did not finish it. It also seems good to me to put down a sketch of the settlement with its houses [see Figure 5]. Although it is no longer relevant, the sketch will be of interest.

Near the settlement they had a palisaded garden, in which the cornstalks they had planted were still standing. The garden was about three almudes [2] in area. This led to a discussion and recollection of the cornstalks that were seen on the seacoast [during the expedition] in 1686, when there was an exploration along the bank of the Río Bravo. The cornstalks must have come from this settlement, and doubtless some flooding of the creek next to the settlement carried them off. In passing through the bay, the currents over a period of time carried them to the other location. [3]

After two days at the settlement, General De León decided to continue the exploration of the bay. The general took the French prisoner as a guide because the Frenchman had said that he knew the bay and had traveled all of it in a boat. With this understanding, and with thirty men, the governor set out with the one in question [Géry], who refused to lead us down the creek because he said that there was no route in that direction. Instead Géry guided the party five leagues to the southwest; and having passed two creeks we traveled three more leagues to the east, as far as the bay, where they camped. [4] The following day we followed the shoreline for about eight leagues and found many lagoons of very salty water and many mudholes, so that it was necessary in some places to lead the horses on foot.

The bay forms a great cove to the north; another, smaller, is to the south, and the better one seems to lead to the mouth of the creek where the settlement was located. At the end of the eight leagues, more or less, we saw the pass where boats can enter, [5] which was about two leagues distant and which we could reach with their horses. The French prisoner affirmed to us that this was the pass where he had entered when he had come from France with Monsieur Philipe de la sala [La Salle].[6]

At the entry of the pass is a very low, small islet, which results in two entrances to the bay. The smaller of them—the one that is toward Veracruz—is the one by which one enters. As far as we could tell, the Guadalupe River enters into this bay by the southern part.[7] However, because it was not possible to enter the area, this could not be verified. The Frenchman affirmed the entrance of the river into the bay.

Along the length of shore that we traced, which, as I have said, was about eight leagues, we saw some ruins of ships, a topmast, a winch, some planking, and staves of barrels and casks, which doubtless were from some ship that had been lost within or on the coast. We could also see one ship's hull.

After reconnoitering the mouth of the bay, they returned along the same route by which they had come. They slept that night on the banks of a creek, near an Indian encampment that, from its appearance, had been abandoned for two months. In it four canoes, although abused, were found; this suggested that the creek entered into the bay.[8] At the Indian encampment a broken powder horn case was found, along with a bit of powder and pieces of very outstanding [quality] paper and a French book. Doubtless, these Indians had been among those who had taken part in the deaths of the French.

When they set out the next day, soldiers came out to greet them before they reached camp. The soldiers said they had received a reply to the letter written to the Frenchmen, for the Indian courier had already arrived.[9] They delivered the letter to the governor. It was written with red ochre and arrived opened. The signature read Larchebec de Bayone, and Bachiller Don Toribio García, priest of Coahuila, saw the signature and concluded that doubtless this meant "the archbishop of Bayonne." However, the priest did not realize two things: first, that Bayonne is not an archbishopric, and [second], that even if it were, it was a very implausible thing that an archbishop would come to a new settlement for no reason. So there was no reason for him to believe this. It seems fitting to me to set down the letter, word for word, because I possess a copy of it, which reads as follows:

Copy of the Letter

Jesus, Mary. I received your agreeable [letter] by which you beg us that you are completely [unintelligible]. We pray to see the goodness [of God]. From among us, two have [unintelligible] farther. I will not fail to send them to search as soon as they have come. We shall not fail to come to make a journey to you, in Christian [unintelligible]. We shall not fail to bring you back among the Christians. We have already been a long time among barbarians who do not even have [unintelligible]. Messieurs, as soon as I receive yours I shall not fail to search for the other gentlemen. Messieurs, I am your very humble and very obedient servant. Larchebeque de Bayone.[10]

When this letter had been read by the royal alferez, Francisco Martínez, who understands French, he said that in substance, its contents were that the Frenchmen who had received what had been written to them were only two in number. Two other Frenchmen had gone farther. The two would wait for them a few days and then would come to the settlement at the bay; they were already tired of wandering among barbarians.

❧

Chapter 39 / The Discovery and Naming of the San Marcos River

ALTHOUGH the governor had decided to wait three or four days for the two Frenchmen because they had written that they would come, he thought that there was a possibility that they would not come either because they might change their minds or because of inconveniences that might develop. Therefore, he decided to break camp on April 26, and at the same time to explore the large river that the French prisoner said was to the north.

Guided by the Frenchman, the governor went with twenty soldiers, and about six leagues away, they found the river. It is very large, seemingly larger than the Río Bravo. They followed its bank upstream to where lagoons blocked the way. It seemed navigable in a small boat. The governor decided—even though it would be difficult—to view the mouth of the river. This finally was accomplished from a little hill that is three quarters of a league from the mouth of the river. The distance from the river mouth to the mouth of the creek where the French came in to settle is the same distance as that from the mouth of the creek to the settlement, namely, about one and a half leagues.

On this day we traveled more than fifteen leagues, the total distance being very near the bay. We shot the sun and found ourselves at 29°3′ (discounting error owing to the bad quality of the astrolabe).[1] To this river we gave the name San Marcos,[2] because it was discovered one day after his feast day.

At 9:00 P.M. we returned to the company where the camp was. The river we explored is north of the settlement. And I do not want to omit, although it may seem a matter alien to the history, some verse that a subject, having witnessed the damage and havoc that the Indians had caused, composed in the French settlement. He recited as follows:[3]

Mournful and sad place,
where gloom alone attends you,
because sad fortune
gave your inhabitants a beastly death.
Here I only contemplate
that you are a fatality and a sad example
of the inconstancy of life
because the wild and murderous enemy,
so cruel and inhuman,
discharged his cruelty with a stubborn hand
against such an innocence,
not pardoning even the youngest child.

Oh beautiful Frenchwomen
who walked over fresh roses in these meadows
and with snowy hands
touched white lily in brief field
and in beautiful drawing
put the finishing touches on Greek ladies
because your ivory [needles]
adorned the seams with profiles
as deceased as you are,
these forests all together look at you
and, not spoiled in vain,
see themselves through your death, and so misused!

And you, cold corpse,
who at one time showed such vigor,

and now by animals
eaten, as your remains show,
I contemplate you tenderly,
and you are a living example of unhappiness.
You enjoy eternal glory,
because you went from this transitory life
to a celestial dwelling,
going with such a wound transcended.
Pray to Eternal God
that he free us from the pains of hell.

The verse was composed in the horror of having found, about a stone's throw from the settlement's last house, a woman killed with arrows. According to the account given later by the two Frenchmen (who will be mentioned in the next chapter), she was fleeing, attempting to escape the enemy Indians, when they shot her down at that location. The sight caused much pity among us, both for her and for the others.

These are judgments of God that we cannot fathom, but it also seems that they are examples and models so that Christians should not immediately oppose the decisions and mandates of the popes. In the one that Alexander VI issued in favor of King Ferdinand and Queen Isabella in 1494, he favored and gifted them with all that the Spaniards had discovered in the West Indies and that they might discover—prohibiting any other king from occupying them, under pain of excommunication. So it may be that because they [the French] had violated this precept, God sent them this punishment.

Before I forget, I shall list at the end of this chapter Indian nations that the French prisoner said were loyal to him. These are the following:

Cuba, Emot, Sanatoo, Poguan, Cosmojoo, Piyai, Piguen, Panaa, Pataoo, Tamireguan, Cagremoa, Agaaunimi, Chile, Cobapo, Huiapico, Etayax, Cuajin, Caomopac, Saurum. These, together with the *five* nations mentioned in Chapter 36, make twenty-four nations.[4] These tribes live dispersed throughout an extent of about seventy leagues. The Frenchman could not state the significance of the meaning that the names of the nations each have in their own language. This can be determined according to our experience with the Indian encampments in this province [Nuevo León] that are congregated on the farms and cattle ranches. For the proof of this I shall set down here the names of some tribes with their meanings, which out of curiosity I have verified. They are as follows:

Ayancuara means "Painted Lines"; *Pantiguara*, "Anointed with Red Ochre"; *Ayanguara*, "Thickets without Thorns"; *Saguimaniguara*, "Field Lacking Wood"; *Maguipamacopini*, "Big Star That Kills Deer"; *Guciacapo*, "Water within the Woods"; *Bayaguera* means "Deer Foot"; *Agustiguara*, "Sharp-Pointed Peak"; *Payamiguara*, "People Who Live in Little Ravines."[5] I do not want to tire the reader with more translations, because those that I have recorded suffice as proof. More important, the meaning of the tribal names are not ideas and concepts worth committing to memory, as there is no purpose for doing so.

❧

Chapter 40 / Governor Alonso de León Locates the Two Frenchmen

AS he was returning from the exploration of the Bay of Espíritu Santo on the second day after leaving the French settlement, the governor decided, in view of the news contained in the letter, to undertake a new journey in search of the two Frenchmen. He ordered the main party to proceed to make camp on the Our Lady of Guadalupe River, and with thirty soldiers he set out in a northerly direction. Having traveled about twenty-five leagues with a guide they took along, they came upon an Indian encampment where there was a Tejas captain, in whose company were the two Frenchmen. The Tejas captain was showing the Frenchmen good care and hospitality as far as was possible from his way of living. There were other Indians with the Tejas captain, but his own land was not there; it was much farther on.

The Tejas captain had a little chapel made of buffalo hides that contained some images and a crucifix, and he held them in great veneration. He maintained a fire in the chapel at all times.[1] As the governor approached, the Tejas Indians, with the two Frenchmen, went out to receive him and they saluted him with pistol shots. The Tejas Indian spoke to God and made it understood by signs that there was a God in heaven.

It seemed fitting to Alonso de León to bring the Tejas captain and some of his people to the main camp [at the Guadalupe crossing] to ingratiate themselves with the Tejas and to distribute to the Indians some of the valuables that still remained. The Tejas captain was an Indian in whom some ability was recognized (although he was a barbarian). The captain was flattered by both the governor's treatment and everything else. The governor gave him and his people everything that remained, with which they were very pleased.

To rest the horses, the camp had to remain two more days on the Guadalupe River. During this time, the Frenchmen were asked about the deaths of their people. They told us that they had been stricken with an attack of smallpox, from which more than one hundred people had died.[2] Those who lived at the settlement were very much at peace with the Indian nations of that area and were very unconcerned about the Indians harming them. A little more than a month later, five Indians came to the settlement under the pretext of selling them some things. They had stopped in the farthest removed of the five houses; and then others came along on the same pretext. Since the French did not suspect them, they all went to see them, unarmed. When they were inside the house, a large number of Indians came and seized them, and another ambush came out of the creek at the same time. So the settlers could not defend themselves. The Indians stabbed or clubbed them all to death, among them two priests and a cleric, and they sacked all the houses.

The Frenchmen said that they had not been present at this occurrence because they had gone to the Tejas Indians, from whom they heard this news. Later, four of them returned and found their companions dead—about twenty, more or less, with some women. They had buried up to fourteen that they found, and burned almost a hundred quintales[3] of gunpowder so that the Indians would not carry it off. They said that the settlement was well equipped with all kinds of firearms, swords, and cutlasses, and very good ornaments for the church, including three chalices. They also had a number of well-bound books.

One of the Frenchmen (the youngest, who was scarcely twenty-two years old) said that he was called Juan Larchebec de Bayone, and the other, Jácome. The first was a native of Bayonne, and the second of La Rochelle. The governor took down their declarations in secret to send to His Excellency.[4]

Before the camp was moved from the Our Lady of Guadalupe River, the governor urged the Tejas captain to come along with his people; but the Indian leader, using a native cunning, said that he would not go until he saw that we had crossed the river. No arguments could sway the Tejas leader, and he watched us cross [the river] and did not move until we were out of view. We were amazed that a barbarian should have so much prudence.

The next day, when camp had been made, we were overcome by curiosity and asked the two Frenchmen about their life among these barbarous people, including about the Indian settlement and mode of government. As individuals who had lived among the Indians, they could answer from personal experience. They said that the Tejas nation had a community far from where we had found them (but they could not say how many leagues). They said that the Tejas settlement was fifteen leagues long and seven leagues wide (they denoted this distance with a demonstration of the land that we could see). In the community every inhabitant has his house and large garden, enough to plant corn for his use. They said that they also grow beans, squash, and other plants, with which they sustain themselves. The houses are built of poles and are round, with a shack next to it as well. They construct walls or divisions and sleeping quarters or rooms inside. If one neighbor is away on some important business, the governor of the community appoints another in his place who takes care of his house and harvests the crops—so that when he gets back he finds everything gathered and in good condition. This seemed to us a very good government. They affirmed that farther on there are nine more communities, each very well established and in good order.

I also remember that one night when the Tejas Indian was with us, we asked him, through an interpreter and with the help of the two Frenchmen, if possibly he had seen a woman wearing a habit (pointing out that of Fray Damián) or if his ancestors had seen one. To this he responded that he had not seen her, but that he had heard of such a person from his ancestors. He said that on some occasions a lady wearing the habit they showed him had appeared to his ancestors. So it was opined that she was Mother María de Jesús,[5] the nun of Agreda, as she mentions in her writings that she traveled in those provinces, which she calls "Tielas."

Continuing our return trip to the Province of Coahuila, we reached the Nueces River, which is sixty leagues from the presidio [of Coahuila]. On the following day, May 10, it seemed proper to the governor to advance with fifteen men and the two Frenchmen and the royal alferez, Francisco Martínez, to dispatch to His Excellency an account of the exploration of the French settlement and the bay, with the journal and itinerary that he had kept with complete punctiliousness and clarity, including the description and quality of the land. Having arrived at the presidio of the province [of Coahuila] on [May] 13, at the hour of prayer, Francisco Martínez set out on [May] 18 for Mexico City with the two Frenchmen and the dispatches for His Excellency, who must have been very anxious to know the outcome of this expedition—in which, thanks to God, no danger was experienced.

❧

Chapter 41 / Uprisings in Nuevo León in 1689

GIVING an account of the occurrences in the Province of Coahuila is not outside the scope of the history of Nuevo León. For one thing, the [1689] expedition included Coahuila's best soldiers; furthermore, that province and this one [Nuevo León] border one another. Coahuila belonged to this jurisdiction from the time of the exploration of this province by Luis de Carbajal y de la Cueva, who entered it in around 1580. I have seen the agreement by which it was granted, and from this grant they drew the one that His Majesty made with Don Martín de Zavala in 1625. Thus I shall go on from here with whatever occurrences there may be in either Nuevo León or Coahuila, because the jurisdictions are not relevant.

While we were on the journey to the Bay of Espíritu Santo—or rather, soon after returning from it—the Janambre[1] and others from the San Antonio region rose up and killed two shepherds. They also burned the houses in the San Antonio Valley, which obliged some settlers to move away. It was necessary for the governor of Nuevo León to involve himself personally in their punishment. He formed a company and, because of his good efforts, the troops captured some of the aggressors, whom they punished. However, the threat continued as many of the enemy retreated to the mountains while others escaped to the thickest, most impenetrable woods.

Nevertheless, various expeditions continued to be made—but bore little fruit, because these natives are very astute and are seldom found on plains, where we could capture them. Although the governor tried to attract them by peaceful means, he could not. He assigned that side of the province to Major Carlos Cantú, a Pilón Valley settler experienced in militia. Cantú's good efforts enabled him to capture twenty Indians out of those suspected of the crimes that had been committed. The guiltiest were hanged, and they took away the others (accompanying justice with mercy) to exculpate their crimes in the mines of Mazapil and Bonanza—from which they all escaped in a few months.

The Indians continued their uprising; as a result, the mission of San Buenaventura de Tamaulipas was abandoned. The priest went to live at the mission of San Cristóbal, which is six leagues away; the enemy had taken away the few pack animals belonging to San Buenaventura. Although at that time the mission was not abandoned completely, it was necessary to do so soon afterward, so that the Indians would not carry off any more livestock. The animals were moved to the mission of San Cristóbal. The Indians who had burned the priest's dwellings remained unpunished.

When the governor saw that the uprising of the Indians continued and that efforts to reduce them—on the part of General Fernando Sánchez de Zamora, chief justice and lieutenant captain general of the district and mines of Río Blanco—had no effect, he was obliged to go out again in person to see if he could have some effect. He enlisted a company of sixty soldiers and set out in early September. On his journey they reached the San Antonio Valley, from which they dispatched spies and also a letter to General Zamora telling him to collect as many people as he could and come to join His Lordship. This was done; the general arrived with a squadron of fifteen well-armed and well-prepared soldiers. Some of them set out that day with Major Carlos Cantú to see whether, with assistance from the spies, they could capture some of the enemy.

Forty-four men set out on this task. During the engagement, their camp was at a post called San Agustín. Letters arrived at the post from the lieutenant of the Pilón Valley and from Father Domingo Blanco, a missionary from Tamaulipas. The letters told how Domingo Conde, protector of the town of San Cristóbal, had confided in Indians whom he had in his retinue and who most of the time served him in that town. He had decided, with a son-in-law, to go to the Tamaulipas Mountains with an Indian called Juan Bellaco. Juan and the son-in-law had fled back the town with news of how a squadron of Indians of [Bellaco's] people had arrived. When they had sat down to talk with them while they were still at some distance, they grabbed Conde and killed him. This news caused everyone much sorrow. All condemned the decision of the deceased and his trustingness, because they had experience and knew the Indians could not be trusted.

On September 18 the troops that had gone to look for the enemy returned with eighteen prisoners of all ages, whom they had captured in ambush. They recounted an unusual occurrence. The troops had chased an Indian who was about to escape into the woods; the Indian's young eight- or nine-year-old daughter was running along with him. When the Indian saw that the soldiers were about to catch up to him (he was already very near the woods), he recognized that, although he could escape, his daughter could not. The Indian then shot an arrow at her chest. She deflected the arrow with her hand when she saw what her father was doing. Nevertheless, the arrow entered her at an angle, about four finger-widths into the left side of her chest. The Indian had time to reach the woods, although he was already wounded. The child was brought back with the others. Care was taken to heal her, and in four or five days she recovered from the wound.

It seemed fitting to the governor to set the captives free to see if by this liberality (and by having given the Indians woolen cloth, small blankets, and other things) he could induce them to have their companions come down in peace—promising them, by means of those who were set free, that they would be received with all affection. But neither these nor other efforts sufficed to achieve it, and the uprising continues as this is being written.

The governor sent out a squadron of soldiers to look at the body of the deceased Conde; they found it devoured by animals, with his bones strewn about. Seeing that nothing advantageous could be achieved, the governor ordered us to come to the city of Monterrey, as was done, with the fruitlessness that has been seen previously.

The land remained in a worse state than before, although General Zamora, as a neighbor and the nearest to the allies, promised to make all possible efforts to bring about peace. But peace has not been achieved; and two missions, San Bernardino and San Antonio, have been depopulated and their missionaries are in other monasteries keeping watch for when His Divine Majesty may be pleased to have peace take effect.

Chapter 42 / The Exploration and Settlement of the Río Blanco

I HAVE brought the history of the Province of Nuevo León to the present, and have given an account of things that occurred. While the news is arriving of the new expedition to the province of the Tejas [Indians] by order of the viceroy, under the command of Governor Alonso de León (and in due time the new motives that existed therefor will be told), it seems fitting to me to augment the account with the exploration of the Río Blanco. This is a mining district that, when it was in its full vigor, afforded His Majesty many assets because of the silver that was extracted and because the mines belonged to this province's government. This post is fifty leagues southeast of Monterrey, seven leagues from the San Antonio de los Llanos mission.

There are three routes from Monterrey to there. One is called El Pilón Chico and crosses the river thirty-seven times. This comes out between two high, inaccessible mountain ranges, and on it is a bridge called Puente de Dios [God's Bridge] because it was made by nature. The river passes under the bridge; its bed seems to lie about twenty estados [about 110 feet] below. From there one comes upon a post called Labradores, five leagues from a valley called Pablillo; from there one continues to the Río Blanco.

The second route is called Los Pastores, which has no river to cross. However, there is a small, narrow pass five leagues long. This is very dangerous for transporting sheep, because the pass is so narrow that, if there were a downpour, no sheep could escape.

The third route is via the San Antonio mission. To reach the settlement of Río Blanco, the Río Blanco is crossed forty-four times. Despite these inconveniences, these routes are ordinarily traveled by the shepherds, and by means of them flocks are taken to New Spain.

During the expedition that this province's governor made in search of the warlike Indians—to which I referred in the last chapter—I was in contact with General Zamora and told him that I was writing this history. He told me that he had a little notebook of observations he had made of the Río Blanco district. I requested that he send it to me, and I quote it to the letter.[1]

Chapter 43 / The Exploration of the Province of the Tejas Continues

I HAVE noted that an account would be given of the new expedition that was arranged to explore the province of the Tejas and that the motives that necessitated it would be disclosed. These arose because of the letter Governor Alonso de León wrote to His Excellency in which he told of the necessary preparations for the expedition and the need to establish presidios in the locations that the governor designated. These presidio locations were on the Río Bravo [Rio Grande], the Río Zarco [Leona], and the Río de Guadalupe, with another on the bay. To settle the province of the Tejas, another was needed with as many soldiers as in the others.

His Excellency discussed the proposal not only with His Majesty's ministers, but also with the religious prelates so the priests would see that they could attend to the conversion of as many souls as might ask for baptism. They were to be under Fray Damián Massanet and attended by soldiers of complete acceptability, valor, and moral qualities.

Then His Excellency ordered the governor to solicit however many might be necessary for the second expedition and named a leader who was completely acceptable to the priests to assure that there would not be any disputes between the groups, nor any bad example for the Indians. He ordered the governor to try, in the interim, to continue the communication with the Tejas governor and to notify them of His Excellency's proposal that the Tejas should agree to friendship with us and should desire to embrace religion. The governor was to tell the Tejas governor that in His Majesty's name he would do him many honors and favors and would send him valuables of the kind that the Tejas Indians esteemed most. His Excellency ordered the governor to notify him of the most appropriate time to carry out the journey and the route to follow, with all the requirements and necessary preparations.

The governor responded to all the basic questions. Therefore, His Excellency decided to dispatch an order to the magistrate at Zacatecas and to Sombrerete to enlist ninety men, and, if that number could not be raised, the balance to be enlisted in Nuevo León and Saltillo. Once these preparations

FIGURE 6. *To secure his allegiance to the Spanish crown, Alonso de León presents a*

cane of authority to the chieftain of the Tejas in East Texas on his 1690 expedition.

were complete and His Excellency's order was dispatched for twenty soldiers from the presidios of Vizcaya, the journey was set for February. However, this date proved too early because of the lack of horses, which could be found only outside of the region.

In addition, the twenty soldiers from Vizcaya had been delayed, and only forty soldiers were gathered and enlisted in Zacatecas and Sombrerete. There were twenty from Nuevo León, including four from the presidio of Cerralvo. They set out from Monterrey on March 15, 1690, and from the province of Coahuila twelve days later, March 27. Although the twenty soldiers from El Parral had not arrived,[1] Alonso de León decided to set out and left the men from El Parral to catch up with the company whenever they might arrive.

The twenty soldiers from El Parral reached Saltillo and then went on to Coahuila, and, because of certain differences that two soldiers had with a settler, swords were drawn.[2] The lord mayor learned of it, took the soldiers captive, and made peace. However, since the ill-intentioned are never lacking in republics (thus it was divulged), they advised the head of the soldiers, one Antonio Martincho, that he had allowed his soldiers to be taken captive even though the lord mayor was not their judge. Although the case had already been settled and the disputants had made friends, Martincho, accompanied by six soldiers, went to the royal house. Some of them were left to guard the doors while the others went inside—where they found the lord mayor, Don Alonso Ramos de Herrera y Salcedo, lieutenant captain general. Seeing Martincho standing at the door and assuming that he was coming to say goodbye, Alonso Ramos asked him when the journey was to take place. The answer he gave was to pull out a dagger and cut Ramos on the head in such a manner that he cut off a piece of skin. Another was cut from his left elbow, with which he had tried to ward off the blow. Thus he would have killed him had a priest not been there to interpose himself. In addition, a mulatto belonging to the lord mayor placed himself in front of him and received another large cut on the head.

When the leader left with his six soldiers and with the lord mayor shouting, the settlers, completely ignorant of the event, appeared. The leader and his soldiers holed up in a house that is about a league from the town, near a farm, and prepared to defend themselves. The soldiers mounted their horses and waited to see if the settlers were going to capture them. In the meantime, many people had collected in the town. The lord mayor named a leader and ordered him to capture the six soldiers and the leader, or to kill them if they refused to surrender. They approached the place where the soldiers were, taking along two priests who, with their powers of persuasion should advise them to surrender. Although they were urged to do so, the soldiers refused to give up. Finally they urged the leader so strongly that he let himself be persuaded and was captured, with four of the group who accompanied him.

They gave the leader a separate jail and put the other four in the public one. Once their statements were taken, the four confessed the crime and the leader denied it. The soldiers said that the leader had put them under penalty of death to accompany him. In light of these statements, the leader confessed openly, saying that his companions had no guilt at all. Because the crime had been so atrocious, the lord mayor, according to military custom, ordered him shot, so that he might serve as an example.

The four soldiers were set free so that they might go with the others to fulfill their duty. They reached Coahuila after the governor left. By means of the trail, however, they reached him on April 30, when the company was on the other [east] side of the Guadalupe River. When two of the soldiers gave an account of how the company members were coming along behind without horses or provisions, the governor sent them relief.

The governor had already reconnoitered the French settlement, which had been explored the previous year. When he saw the artillery that had been buried there, he burned the fort. He had not burned the fort the previous year for reasons that moved him, of which he gave notice to His Excellency.

They left the fort to reconnoiter the bay, where they saw two buoys. Apparently, one was where the San Marcos [Lavaca] River flows into the bay, and the other was to one side and seemingly signaled the same channel. They hoped on this day to observe the latitude of the bay, but unfortunately it was cloudy, so it was not possible to do so. It was hoped that the latitude that was observed the previous year, with the broken astrolabe, could be corrected. However, I always judge that the latitude will be found to be 29°,[3] the reading that all the authors of geographies give.

The general traveled with some company members more than sixty leagues in various directions to see whether they might find Indians from whom to get guidance, but none were found until May 3, after they had crossed the San Marcos [Colorado] River. Here they found an Indian woman and child. Although Alonso de León's party signaled to them by signs, the [Tejas] Indians refused to approach and instead escaped into the woods. So the governor went with two soldiers to the Indians' encampment and, seeing that they were not there, he left tobacco, knives, ribbons, earrings, and a piece of cloth. He camped for the night away from the Indian encampment. The next day an Indian came to meet the governor. After he had ingratiated himself with the Indian and asked repeated questions concerning the governor of the Tejas, the Indian said that he would notify the Tejas governor. So the governor [De León] decided to send him immediately to the governor of the Tejas. The Indian left his wife and a young brother-in-law to guide them.

The governor then dispatched Captain Francisco de Benavides with three soldiers to the camp so that the supply party would come to him. On May 9, having recrossed the San Marcos [Colorado] River, De Leon found two Indians and, a short distance away, Captain Francisco de Benavides with three soldiers. The captain brought an Indian he had found who was conversant with the Mexican [Aztec] language to serve as interpreter. By this means, it was learned that a French boy was at an encampment about two days' march west, and a second boy was in another encampment toward the east. Carrying out the effort for the second day, we found some Indians and one of the French boys, named Pedro [Pierre] Talón,[4] a boy twelve years of age. (At that time the Indians did not have information on any other French boy.)

The following day, news of the second Frenchman was received; he was in another encampment. As the governor was on this [southwest] side of the San Marcos [Colorado] River, and it had rained a good deal upriver, he was fearful of a further rise and recrossed the river that day. On the following day, May 12, the second Frenchman arrived with three other Indians to meet the governor. The Frenchman said that his name was Pedro Muñi.[5]

The company then traveled toward the province of the Tejas. The governor of that nation, having received notice of De León's approach, traveled to a location about twenty leagues this side of his residence to meet the governor. He was accompanied by fourteen members of his tribe, to whom the troops distributed clothing and other goods that they were carrying. The governor of the Tejas and his people were very happy to see the Spaniards, and the Tejas governor said that his people had been awaiting them with anticipation.

Continuing the journey, De León's party reached a very pleasant valley, which he named the Valley of Galve. A very large river passes near it, which they named Río de la Santísima Trinidad [the Trinity River]. It was difficult to cross. On May 22, after the company had passed some very large live oak mottes and five dry creeks, they reached a heavily settled valley, which is the beginning of the land of the Tejas. There they found many houses built in the Tejas style, and nearby were many fields of corn, beans, pumpkins, and watermelon. They named this settlement San Francisco Javier.

To the north of this settlement, beyond a hill covered with live oaks, and about a quarter-league away, was another valley of Indians of the same nation with their houses. The Tejas governor told Alonso de León that his house was nearby, and they went to it. Before they arrived, the Tejas governor's mother, wife, and daughter came out, with many others, to receive the troops. They brought out benches on which they sat—a civility that greatly surprised our troops. Our surprise grew when they very neatly served corn and *atole* tamales.[6]

* * *

Chapter 44 / The Journey to the Tejas Continues

WHEN I consider the explorations that General Alonso de León has made along this Northern Sea [Gulf of Mexico] since 1686, and the honor that should be given him for such innumerable works and services, I think that they are worthy of eternal fame. This should be proclaimed not only in the Indies but also in Spain and all of Europe. However, the same fortune may follow him as has followed other explorers of this New World, namely, that instead of honor, they received ingratitude and rudeness. History is full of similar recompenses.

Our general has made four journeys in these areas (as is mentioned in this history), with the good fortune that has been experienced. On this last one, he explored the heavily populated nation of the Tejas, in which one expects a very full harvest of souls that are to be converted to the brotherhood of our Holy Mother Church, because they are such a docile nation (as has been experienced) and have gained so much affection from the Spaniards.

Our general is worthy of the commendation that Pope Alexander VI made to Don Cristóbal Colón [Christopher Columbus], who first discovered this New World. In the bull that he issued awarding the Indies to the Catholic monarchs—the words of which are as follows: "dilectum virum

Christophorum Columbum virum utique dignum et plurimun comendan-
dum ac tanto negocio actum destinatis non sini maximis laboribus et periculis ut terra firma et insulas remotas et incognitas permare ubi ac temus nav-
igatum non fuerat dilixenter in qui resed, etta."

These words apply to our triumphant general word for word, because in
these, *non sini maximis laboribus et periculis, etta,* he is seen so adequately,
in truth, in the labors and perils that he experienced on these journeys. He
crossed unknown lands and passed through many warlike nations of barbarian Indians with fewer than a hundred men, many of whom were not
experienced in this type of warfare. He maintained in these explorations an
invincible constancy in such immense labors and difficulties. Not lacking op-
position, he prudently resisted the presumptuous ignorance of some and the
malice of others who, with no experience whatever, went against his advice.

Now returning to our history, I shall record that when our companies
had reached the beginning of the province of the Tejas, and when our general
had made camp about a half-league from the Tejas governor's habitation, it
was advised that a good example would be set by having the priests and
officers march in a procession. Thus it was arranged, with innumerable Indians who had already gathered at the camp accompanying it. When they
reached the governor's home, they sang the *Te Deum Laudamus.* After the
gathering had been seated for a long time in his house on benches that the
governor ordered brought out, they took from the same house pots and
casserole dishes, with beans, corn, and *pinole* [1] for lunch. All dined to their
fill and returned to the camp.

The next day, the men constructed a chapel to celebrate the festivity of
the Day of Corpus [Christi], in order to make a good impression on the Indians. After their governor had been consulted, De León ordered the Indians
to gather and distributed clothing and the other goods that had been
brought for that purpose, which His Excellency had given. With a large
number of Indians attending, that day's festival was celebrated with the
greatest solemnity possible, with a procession and the other ceremonies that
could be carried out, as a good example for the natives.

After this celebration the royal standard was raised in the name of His
Majesty, and the governor of the Tejas and his captains gave it their obedience. General Alonso de León, in the king's name, promised to favor them
and to assist them in every way possible. He gave the Tejas governor a title
and nomination with all the formalities and turned over to him a staff as a

symbol and ordered all the Indians to respect him and obey him as their governor and captain general.

Of the four priests who came as missionaries, three remained—Fray Miguel de Fontecubierta, Fray Antonio Bordey, and Fray Francisco de Jesús María. The Indians were told, through an interpreter, that they should obey and respect the priests, with whom there remained only three soldiers. No more were left behind because of the Tejas governor's warning and objection. He was concerned that if many Spaniards remained there without wives, they would appropriate the Indians' women. The Tejas governor was very content with the company of the priests, since he himself had requested that they remain. Possession was given to Fray Damián Massanet, administrator of conversions at this mission, which left the priests very content that there might be so many souls in the brotherhood of our Holy Mother, the Church.

There was present among these Indians one man whom all respected and held as their minister or priest. This man, having seen our priests—be it by divine inspiration, or because one of their ancestral customs was the veneration of priests—told the Indians (while he pointed to the priests) that those were the true ministers and that they were to obey them from then on. They were to give the first fruits of the harvest to the priests from then on so that they might offer them to God. All this was understood by means of an Indian called Tomás,[2] who was conversant with the Mexican [Aztec] language and knew the mother tongue of the Tejas. He declared that he had come to the area initially with two priests from El Parral two years before; the priests had stayed far away, and he had come on to these parts, where he had remained. So our people had some relief because he was knowledgeable in the Tejas language.

The governor of the Tejas told our governor that some Frenchmen had asked to settle among his people,[3] and that he had told them that they should not come because he had a great friendship with other Christians and was awaiting them. With this answer they again sent a messenger, who told him not to admit such people, for they were very bad and would take away their wives and children. If the governor had not been so satisfied with our people and our kindness, this ill advice might have corrupted him. God, Author of all things, disposed his heart not to give credence to the requests of the French—in which it is known that the demon, envious of the fruit that is to be brought forth from the reduction of these people, desired to impede it.

These wiles are not to prevail because of the constancy that has been recognized in that nation [Tejas] for embracing evangelical law with the help of the priests who remained there.

❧

Chapter 45 / The Expedition to the Tejas Concludes

WHEN matters were arranged in the manner mentioned, it seemed fitting to our general to search for the location most appropriate for establishing the priests' mission. After consulting with the Tejas governor, our governor set out with him, the priests, and some officers in a northeasterly direction, where they saw three very agreeable (although small) valleys in which the Indians said that two of the Frenchmen who had wanted to settle there had died.[1] This was verified by the two graves that could be seen.

They came to a large river, but found no ford. The natives, however, crossed on a tree that had been cut near the bank and that reached to the other side.[2] In order to cross safely, they used a thick rope that one could hold onto that went along the trunk. De León gave this river [the Neches] the name of San Miguel Arcángel.

At this location it was arranged that a residence for the Apostolic Fathers should be built. As far as we could determine, it turned out to be in the middle of the principal settlement of the Tejas. They spent six days constructing the church and convent cells as best they could. Possession of the post was given to the priests and Mass was sung with all magnificence in the church; it was said by the administrator, Fray Damián Massanet. The governor and many of his people attended it with great devotion, and they continued at these functions for the six-day period. On June 1, leaving three soldiers with the priests, De León's company set out on their return trip to Coahuila.

The governor did not leave more soldiers because the Tejas governor objected that the Spaniards would be without women to attend them, which would cause them to harass the Indian women; this was the reason no more soldiers remained. At the beginning of any settlement—and still more when it is as important as this one is—much care is necessary, to the point that when the ways of the people are recognized, one arranges things to their taste. If there is unpleasantness at the beginning, the goal of the reduction of the Indians will never be attained. Our governor assured the governor of the Tejas and all his people that they might live in great peace and love with us, at which news they remained very content. The priests were provided with everything necessary for one year.

The company took the road back toward the Province of Coahuila and reached the River of the Santísima [Trinidad]. On the trip to the Tejas, the river was crossed very easily but they now found it so swollen that it detained them for eight days. When the governor realized this, he ordered rafts built, and the river was crossed in this manner, with substantial difficulty. After reaching this side [the west bank] of the San Marcos [Colorado] River, our governor set out with sixteen soldiers first northeastward in search of two French boys and a Frenchwoman. Some Indians had said that they were at an encampment four leagues away. This distance seemed wrong because the party moved more than seventeen leagues that day, finding various encampments of Indians to whom they gave gifts. The Indians were very friendly, and some even guided our people the next day for fifteen leagues. Continuing in an easterly direction in search of the boys, they came upon a large nation of Indians to whom they showed kindness and who gave the party four Indians as guides, and these Indians escorted the troops fourteen leagues.

Having crossed a creek that the Indians called Canoas, and having left last year's French settlement behind, they set out toward the southeast and found two Indians on horseback, who were coming from the land of the Indians who held the French youths. These Indians took our soldiers to their encampment, which was on the point of a cove, where the two French boys and the Frenchwoman were. The governor, treating the Indians pleasingly and ingratiating himself with them in order to obtain the youths' release, negotiated with the Indians. Since the Indians were given all that they asked for, and as they did not see more than sixteen of our men, they were emboldened to kill our troops. With great daring the Indians began to request, in exchange for the rescue, all the horses our people had and even the clothes they were wearing. They delayed by saying that they were going to look for one of the other French boys, who was two leagues from there, and in fact they brought him.

Continuing their audacity—each one bringing many arrows, with his bow and his leather shield—they asked for exorbitant things and threatened to kill all of the troops if their demands were not met. They then immediately attacked, shooting arrows with great vehemence. At this our troops went on the defensive, killing four Indians and wounding two others; they [the Indians] then withdrew. The Indians also wounded two horses. Our troops, having taken the two French boys and the Frenchwoman, continued the attack. In this fray the Indians shot two arrows at our governor. They knocked off his hat with one arrow and the other glanced to one side, doubtless because of the good armor he wore.

After this victory, the company moved to the Guadalupe River. From there, continuing the return trip to Coahuila, the company reached the Rio Grande on July 4. It could not be forded because it was very swollen, which required them to remain there more than twelve days. It was necessary to build rafts out of buffalo hides so that some of the soldiers who could not swim could cross. Nevertheless, one of them fell in the river accidentally and drowned.

Before the company crossed the river, our governor ordered the dispatching of news because of His Excellency's concern about the delay. This was done by Captain Don Gregorio Salinas [Varona], a person who was on the journey by order of the viceroy. The trip lasted from March 15 to July 30, and the delay caused much concern. However, two things were mentioned that caused the delay, namely, having taken along weak horses, caused by the great drought at the time of the departure, and having been detained by one of the many large rivers in those areas. To this, one may add, the distance that was added to the expedition of last year—from the settlement of the French to the province of the Tejas—which was a distance of one hundred leagues. If a computation be made of the distance traveled on this journey, from when they left the presidio of Coahuila [Monclova] to when they reached Monterrey, it is nearly seven hundred leagues. One may consider the difficulties that were occasioned on such a long journey.

I almost forgot to mention the latitude at which the province of the Tejas is located. Based on what was observed with the astrolabe that Don Gregorio de Salinas [Varona] and Francisco Martínez carried, it is at 34°7′ north.[3]

That which may occur henceforward, God willing, will be noted. I do not doubt that, with the conquest of the Tejas continuing, a greater volume will be written. May Our Lord wish that all be for His greater honor and glory.

September 7, 1690.

Appendix A / Governor Alonso de León's Revised 1690 Expedition Diary

JOURNEY made by Governor Alonso de León, by order of the Most Excellent Count of Galve, viceroy of New Spain, in the company of Captain Don Gregorio de Salinas Varona, from the Province of Coahuila to the Bay of Espíritu Santo and the Province of the Tejas, on March 26, 1690.[1]

Sunday, March 26

The droves of pack animals loaded with supplies left the villa of Santiago de la Monclova and stopped one league beyond the Indian community, a league and a half north of the villa. / 1.5 leagues

Monday, March 27

The party moved out in a northeast by east direction and traveled three leagues to camp below the hills on the bank of the Coahuila River.[2] 3 leagues

Tuesday, March 28

We set out from the camp east-northeast and downriver; leaving the river behind we entered Baluartes Pass.[3] From the pass we turned aside for a distance of one league, coming to a stop on the riverbank on which we had camped on the twenty-seventh—having marched eight leagues. / 8 leagues

Wednesday, March 29

The party continued downriver east by northeast for a little more than one league past El Alamo.[4] There the party, having marched five leagues, stopped at a camp on the bank of the river surrounded by flat land with some chaparral and lechuguilla. / 5 leagues

Thursday, March 30

The party set out along an east by northeast route, downriver, moving toward the junction with the Sabinas River; there, having marched through flat land with some mesquite brush and lechuguilla, we stopped on the river-bank. Here we were joined by the troops of the Kingdom of León and the missionary priests. On this day we traveled four leagues. / 4 leagues

Friday, March 31
The party set out downriver and, climbing the hill that was ahead by an easterly route, we reached the Sabinas River, having marched about two leagues. After crossing the river, the party stopped. / 2 leagues

Saturday, April 1
We marched in a northeasterly direction six leagues, crossing plains without water. This was quite difficult country because of the many mesquite trees, although it was flat. The party stopped when we came to a pond. / 6 leagues

Sunday, April 2
We headed northeast by north and crossed some little hills covered with chaparral and some flat land. We came to rainwater ponds, where the party camped, having marched five leagues. / 5 leagues

Monday, April 3
We set out in a northerly direction through flat land with very little chaparral and traveled as far as the bank of a creek, where we found the Frenchman's Indians,[5] to whom we gave tobacco and clothing. Here the party stopped to camp, having marched four leagues. / 4 leagues

Tuesday, April 4
We set out in a northerly direction in search of the Rio Grande, through flat land with some mesquite. After finding the river crossing, the party stopped on the bank. Bison were found nearby. On this day we marched five leagues. 5 leagues

Wednesday, April 5
We remained at the camp so that members of the party might confess and fulfill their obligations to the church before crossing the river.

Thursday, April 6
We crossed the river and marched north by northeast to camp on the bank of a dry creek, having traveled eight leagues. The party went to sleep without water after crossing some hills and marched through scrub mesquite growths. / 8 leagues

Friday, April 7

The party moved out in a northeasterly direction through flat land and camped on Ramos Creek, where there is a large live oak and some scrub mesquite. We traveled three leagues. / 3 leagues

Saturday, April 8

The party headed out northeast by north through flat land dotted with mesquite trees and arrived at a creek. Because of the difficult crossing, most of the day was spent preparing to cross the stream and leading the pack animals across. There the party stopped, having marched three leagues; the camp was given the name Caramanchel.[6] / 3 leagues

Sunday, April 9

The party set out in a northeast by north direction across plains and through two tree-lined ravines. We then entered a growth of mesquite, and after traveling about half a league we came upon the Nueces River, where there are many flint rocks. The party, having traveled five leagues, camped on the banks of the river in a large meadow formed by the river. / 5 leagues

Monday, April 10

We crossed the river and moved east through a ravine with thick groves of pecan and mesquite trees, until we reached a hill, after marching about two leagues. Then we continued in a northerly direction about another two leagues. Then we turned to the east through flat land full of mesquite and came upon the Sarco River.[7] Having crossed it, the party camped on the far side, having marched seven leagues. / 7 leagues

Tuesday, April 11

The party set out in a northerly direction across plains interrupted in places by mesquite, little hills, and ravines. We came upon the Hondo [Frio] River, where the party camped, having marched six leagues. / 6 leagues

Wednesday, April 12

The party was detained in camp to search for two members of the company who were lost on the march the day before.

Thursday, April 13

We received notice that six leagues from the camp was a settlement of Indians to which a Frenchman had come.[8] I set out for the settlement in the afternoon with twenty men, including Captain Don Gregorio de Salinas

Varona,[9] in a westerly direction along the bank of the [Frio] river, on the far side. After traveling about five leagues, I made camp for the night. / 5 leagues

Friday, April 14

At dawn I continued my march along the same route about a half league, and then I followed a northerly route, through a plain dotted with many oak trees, to the riverbank. There we found the settlement, about a half-league away, where many Indian men, women, and children came out to meet us. We gave them gifts of tobacco; they told us that two Frenchmen were living on the other side of the Guadalupe River. One Indian had a French musket. From there we returned to the base camp with many Indians who accompanied us the full distance. At the camp we gave them clothing, flour, and tobacco. On this day the two missing soldiers caught up with the party. Today we marched seven leagues. / 7 leagues

Saturday, April 15

The party set out in an easterly direction downriver through ravines with mesquite trees, and we arrived at the ford of the [Frio] river. Here the party, having marched five leagues, stopped to prepare for the crossing. / 5 leagues

Sunday, April 16

We crossed the Hondo [Frio] River, along an east by northeast route through flat land, where we came upon a creek.[10] It was necessary to prepare for the crossing and clear the nearby growth. From there we continued our journey as far as some rainwater ponds, where the party camped, having marched eight leagues. / 8 leagues

Monday, April 17

The party set out toward the northeast, but the woods that were to be crossed made it necessary to detour north by northeast and east. We came upon Robalos Creek,[11] where the party camped, having marched five leagues. / 5 leagues

Tuesday, April 18

The soldiers dispersed in various directions to search for 120 horses that had stampeded; they were recovered in the afternoon. The party set out and, in a short distance, the guide lost his sense of direction and we followed a northerly route to search for the Medina [San Antonio] River. It was late in the day, and the party camped on a little hill, which we named the Encampment of El Rosario. We had marched four leagues through flat land with, in places, oaks and mesquites. / 4 leagues

Wednesday, April 19

The party, traveling through woods of oaks, live oaks, and mesquites, continued in a northerly direction in search of the Medina [San Antonio] River. At the gorge of the river the party camped at a location upriver from the crossing, having marched seven leagues. / 7 leagues

Thursday, April 20

We moved out in an easterly direction, and at a distance of two leagues we found the ford. There the party stopped because it was necessary to prepare for the crossing.[12] / 2 leagues

Friday, April 21

We crossed the [San Antonio] river and marched in an easterly direction through flat land with some oaks, live oaks, mesquites, and willows. We arrived at León [Cibolo] Creek,[13] where the party stopped; on this day we marched five leagues. / 5 leagues

Saturday, April 22

The party traveled in an easterly and sometimes in a northeasterly direction through flat land with live oaks and other oaks until we came upon a creek of salty water.[14] There the party camped, having marched six leagues.
6 leagues

Sunday, April 23

The party continued east by northeast through flat land and hills with mottes of live oaks and other oaks. Having marched five leagues, we arrived at a location close to the Guadalupe River near a tributary creek. / 5 leagues

Monday, April 24

The party moved down river until we reached the crossing,[15] which was sounded. Most of the day was spent fording the river. The party stopped to camp on the other side; on this day we marched two leagues. / 2 leagues

Tuesday, April 25

I set out with Captain Don Gregorio de Salinas Varona and twenty soldiers along a pathway to the southeast[16] to reconnoiter the Bay of Espíritu Santo. We continued about fourteen leagues, through flat and fertile land with

some live oaks and other oaks; having reached a rainwater pond we camped.
14 leagues

Wednesday, April 26

We continued our journey to the old French settlement, and at about five
leagues, we found the place by following the road toward the southeast.
There we stopped to burn the fort. After it was burned, we went on to reconnoiter the bay about two leagues [from the fort]. There we saw two buoys
marking channels, one at the mouth of the San Marcos [Lavaca] River and
the other at the mouth of the Guadalupe River. The sun was not observed
because it was overcast. From there we turned back upstream along the
Frenchmen's river [Garcitas Creek] to see if we could find any Indians in
their old settlements. We were unable to find any, and because it was already
late, we stopped to camp on the riverbank; on this day, going and returning,
we marched fourteen leagues. / 14 leagues

Thursday, April 27

We returned to the base camp; on this day we traveled twenty leagues upriver
watching for Indians, but found none. / 20 leagues

Friday, April 28

I set out with eight soldiers and moved up the Guadalupe River about six
leagues and sending smoke signals to see if I could meet any Indians. Because I received no response I returned to the base camp, having marched,
going and returning, twelve leagues. / 12 leagues

Saturday, April 29

The party moved out in an easterly direction, about three leagues, and then
we turned northeast about another three leagues through flat land, with
ravines and thick mottes of live oaks and other oaks. After reaching some
rainwater ponds, the party stopped to camp at the foot of a hill, which we
named San Pedro Mártir. / 6 leagues

Sunday, April 30

After mass two soldiers arrived from the presidios of El Parral, who were
their companions. I set out with sixteen soldiers to clear some woods and to
see if I might find Indians to guide us to the province of the Tejas. Upon
reaching some abandoned Indian settlements, I made camp; on this day I
marched nine leagues. / 9 leagues

Monday, May 1

I continued my journey and reached a high hill, where I stopped because it was already late; on this day we traveled twelve leagues. / 12 leagues

Tuesday, May 2

I continued my journey and reached a meadow near the banks of the San Marcos [Colorado] River. Because the river was deep, I was unable to cross. On this day we traveled fourteen leagues. / 14 leagues

Wednesday, May 3

I continued my journey upriver as far as the ford,[17] which I found very good. There I crossed and continued my journey, and about five leagues beyond the river, on the edge of a wood, we saw two Indians. When we called to them, they refused to come. Instead they went into the woods, so I camped there for the night to see if they would come to me; on this day I marched seven leagues. / 7 leagues

Thursday, May 4

In the morning, one of the Indians came to see us, and when we had talked with him by signs, he told us that he was of the Tejas tribe[18] and that today we would reach a settlement. Continuing to guide us for about three leagues, he told us that the settlement was very far off, and that if I would give him a horse he could tell the Tejas captain. So I sent him off and returned to the previous night's camping place, because he had told me to wait there for him—having marched on this day, going and returning, six leagues. On this same day the twenty soldiers from the presidios of El Parral arrived to join the supply party that I left at the San Pedro Mártir encampment. / 6 leagues

Friday, May 5

In the morning, I dispatched four soldiers to the supply party to tell them to move out, and at about five in the afternoon the Indian whom I had sent to the Tejas captain returned. He said that because the horse had run away, he could not continue, and he had come to notify me of this.

Saturday, May 6

I sent four members of the company out on the trail to see if anyone had met some of the Indians, and they found another Indian, whom they brought to me. When I offered him clothing to induce him to go to the Tejas to notify the governor that I was there, the first Indian, jealous of the offer, told me that if I would give him another horse, *he* would go to the Tejas. Therefore, I dispatched him. On this same day the four soldiers that I sent back reached the supply party.

Sunday, May 7
The supply party set out from the San Pedro Mártir encampment and followed the route about three leagues [ ] by northeast[19] through thick woods of oaks and live oaks, which in spots it was necessary to clear. They traversed a few plains, including meadows surrounded by live oaks and other oaks, and crossed two dry creeks. Next they followed a westerly and at times northerly route, finding the same woods and scrub growths of live oaks that it was necessary to clear. Next they crossed some plains and four creek beds that carried very little water. The party stopped to make camp on the bank of one of the creeks, which they named La Aparición de San Miguel Arcángel. On this day the supply party marched nine leagues. / 9 leagues

Monday, May 8
The supply party set out from the encampment in a northerly direction over hills and ravines and crossed eight dry creeks and some thick patches of live oaks and other oaks, where the party reached a creek that carried very little water. There it stopped in a clearing shaped like a half-moon and found in a northeasterly direction. The supply party named it San Gregorio Nacianceno encampment. On this day they marched nine leagues. / 9 leagues

Tuesday, May 9
The supply party set out from San Gregorio Nacianceno toward the north over hills and ravines and some woods of live oaks, other oaks, mulberries, and grapevines so thick that it was necessary to clear about one league. Having crossed six dry creeks and reaching a flowing creek, the party stopped at a hill. It was named Jesús, María y Joseph de Buena Vista.[20] On this day we had marched seven leagues. / 7 leagues

On the same day, at nine in the evening, I reached the supply party. I immediately set out again with eight men (among them Captain Don Gregorio de Salinas Varona) in search of a young Frenchman who was in an Indian settlement to the southwest. Having marched about twelve leagues, I camped at the edge of a hill, as it was dark. / 12 leagues

Wednesday, May 10
We set out before dawn, continuing by the same southwesterly route for

about nine leagues to a hill, before entering the woods. From there we followed a westerly route through very thick stands of oaks, live oaks, many grapevines, and mulberries, to some clearings at the edge of the woods, for about five leagues. At the end of the clearing, we met a young Frenchman, Pedro [Pierre] Talon, who was moving along with a group of Indians.[21] From there we returned, following the same route, to a camp near the same hill where I had slept the previous night. On this day we had marched, going and returning, twenty-seven leagues. / 27 leagues

Also on May 10, Captain Francisco Martínez continued with the supply party in a northerly direction, over hills and ravines, to cross the San Marcos [Colorado] River. He crossed it and continued his journey, in the same direction, as far as a hill where he encountered the soldiers I had left behind. There, having marched eight leagues on this day, he stopped to make camp. This camp was named San Ildefonso. / 8 leagues

Thursday, May 11

We started our journey before dawn, continuing in a northeasterly direction for about twelve leagues, until we reached a high hill that has mottes of very tall pecan trees. There I came upon a settlement of Indians who told us of another Frenchman who was nearby at another Indian settlement. I sent an Indian to search for him, and at the same time I dispatched two soldiers to the supply party to have four men come with provisions so that, in case the Frenchman did not come to us, we might go search for *him*. At this time we crossed the San Marcos [Colorado] River before it rose, because it had rained a good deal this afternoon. We marched sixteen leagues on this day. 16 leagues

Also on May 11 the campsite of the supply party was improved by moving it to another, more advantageous location, about three leagues in a northeasterly direction, where the supply party stopped on a hill that was named San Joseph. / 3 leagues

Friday, May 12

The Frenchman [Pierre Meunier] arrived in the morning, with three Indians and the soldiers from the supply party. We then continued our journey until we reached the party, which was six leagues from the river, in a northerly direction. / 6 leagues

Meanwhile, the supply party had stopped to wait for us to arrive with the Frenchmen.

Saturday, May 13

The united party set out from the San Joseph encampment and moved in an easterly direction about three leagues, and then marched three more leagues northeast over hills and ravines and crossed three creeks with little water. There the party stopped on the bank of another creek at the edge of a small woods. It was named San Francisco de Asís. / 6 leagues

Sunday, May 14

The party set out from San Francisco de Asís over a hill and across a ravine in a northeasterly direction, in search of the Colorado [Brazos] River, which had heavy woods along its banks. There the party stopped and named the river Espíritu Santo.[22] On this day we marched six leagues. / 6 leagues

Monday, May 15

The party set out from the encampment on the Espíritu Santo [Brazos] River in an easterly direction and traveled about three leagues through very thick woods, which were cleared for the pack animals. Afterward we continued in a northeasterly direction about one league through some narrow clearings interspersed with small wooded areas. Then we moved in a northerly direction about another league, where the party camped at a creek [the Navasota River] that was named San Juan. / 5 leagues

Tuesday, May 16

The party traveled from the San Juan [Navasota] toward the northeast about two leagues, as far as a boggy creek. Then there followed another creek with a good crossing, from which we continued northeast by north about another two leagues. There we found some ponds. The party, having marched four leagues, stopped and named the campsite El Beato Salvador de Horta. 4 leagues

Wednesday, May 17

The party left El Beato Salvador de Horta and moved northeast by north through flat land and camped at a creek, which they named San Diego de Alcalá. On this day we marched six leagues. / 6 leagues

Thursday, May 18

The party, traveling northeast by east over flat land, moved out from the encampment, although in places it was necessary for soldiers to prepare for the crossing of creeks and to clear tree limbs that interfered with the crossing.

On this day we met the Tejas captain, accompanied by fourteen Indians, on the bank of a creek.[23] I gave them clothing and other dry goods. From there we continued the journey and entered a very pleasant valley, which we named Santa Elvira, and then we came upon another creek. There the party stopped, on the creek bank, and we named the encampment Santa Elvira. On this day we marched eight leagues. / 8 leagues

Friday, May 19

The party left the encampment of Santa Elvira and moved north by northeast through a small woods, where we came upon another very large and pleasant valley. It was given the name Galve. On leaving it we came upon a large grove of trees and a large, deep river, which we named the Río de la Santísima Trinidad [the Trinity River]. It was necessary to make preparations to cross it, and the greater part of the day was required to transport the pack animals across. On the other side we found another very pleasant valley, which we named Monclova. There the party stopped near the bank of the river, and we named the encampment San Sebastián. On this day we marched about one and a half leagues. / 1.5 leagues

Saturday, May 20

The party traveled northeast by east from the Monclova Valley and the San Sebastián encampment through woods of oaks, pecans, and grapevines, for a distance of four leagues. On leaving the woods, we found another valley, which we named San Sebastián. In the woods that are in an easterly direction facing the road, we came upon four Indian houses, which we named San Bernardino. These Indians had corn planted, and their houses were very clean. We treated them in a friendly manner and from there we continued our journey in a northeasterly direction through another oak woods—the trees being sparse but large—and across two creeks that carry very little water. Farther on we found some clearings where we came upon several freshwater ponds. There the party stopped to camp on the shore, and we named it the encampment of San Bernardino; on this day we marched seven leagues. 7 leagues

Sunday, May 21

The party traveled northeast by east from San Bernardino through woods of oaks, live oaks, some pines, and small grapevines with bunches of grapes on both sides of the road. We crossed four deep, dry creeks with difficult crossings and some small hills of unproductive land covered with oaks. The woods were very sparse. Having reached another creek, the party stopped and camped in the woods where it forms a clearing and named it San Carlos encampment; on this day they marched six leagues. / 6 leagues

Monday, May 22

The party set out from San Carlos toward the northeast by east through the same woods of oaks and some pines and, in spots, grapevines along the road on both sides. Having crossed five dry creeks and two little hills, both of them with veins of metal and growths of scrub live oak and large oaks, we came to a valley with many Tejas Indian houses. Around them were their planted fields of corn, beans, pumpkins, and watermelons. From there we made another turn to the north, over a high hill with the same type of scrub, and descended into another valley of Indian houses and planted fields. Here the Indian governor said that we were very close to his house and that we should stop on the edge of the valley near a creek. Here the party, having marched five leagues, camped and named it La Madre Jesús María de Agreda Valley and encampment. / 5 leagues

The name of the first valley is San Antonio de Padua, the second is Santa Juana, the third Santa Margarita, and the fourth, San Carlos. On May 25 the latitude of the settlement of the Tejas was measured; it is at 34°7′.

On the twenty-seventh, twenty-eighth, twenty-ninth, thirtieth, [and] thirty-first, they worked on building the church and the residence of the apostolic missionaries. They took possession of the house and the church on the thirty-first.[24]

Thursday, June 1st

The church was blessed, and the Reverend Father Administrator Damián Massanet sang the Mass after the blessing of the church, which was done with a procession. In the afternoon, the supply party set out from the San Francisco de los Tejas encampment to return to the Province of Coahuila by the same route we had taken earlier. On this night, having marched five leagues, it stopped at the Encampment of San Carlos. / 5 leagues

Friday, June 2

Governor Alonso de León, Captains Don Gregorio de Salinas Varona and Francisco Martínez, the Reverend Father Administrator Fray Damián Massanet, and four soldiers set out following the supply party from San Francisco de los Tejas. We met up with the party at their encampment. From there we continued our journey with the unified party as far as the valley that is about half a league on this side of the Encampment of San Bernardino. Here the party camped. We marched on this day six and one-half leagues. 6.5 leagues

Saturday, June 3

The party moved out from San Bernardino and, crossing the valley of San Sebastián and the Monclova Valley, reached the Santísima Trinidad [Trinity] River. Because it was swollen and could not be forded, we camped near its bank in the Monclova Valley; on this day we marched seven leagues. 7 leagues

Sunday, June 4

We remained in camp waiting for the river to recede, and we did the same on Monday the fifth, Tuesday the sixth, Wednesday the seventh, Thursday the eighth, and Friday the ninth. On Saturday the tenth a raft was built and we began to cross the river.

Sunday, June 11

We completed the crossing at about two in the afternoon, and the party set out across the Galve Valley, as far as Santa Elvira. There, having marched three leagues, we camped near some freshwater ponds. / *3 leagues*

Monday, June 12

The party moved out from the encampment and traveled about two leagues past the San Diego de Alcalá camp, to halt near some rainwater ponds; on this day we marched nine leagues. / *9 leagues*

Tuesday, June 13

The party set out from the encampment, marched past the Encampment of El Beato Salvador de Horta, and reached that of San Juan [Navasota River]. Here the party, having marched eight leagues, camped. / *8 leagues*

Wednesday, June 14

The party moved out and crossed the Espíritu Santo [Brazos] River. We reached a little hill next to a live oak tree with four branches extending out from the trunk. There the party stopped at a pond; we marched nine leagues on this day. / *9 leagues*

Thursday, June 15

The party set out and marched past San Francisco de Asís. We reached a creek at the foot of a hill; there, having marched seven leagues, we camped next to a small motte of trees. / 7 leagues

Friday, June 16

The party left the encampment and passed by those of San Joseph and San Ildefonso. We arrived near a creek at the foot of a low hill that has some small oaks and live oaks on the eastern side, and the creek on the west. There [the party], having marched seven leagues, stopped. / 7 leagues

Saturday, June 17

The party set out from the camp to cross the San Marcos [Colorado] River and continued until we reached the location and encampment of Jesús, María y Joseph de Buena Vista, where we stopped to camp; on this day we marched five leagues. / 5 leagues

At this encampment there were many Indian nations, including the Cantoná [Cantona], Thoagá [Tohaha], Chaná [Sana], and Cabas [Cava].[25]

Sunday, June 18

The supply party moved out to continue the journey.[26] Governor Alonso de León, Captain Don Gregorio de Salinas Varona, and sixteen soldiers set out in a northeasterly direction in search of two young Frenchmen and a Frenchwoman. We moved about four leagues across some plains until we reached a small wooded area, which we crossed. Then we continued in an easterly direction about three more leagues, where we found another Indian settlement in a small woods. These Indians are called the Thoó.[27] From there we continued in a southeasterly direction until eight in the evening, across some plains where there was an infinite number of bison, to the bank of a creek the headwaters of which are in a thick motte of trees. There we camped; on this day we marched about sixteen leagues. / 16 leagues

Monday, June 19

At dawn we continued our journey along the bank of the creek, which had trees on both sides. Having crossed it and marched about two leagues, we came upon a nation of Indians called the Cóoc,[28] whom we treated in a hospitable manner, and they became friendly. From there we continued our journey in a southerly direction across some plains, and in about one league we came upon another nation of Indians; these are called Thoó. From there we continued for about four leagues in a southerly direction across a plain, where there were countless bison. We entered a small woods and continued our journey, moving toward the west. After crossing a large creek in a woods, we came upon a very large nation of Indians who numbered more than three thousand. These are called the Naaman,[29] whom we treated graciously. They became our friends and provided Indians to guide us as far as the next Indian settlement. We continued across some plains, but as it was already late at night, we stopped to camp on the bank of a creek; on this day we marched about fifteen leagues. / 15 leagues

Tuesday, June 20

We continued our journey in an easterly direction and came upon a nation of Indians who are called Caisquetebana,[30] whom we treated with hospitality. They provided four Indians to guide us to the young Frenchmen. We set out in the same direction to cross Frenchmen's Creek.[31] Having crossed it, we continued to the former settlement of the French. From there we continued southward to Canoe Creek,[32] and having crossed it, we came to another creek where we camped; on this day we marched fourteen leagues. 14 leagues

Wednesday, June 21

We set out in a southeasterly direction, and after about one league we came upon two mounted Indians who were members of the tribe that held the young Frenchmen. These Indians led us to their settlement, which was at the head of a small bay. The nation is called the Cascosis.[33] There we found the young French youths, Roberto and Madalena Talon,[34] whose release we discussed with the Indians. Although we had been friendly to them and had recovered the two captives, the Indians behaved in a thousand insolent ways, asking us to give them all our horses and even the clothing we wore. Meanwhile, other Indians went to look for another French boy, who was held two leagues away among natives of the same nation. After bringing him to us, the Indians increased their threats and displayed bows and arrows. A large number of Indians came with leather shields and made exorbitant demands. They said that if we did not meet their demands, they were going to shoot all of us full of arrows and kill us. No sooner did they say this than they started to shoot arrows. Therefore, we fired at them, killing four of them and wounding two. Then, having wounded two of our horses, they retreated. We departed and camped about four leagues away, where we had slept the previous night. On this day we marched a total of twelve leagues, [the return being] in a northerly direction, and we stopped on a plain near the bank of a creek. 12 leagues

Thursday, June 22

At dawn we set out in a northerly direction across some plains along the bank of the Guadalupe River, where we found some thick patches of brazil-wood. At about 10 o'clock in the evening we stopped to camp near a small woods; on this day we marched fourteen leagues. / 14 leagues

Friday, June 23

We rode out in a northerly direction about two leagues, where we came upon the tracks of the supply party that had gone on ahead. About three leagues farther on, we came upon the camp of the supply party near the ford of the Guadalupe,[35] where we stopped; on this day we marched five leagues. 5 leagues

Saturday, June 24

The party moved out from the fording area to cross the Guadalupe River; and having crossed it, we continued our journey as far as a creek before the Encampment of Agua Salada.[36] There the party stopped; on this day we marched seven leagues. / 7 leagues

Sunday, June 25

The party set out, continuing its journey, and passed the Encampment of Agua Salada. Having marched seven leagues, we camped on León [Cibolo] Creek. / 7 leagues

Monday, June 26

The party broke camp and continued its journey until it crossed the Medina [San Antonio] River. There we stopped and made camp; on this day we marched six leagues. / 6 leagues

Tuesday, June 27

The party left the camp on the river and moved through woods of oaks and mesquite brush toward the south and southeast until we reached a creek, where the party camped, having marched seven leagues. / 7 leagues

Wednesday, June 28

The party traveled about four leagues from the campsite in a westerly direction through oak woods and plains, and then we followed a southerly route about one league. There we came upon a freshwater pond and, in the vicinity, some clumps of mesquite brush and of prickly pear. Here there was also a settlement of Indians called Thooé.[37] The party, having marched five leagues, stopped to make camp. / 5 leagues

Thursday, June 29

(Saint Paul the Apostle's Day). The party moved out from the camp and, after crossing near the Aire ponds and a ravine, it stopped at some rainwater ponds. On this day the tired horses, numbering 207, were left with twenty-five men so that they could follow more slowly. On this day we marched about four leagues. / 4 leagues

Friday, June 30

The party set out from the campsite to cross the Hondo [Frio] River. After we crossed it, it stopped.[38] We went on about three leagues, as far as the Las Cruces ford;[39] there the party stopped on the bank of the river [the Frio]; on this day we marched nine leagues. / 9 leagues

Saturday, July 1st

The party left Las Cruces ford to cross the Frío [Leona] River. Having come upon the river, the party stopped; on this day we marched five leagues. 5 leagues

Sunday, July 2

We crossed the [Leona] river, and the party continued its journey to cross the Nueces River. Having reached the [Nueces] river, we crossed it and continued as far as some ponds that are before Caramanchel [Comanche] Creek. Having marched eight leagues, we stopped to make camp. / 8 leagues

Monday, July 3

The party set out from the encampment and, after crossing the creek and passing by the Encampment of Caramanchel, we reached the Ramos ponds. We continued our journey as far as the encampment where we earlier had slept without water. Here the party stopped—the ponds now contained water. On this day we marched eight leagues. / 8 leagues

From July 4 until Wednesday, July 12, I was detained.[40] In the afternoon, although the river [the Rio Grande] was very swollen and no one dared to ford it, I entered the river to cross it, with the horse swimming, and the water came up to below my chest. I crossed it so that I could notify His Excellency of our expedition. Then the Father Administrator Damián Massanet with four soldiers and the young Frenchman called Pedro Moñe [Pierre Meunier], followed me.

Thursday, July 13

I marched as far as the Agua Verde ponds,[41] which are on this side of the mentioned river [the Rio Grande]. / 14 leagues

Friday, July 14

Before dawn we set out to continue our journey and crossed the Sabinas River, where we arrived upriver from the junction of the two rivers [the Sabinas and Nadadores]. There we stopped to camp, having marched seventeen leagues. / 17 leagues

Saturday, July 15

We moved out, continuing our journey to our destination, the villa of Santiago de la Monclova; on this day we marched twelve leagues. / 12 leagues

Indian tribes encountered: Cantoná, Toagá, Chaná, Cabas, Thoó[2], Cooc, Naaman, Caisquetebana, Caocosis, Mojoman.[42]

Appendix B / Indian Tribes Reported in Captain Alonso de León's *Discourses*, Juan Bautista Chapa's *Historia*, and General Alonso de León's Revised 1690 Expedition Diary

THIS appendix lists alphabetically the names of eighty-six Indian tribes or bands reported by Captain Alonso de León in his *Discourses* on the Kingdom of Nuevo León, by Juan Bautista Chapa in his *Historia* (except the 250 tribes listed in Chapters 28 and 29), and by General Alonso de León in his revised 1690 expedition diary. Each entry includes information on when (chronologically) and where the tribe was seen or reported and a description of the circumstance of each encounter. Brief citations are given to references to the tribes in other Spanish and French colonial documents, including the 1675 diary of Fernando del Bosque (Bolton, *Spanish Exploration*, 291–309), the journal kept by La Salle's post commander at Matagorda Bay, Henri Joutel (Margry, *Découvertes*, 3:91–534), Fray Damián Massanet's unpublished 1690 letter to the viceroy (AGI México, 61-6-21, 75–84), and the unpublished 1690 interrogation of Pierre Meunier and Captain Gregorio de Salinas Varona in Mexico City (AGI México, 61-6-21, 53–64). References to the tribe included in the *Handbook of North American Indians* (*HONAI*) and the tribal entries in the *New Handbook of Texas* (*NHOT*) are also noted.

Agaaunimi

Chapa includes the Agaaunimi tribe in his list of Indian nations that the French prisoner Jean Géry identified as loyal to him. Géry said that they lived dispersed throughout an area that extended about seventy leagues southwest of Matagorda Bay.

Aguata

A 1632 request (*requerimiento*) presented to the city and provincial authorities in Monterrey identified the Aguata tribe as one of several that had been involved in uprisings in Nuevo León during the preceding thirty years and had recently been involved in additional damaging revolts against local Spanish authority. In 1633 the tribe, along with allied tribes, including the Icaura, Sucuyama, Iguaracata, and Tepehuan, attacked and killed fifty-six Cataara Indians (who were friendly to the Spaniards) in a village located about three leagues from Cerralvo. In the early 1640s tribal members were suspected of killing a friendly Indian herder near the Great Salt Lick. Chapa includes them in his list of tribes who lived near Monterrey in the middle seventeenth century (*HONAI*, 10:356).

Agustiguara

In his account of the 1689 De León expedition, Chapa lists the Agustiguara tribe (along with seven others) as living in *encomiendas* in Nuevo León and he gives the Spanish translation of the tribal name as "sharp-pointed peak."

Alasapa (Alazapa)

Between 1639 and 1647 the Alasapa tribe was involved in several attacks on Spaniards near Monterrey, at the mines near Cerralvo, and at locations on the Salinas, Alamo, and Pilón rivers. These uprisings resulted in the deaths of several Indian and mulatto shepherds, the loss of numerous horse herds, and the delay of General Juan de Zavala's 1644 expedition. Chapa lists the tribe as living within ten to twelve leagues of Cerralvo in the middle seventeenth century. In his 1690 letter to the viceroy, Padre Massanet reports that members of the tribe lived ten leagues south of the Río de los Sabinos in Coahuila. Alvares Barreiro includes the Alasapa in his list of tribes who lived in Nuevo León in the 1720s. See Thomas H. Naylor and Charles W. Polzer, *Pedro Rivera and the Military Regulations for Northern New Spain, 1724-1729*, 222. In *HONAI* (10:356), T. N. Campbell lists the Alasapa among the several tribes who lived near present-day Lampazos, close to the present-day northeastern boundary line between Nuevo León and Coahuila.

Amapola (Amapula)

In 1638 the Amapola tribe (along with the Camalucano, Carana, and Cataara) brought to Cerralvo the news that Dutch soldiers had landed on the coast forty to fifty leagues east of the town. Chapa (Chapter 28) includes the tribe among those who had lived ten to twelve leagues from Cerralvo (*HONAI*, 10:356).

Ancacuara (Ayanguara?)

In 1648 the Ancacuara (along with the Icaura, Guaracata, Inquro, Camahan, and Icuano) engaged in numerous attacks against Spaniards throughout the province, including one raid in the Papagayos Mountains. Chapa translated the tribal name Ancacuara as "Thickets without Thorns" and added that they resided at the time (the 1680s) at an *encomienda* in Nuevo León (*HONAI*, 10:356).

Bayaguera

According to Chapa, Bayaguera means "Deer Foot." The tribe resided in an *encomienda* in Nuevo León in the 1680s.

Bobole (Bobol)

In 1665 over one hundred Bobole joined Fernando de Azcué's expedition against the Cacaxtle. In his 1675 expedition, Fernando del Bosque encountered Bobole south of the Rio Grande (Bolton, *Spanish Exploration*, 308).

Borrodo

The Borrodo tribe was identified as one of several Indian nations that revolted against Spanish authority near Monterrey during the 1600–1630 period. Chapa wrote that in 1665 two Borrodo Indians were convicted of stealing livestock. In 1667 members of the tribe from the Tamaulipas Mountains began carrying away horses and attacking shepherds. See also the entry "Borrodo" in Foster, *Spanish Expeditions into Texas*, 269, which lists specific encounters between the tribe and Spaniards in Nuevo León between 1727 and 1767 (*NHOT*, 1:652; *HONAI*, 10:329, 331, 352, 353).

Cacaxtle

The Cacaxtle tribe was attacked by Spanish forces under Major Juan de Garza near the Rio Grande in late 1663 or early 1664 and under Fernando de Azcué near the Nueces in South Texas in 1665. See also the entry "Cacaxtle" in Foster, *Spanish Expeditions into Texas*, 269, which describes the tribe's encounters with Governor Salinas Varona during his 1693 expedition as he crossed the Rio Grande and later the Colorado River (*NHOT*, 1:844; *HONAI*, 10:329–337).

Cagremoa

Jean Géry claimed that the Cagremoa tribe was one of nineteen tribes loyal to him and dispersed within about seventy leagues of Matagorda Bay. His claim was supported by the fact that Chapa and De León had witnessed and recorded the warm reception that Géry received from numerous tribes they encountered between the Rio Grande and the Colorado River.

Caisquetebana

De León met the Caisquetebana tribe near the Victoria-Jackson county line on June 20, 1690. See Appendix A.

Camahan (Camasan)

In 1648 the Camahan tribe, along with five others, was engaged in several uprisings throughout the province. Salinas (*Indians of the Rio Grande Delta*, 88) notes that in some Spanish documents the tribe was referred to as Borrado, a name that was applied to several tribes that lived in northern Nuevo León in the seventeenth century (*HONAI*, 10:356).

Camalucano

In August 1638 the Camalucano tribe (with three others) informed officials in Cerralvo that Dutch soldiers had landed on the nearby Gulf Coast. Soon thereafter the Spanish expedition that was sent to respond to the Dutch landing was itself surrounded and attacked by the same tribe. Chapa (Chapter 28) includes the tribe among those who lived ten to twelve leagues from Cerralvo (*HONAI*, 10:356).

Cantona

On June 17, 1690, Governor De León's party met the Cantona tribe near the crossing of the Colorado and the high hill called Jesús, María y Joseph de Buena Vista. See Appendix A. The Cantona were with the Tohaha, Sana, and Cava, some of whom Jean Géry said were loyal to him. See also the entry "Cantona" in Foster, *Spanish Expeditions into Texas*, 270, which identifies other encounters by Spanish expedition leaders with the tribe (*NHOT*, 1:962–963).

Caomopac

Jean Géry identified the Caomopac tribe to Chapa as one that was loyal to him and that resided within seventy leagues of Matagorda Bay (Chapter 39).

Carana (Caraña)

In 1638 the Carana were among the four tribes that informed the Spaniards in Cerralvo that the Dutch had landed on the Gulf coast. Chapa included the Caraña in his list of tribes found within ten to twelve leagues' circumference of Cerralvo (*HONAI*, 10:356).

Cascosi (Caocose)

On June 21, 1690, Governor de León recovered three French children from the Cascosi at the head of San Antonio Bay (see Appendix A). Although the tribal name is written twice in the manuscript and appears rather clearly as Cascosi (Cascosis, plural), Bolton has rendered the name as Cascossi. On Governor Alarcón's visit to Matagorda Bay in 1718, he met at the bay shore a number of local Indians who identified themselves as "Caocose," according to Céliz, *Diary of the Alarcón Expedition*, 101 n138. Pierre Meunier refers to the tribe living at Matagorda Bay as the "Cauquesi," according to Captain Gregorio de Salinas Varona's interrogation in Mexico City on August 19, 1690; however, the captain personally refers to the same tribe as the "Caocosi." Although we have at least four independent sources referring to the tribe with the same or a similar name—Cascosi—contemporary anthropologists and writers most frequently identify the tribe under the generic designation of Karankawa. See Robert A. Ricklis, *The Karankawa Indians of Texas,* 4–10.

Cataara

The Cataara tribe, usually an ally of the Spaniards, lived in a village about three leagues from Cerralvo. In 1632 they were acting as herdsmen for the governor's horse herd when they were attacked by the Tepehuan near the Papagayos Mountains. Chapa says the tribe lived ten to twelve leagues from that city. In 1643 Martinillo, a tribe member, served as a guide for a military exercise conducted near the San Juan River (*HONAI*, 10:356).

Catujane

The Catujane tribe was found on a mesa called Los Catujanes near La Caldera, about twenty-five leagues from Monterrey, according to Chapa. On Fernando del Bosque's 1675 expedition, he encountered the chief of the Catujano and some of his tribe along with some Tilija, Ape (Hape), and Pachaque north of the Rio Grande (Bolton, *Spanish Exploration*, 304).

Caurame

On July 2, 1686, General Alonso de León's expedition was joined by forty-four Caurame, and the expedition party passed their encampment on their return march on July 24.

Cauripan

In 1637 the Cauripan, along with the Cuepane and several other tribes, planned an attack on Cerralvo and Cadereyta, but companies led by Captain Alonso de León made a preemptive strike against the tribes. In 1642 Captain de León also attacked a band near Cerralvo (*HONAI*, 10:356).

Cauxagua (Cayaguagua?)

In 1643 Captain de León's company, operating out of Cerralvo, pursued a

band of Cauxagua (and Guajolote) who had killed many horses and two Indians. Genaro García renders the name as Caujagua. Chapa says the
Cayague Indians were located ten to twelve leagues from Cerralvo (Chapter
28). This was one of several tribes identified as rising up against Spanish
authority in Nuevo León in the early 1600s. See also "Cayague" in *HONAI*,
10:356.

Cava (Cuba, Caba)

Jean Géry identified the Cuba as loyal to him and living within seventy
leagues of Matagorda Bay. He may have been referring to the Cava, whom De
León met on the west side of the Colorado crossing in June of 1690. See also
entry "Cava" in Foster, *Spanish Expeditions into Texas*, 271.

Chichimeca

In the 1640s, when Captain Alonso de León was on his return trip from a
trading expedition to the Gulf Coast, he dispersed a large band of Chichimeca Indians who had encircled and threatened a community in Tamaulipas. Chapa apparently uses the term "Chichimeca people" not only as a
tribal name but as a descriptive term to identify a group of tribes or tribal
members who were rebellious, as the Chichimeca Indians had been earlier in
Central Mexico (*HONAI*, 10:329–331).

Chiles

Jean Géry reported to Chapa that the Chiles lived within seventy leagues of
Matagorda Bay and were loyal to him (Chapter 39).

Cobapo

The Cobapo was one of several tribes that was loyal to Jean Géry and
that was living in the 1680s within seventy leagues of Matagorda Bay
(Chapter 39).

Cóoc (Coco)

On June 19, 1690, Governor de León met members of the Cóoc tribe in northern Lavaca County (see Appendix A). See also entry "Coco" in Foster, *Spanish Expeditions into Texas*, 272–273.

Comocaura

In the 1640s, Captain Bernardo García, operating out of Cerralvo, attacked a village of Comocaura. Chapa (Chapter 28) identifies them as a tribe who had lived near Cerralvo (*HONAI*, 10:356).

Cosmojoo

Jean Géry identified the Cosmojoo tribe as one that was loyal to him and living within seventy leagues of Matagorda Bay (Chapter 39).

Cuajin

The Cuajin tribe was living in the 1680s within seventy leagues of Matagorda Bay, and Jean Géry reported that they were loyal to him (Chapter 39).

Cuauguijo

In 1669 General De León captured Juanillo, the captain of the Cuauguijo tribe, which was described as very warlike (Chapter 17).

Cucuyama

The Cucuyama tribe is described as one that, in the early 1600s, rebelled against Spanish authorities in Nuevo León (Chapter 19).

Cuepane (Cuepano)

In 1637, the Cuepane tribe, along with their allies the Cauripan and several other tribes, planned to attack Cerralvo and Cadereyta, but a Spanish strike preempted the Indian raid. One tribal leader was captured and hanged in Cerralvo. Chapa (Chapter 28) lists the tribe as living within ten to twelve leagues of Cerralvo (*HONAI*, 10:356).

Emet (Emot)

Jean Géry reported to Chapa that the Emot tribe was loyal to him and was living within seventy leagues of Matagorda Bay (Chapter 39). De León visited an Emet encampment on his 1689 expedition. See entry "Emet" in Foster, *Spanish Expeditions into Texas*, 274 (*NHOT*, 2:861).

Etayax

The Etayax tribe was reported to be loyal to Jean Géry and to be living in the 1680s within seventy leagues of Matagorda Bay (Chapter 39).

Guachichil (Hutachichil, Cuachichil)

In 1626 a Guachichil tribal captain named Cuaujuco sold the Spaniards many Indians whom he had captured near the Pilón River. About the same time, the tribe attacked Spaniards living near Monterrey, and the uprising spread throughout northern Nuevo León. Chapa lists the tribe as having lived near Monterrey (Chapter 28). Although the manuscript of De León's *Discourses* and Chapa's *Historia* give the tribe's name as Guachichil, Genaro García renders it as Huachichil or Hutachichil in his 1905 edition. Earlier, this well-known tribe was in Zacatecas (1560s) and in San Luis Potosí (1610s) (Naylor and Polzer, *The Presidio and Militia in New Spain*, 121, 414 n16; *HONAI*, 10:337–342).

Guajolote

In 1643 near Cerralvo, the companies of Captain Bernardo García and Captain De León attacked a band of Guajolote and Cauxagua who had killed many horses and two Indians. Chapa (Chapter 28) wrote that the tribe lived within ten to twelve leagues of Cerralvo (*HONAI*, 10:357).

Gualahuis (Hualahuis, Gualeguise, Gualegua)

In 1635 the Gualahuis tribe lived near the Boca de Pilón, and members of the tribe cooperated in the capture and sale of young Indian children. During the same period the tribe joined in an uprising against the Spaniards. Chapa reports that in the late 1650s the Spaniards captured a large number of Hualahuis in southern Nuevo León; twenty-two were taken to the Pilón River Valley and hanged. In 1665 Captain Alonso de León engaged in a limited reprisal attack on a raiding band at Labradores near the Pilón River. Chapa lists the tribe as residents of the area near Cerralvo. Alvarez Barreiro includes the tribe in his list of those living in Nuevo León in the 1720s. See Jackson and Foster, *Imaginary Kingdom*, 46 n, 49, 56 (*HONAI*, 10 : 357).

Guaracata

In 1648 the Guaracata tribe (along with their allies the Icuara, Ancacuara, Incuro, Camahan, and Icuano) engaged in several attacks on Spaniards throughout the province (*HONAI*, 10 : 357).

Guciacapo

The tribal name means "Water within the Woods," according to Chapa (Chapter 39), who says they were living at an *encomienda* in Nuevo León in the 1680s.

Guinaimo

The Guinaimo tribe was reported to be one of several identified as rebelling against the Spaniards in Nuevo León in the early 1600s (Chapter 19).

Hape (Ape, Api)

Chapa reports that on March 31, 1689, Governor De León's party met an encampment of over 490 Indians, including the Hape, near the Rio Grande. Also present were the Mescal, Jumano, and Ijiaba, all known to the Frenchman Jean Géry. See also the entry "Hape" in Foster, *Spanish Expeditions into Texas*, 274.

Huiapico

The Huiapico tribe was loyal to Jean Géry and lived in the 1680s within seventy leagues of Matagorda Bay, according to Chapa's report (Chapter 39).

Icaura (Icuara)

In 1648 the Icaura tribe joined the Icuano and several other tribes in a general uprising. The tribe lived near Cadereyta and in the Papagayos range. They spoke the same language and had the same customs as the Ancacuara and the Incuro. An Icaura captain of this tribe was near Cadereyta and gave aid to the Indians who attacked General De León's residence in 1651 (*HONAI*, 10:357).

Icabia

The Icabia was one of several tribes that in the early 1600s were inciting rebellion against the Spaniards in Nuevo León (Chapter 19).

Icuano

In 1648 the Icuano tribe, along with its allies the Icuara, the Guaracata, the Ancacuara, the Incuro, and the Camahan, participated in an uprising that extended throughout the province (*HONAI*, 10:357).

Iguaracata

In 1633 the Iguaracata tribe along with four other tribes attacked (near Cerralvo) a village of Cataara, who were friendly to the Spaniards (*HONAI*, 10:357).

Ijiaba (Xiabu)

De León met the Ijiaba tribe near the Rio Grande crossing on his 1689 expedition, according to Chapa. De León refers to them as the "Xiabu." See entry "Xiabu" in Foster, *Spanish Expeditions into Texas*, 289.

Incuro (Inquro)

In 1648, the Incuro tribe and allied tribes joined in an uprising that spread throughout the province (*HONAI*, 10:357).

Janambre

In 1645, near the Tamaulipas Mountains, the Janambre tribe twice attacked a trade expedition between Cadereyta and the coastal port city of Tampico in the Province of Huasteca. Soon after Chapa returned from the 1689 expedition into Texas, the tribe struck settlers living in the San Antonio Valley. Salinas comments on the language spoken by the Janambre Indians of southwestern Tamaulipas in *Indians of the Rio Grande Delta*, 146 (*HONAI*, 10:329).

Jumano (Jumane, Chomene)

When he was near the crossing of the Rio Grande on his 1689 expedition, General De León met the Jumano tribe, which was friendly to Jean Géry. In his 1690 letter to the viceroy, Padre Massanet wrote that some tribal members lived near the crossing of the Rio Grande. See entry "Jumano" in Foster, *Spanish Expeditions into Texas*, 276.

Maciguara

In 1635 a member of the Maciguara tribe who was also referred to as a Borrado Indian, was killed near Monterrey by the Tepehuan. Chapa (Chapter 28) notes that the tribe lived within ten to twelve leagues of Cerralvo (*HONAI*, 10:357).

Macorajora

A member of the Macorajora tribe was a workman for Captain Alonso de León [the elder] near Cerralvo (*HONAI*, 10:357).

Maguipamacopini

Chapa translates the tribal name as "Big Star That Kills Deer" and writes that they were living at an *encomienda* in Nuevo León in the 1680s.

Matolagua

The Matolagua tribe was identified by officials in Monterrey as being in rebellion in Nuevo León in the early 1600s (Chapter 19).

Mescal

The Mescal were with the Jumano and three other tribes near the Rio Grande crossing when Governor De León approached the river on his expedition in 1689. In his 1690 letter to the viceroy, Padre Massanet confirmed that the tribe lived near the crossing of the Río del Norte (*NHOT*, 4:640).

Mojoman

Governor De León identifies the Mojoman tribe at the close of his 1690 diary as among the tribes he had encountered on the expedition, but he does not note where he saw the tribe. See Appendix A.

Naaman (Manam?)

On June 19, 1690, Governor De León encountered a large encampment of over three thousand Naaman in central Lavaca County. In his 1690 letter to the viceroy, Padre Massanet writes that the Manam lived near the Guadalupe River (*NHOT*, 4:921).

Otomí

Members of the Otomí tribe served as friendly herders or workmen for Spaniards in Nuevo León, but the members apparently were brought into the area from outside, perhaps from present-day Durango. Although some Otomí became pacified, others living in the Río Verde area in southern San Luis Potosí remained unpacified into the seventeenth century (Naylor and Polzer, *The Presidio and Militia*, 38, 47 n9; *HONAI*, 10:329).

Pajarito

The Pajarito were met by Governor De León on July 23, 1686, about twelve leagues east of the lower San Juan River. On his 1675 expedition, about six leagues north of Monclova, Fernando del Bosque arrived at a place called Pajarito on the Río de Monclova (Bolton, *Spanish Exploration*, 291).

Panaa

Jean Géry claimed that the Panaa tribe lived within seventy leagues of Matagorda Bay and was loyal to him (Chapter 39).

Pantiguara

Chapa translates the tribal name as "Anointed with Red Ochre" and says they were living at an *encomienda* in Nuevo León (Chapter 39).

Pataoo (Petao?)

The Pataoo tribe was loyal to Jean Géry, according to Chapa's report (Chapter 39). Chapa writes that they were residents of an area within seventy leagues of Matagorda Bay. Henri Joutel includes the Petao in his list of tribes that lived west of the Colorado River (called the Maligne by the French). Campbell mistakenly locates the Petao between the Brazos and Trinity rivers. See entry "Petao Indians" in *NHOT*, 5:165–166.

Payamiguara

Chapa translates the tribal name to mean "People Who Live in Little Ravines." They were living in the 1680s at an *encomienda* in Nuevo León (Chapter 39).

Pelon

The Pelon tribe, from the Papagayos Mountains, stole horses and other livestock from Spanish settlers in 1667.

Piguen

The Piguen were loyal to Jean Géry and apparently lived within seventy leagues of Matagorda Bay in the 1680s (Chapter 39).

Piyai

Chapa lists the Piyai tribe as one of many that were loyal to Jean Géry and lived in an area within seventy leagues southwest of Matagorda Bay (Chapter 39).

Poguan

The Poguan tribe was loyal to Jean Géry and resided generally in the area within seventy leagues southwest of Matagorda Bay (Chapter 39).

Quem

A member of the Quem tribe, which lived near the Rio Grande, helped guide De León's 1689 expedition to the French settlement at Matagorda Bay (*NHOT*, 5:385).

Quien

The Quien tribe was identified as one of several that was in revolt against the Spanish settlements in Nuevo León in the early 1600s (Chapter 19).

Quibonoa

Members of the Quibonoa tribe rose against Spanish authorities in Nuevo León in the early 1600s (Chapter 19).

Saguimaniguara

Chapa translates the tribal name as "Field Lacking Wood" and writes that they lived on an *encomienda* in Nuevo León in 1689 (Chapter 39).

Sana (Chana)

De León met the Sana tribe with the Tohaha, Cantona, and Cava near the Colorado crossing on June 18, 1690 (*NHOT*, 5:792).

Sanatoo (Sanaque?)

Géry reported that the Sanatoo tribe was loyal to him and lived within seventy leagues southwest of Matagorda Bay (Chapter 39). In his 1690 letter to the viceroy, Padre Massanet writes that the Sanaque lived near the crossing of the Rio Grande.

Saurum

Jean Géry told Chapa that the Saurum tribe was loyal to him and that it roamed in an area that extended about seventy leagues southwest of Matagorda Bay (Chapter 39).

Sucuyama

Near Cerralvo the Sucuyama, along with their allies, attacked a village of Cataara Indians who were friends of the Spaniards (*HONAI*, 10:357).

Tacuanama

The Tacuanama tribe was in rebellion against Spanish authority in Nuevo León during the 1600–1630 period. A member of the tribe served as a scout and perhaps spy for Governor Martín de Zavala in 1651 to identify tribes that were stealing horses from the Spaniards (Chapter 19).

Tamireguan

Chapa writes that Jean Géry said that the Tamireguan tribe was one of many loyal to him and living within a distance of seventy leagues southwest of the Matagorda Bay area (Chapter 39).

Tepehuan

In 1633 the Tepehuan tribe joined other local tribes in attacking a village of Cataara Indians who were friendly to the Spaniards. Later that year, over three hundred Tepehuan attacked the charcoal camp at San Gregorio and killed fourteen persons. In 1635 they killed a mestizo shepherd and a young Maciguara Indian boy who was living near Cerralvo with a local priest. The tribe continued its raids throughout the 1640s. The raiding bands may have originated in present-day Chihuahua or farther south. For a description of the Tepehuan, a "large and bellicose tribe" that rebelled near the city of Durango in 1616 and later was found in Vizcaya, see Naylor and Polzer, *The Presidio and Militia in New Spain*, 414, 440–441. Members of the tribe rebelled against Spanish authority in Nuevo León during the 1600–1630s period. In 1600 they were also reported to be raiding Spanish locations near Santa Bárbara in Nueva Vizcaya (Simmons, *The Last Conquistador*, 91). Alvarez Barreiro lists the tribe in Nueva Vizcaya in the 1720s. Alvarez says that the Tepehuan were second in size to the Tarahumara (in Nueva Vizcaya), who numbered 37,523. See Naylor and Polzer, *Pedro Rivera*, 214, 215; *HONAI*, 10:306, 331.

Tejas

In 1689, De León met a Tejas captain and several tribesmen who had two Frenchmen at an encampment located about twenty-five leagues north of De León's Guadalupe camp in DeWitt County. The Tejas returned to De León's camp on the Guadalupe for a three-day meeting. De León reports that on May 18, 1690, his party again met a Tejas captain and some of his men six to eight leagues west of the Trinity (probably in Leon County), where the Spanish party was escorted about fifteen leagues to the principal Tejas community. See also the entry "Hasinai" in Foster, *Spanish Expeditions into Texas*, 274–275.

Tetecuara (Tetecore)

In 1667, the Tetecuara tribe was identified as stealing horses near Monterrey. They continued their raiding practices near Cerralvo in 1669 and in 1671. On his 1675 expedition, Fernando del Bosque met some Tetecore on the south side of the Rio Grande (Bolton, *Spanish Exploration*, 307).

Thoaga (Tohaha, Toaha)

On June 17, 1690, Governor De León met the Thoaga (probably the Tohaha) at the Colorado crossing in Fayette County (see Appendix A). The tribe (listed as Tohaha) is included in Henri Joutel's list of tribes living on the west side of the lower Colorado River (called the Maligne by the French) (Margry, *Découvertes*, 3:288). Father Francisco Casañas lists the Toaha as a tribe friendly to the Tejas and living to the south and west of the Tejas (Bolton, *The Hasinais*, 58 n10).

Thoó (Toho, Tohau)

On June 18, 1690, Governor De León's party saw the Thoó tribe about seven leagues south of the Colorado crossing; the next day he encountered the tribe again, and on June 28 the governor met another encampment of the tribe between the San Antonio River and the Nueces. The Tohau are included in Henri Joutel's list of tribes that lived on the west side of the Colorado (called the Maligne by the French) (Margry, *Découvertes*, III:288).

Tlaxcala (Tlaxcalteca)

A friendly settlement of Tlaxcala Indians was located near Cadereyta. Chapa reports that a company of Tlaxcalteca accompanied the Spaniards on their 1663–1664 expedition to locate and attack the Cacaxtle, who were found seventy leagues from Monterrey (*NHOT*, 6:510).

Zacatil

A Zacatil captain joined Governor De León on his 1686 expedition to the mouth of the Rio Grande in search of La Salle's settlement (Chapter 31).

Notes

Introduction

1. Chapter 14 of Chapa's *Historia*, "In Which Occurrences and Prodigies That Have Taken Place in Various Parts of the World Are Considered," is omitted because it is not relevant to the history of Nuevo León.
2. Genaro García, ed., *Historia de Nuevo León*, 7.
3. *Caverns of Oblivion*. Also to be noted, Harbert Davenport translated a short passage of De León's *Discourses* that describes the Indians of Nuevo León. See "The Expedition of Pánfilo de Narváez," 291–295n6.
4. Herbert E. Bolton, ed., *Spanish Exploration in the Southwest, 1542–1706*, 350.
5. Ibid., 405–423.
6. See Vito Alessio Robles, *Coahuila y Texas en la época colonial*, and Eugenio del Hoyo, *Historia del Nuevo Reino de León (1577–1723)*.
7. See Thomas N. Campbell, "The Coahuiltecans and Their Neighbors." In commenting on sources for the history of Nuevo León, Robert S. Weddle writes, "Alonso de León's account [*Historia de Nuevo León*] of the exploration he himself conducted is an indispensable source, especially since documentary material for the region and period of which he wrote is meager. The narrative is taken beyond León's ending in 1648 by Juan Bautista Chapa" (*Spanish Sea: The Gulf of Mexico in North American Discovery, 1500–1685*, 368).
8. Peter Gerhard, *The North Frontier of New Spain*, 356.
9. The commemorative edition was published by the Gobierno del Estado de Nuevo León in Monterrey.
10. All or part of the following forty counties were included in the kingdom of Nuevo León: Cameron, Hidalgo, Starr, Kenedy, Brooks, Jim Hogg, Zapata, Nueces, Jim Wells, Duval, Webb, San Patricio, Bee, Live Oak, McMullen, La Salle, Dimmit, Maverick, Karnes, Wilson, Atascosa, Frio, Zavala, Gonzales, Guadalupe, Béxar, Medina, Uvalde, Kinney, Caldwell, Hays, Comal, Kendall, Kerr, Bandera, Real, Edwards, Valverde, Willacy, Kleberg.
11. Bolton, *Spanish Exploration*, 391.
12. Vito Alessio Robles calls the 200-league-square area measured from Pánuco the

tragic square (*Coahuila y Texas en la época colonial*, 89–95. See also Alessio's map, 90).

13. *Crónica de los colegios de propaganda fide de la Nueva España*, 761.

14. See Jean M. Grove, *The Little Ice Age*; Susan H. Swain, "Mexico and the Little Ice Age"; James E. Fitting, "Regional Cultural Development, 300 B.C. to A.D. 1000," 44; Merlin P. Lawson, *The Climate of the Great American Desert*, 77–85.

15. Charles B. Heiser, Jr., writes that, "although many plants were used as hallucinogens in Mexico, only a few were employed in northern North America." One was the mescal bean, *Sophora secundiflora*, found naturally in Texas ("Ethnobotany and Economic Botany," 202).

16. See Robert S. Weddle's treatment of Carvajal in *Spanish Sea*, 331–345.

17. For a translation of Castaño's 1590–1591 journal with commentary, see Albert H. Schroeder and Dan S. Matson, *A Colony on the Move*. David J. Weber also traces Castaño de Sosa's journey across the Rio Grande near present-day Del Rio and up the Pecos River to the Rio Grande Valley in New Mexico (*The Spanish Frontier in North America*, 79–80). The impact of Castaño's 1590 venture from Nuevo León into modern New Mexico on Juan de Oñate's 1598 expedition to colonize the upper Rio Grande is described in Marc Simmons, *The Last Conquistador: Juan de Oñate and the Settling of the Far Southwest*, 60–61, 101–109.

18. A translation, with commentary, of Hernán Gallego's journal, or *Relation*, of the Chamuscado-Rodríguez expedition and Diego Pérez de Luxán's account of the Espejo expedition into New Mexico is found in George P. Hammond and Agapito Rey, *The Rediscovery of New Mexico, 1580–1594*.

19. For a detailed assessment of Spanish developments leading to the settlement of New Mexico, see Weber, *Spanish Frontier*, 78–82.

20. T. N. Campbell, *The Indians of Southern Texas and Northeastern Mexico: Selected Writings of Thomas Nolan Campbell*, 12.

21. Basil C. Hedrick and Carroll L. Riley, *The Journey of the Vaca Party: An Account of the Narváez Expedition, 1528–1536, as Related by Gonzalo Fernández de Oviedo y Valdés*, 48–51.

22. William C. Foster, *Spanish Expeditions into Texas, 1689–1768*.

23. In Chapter 5 of the Oviedo account, the author records the daily movements of Cabeza de Vaca's party from the first of August to the end of the month, when they crossed the large river (the Rio Grande). The seven travel days included the first day (August 1), 7 leagues; August 2, estimated 6 leagues; August 11, 6 leagues; August 12, estimated 6 leagues; August 28, 2 leagues; August 29, 2 to 3 leagues; August 30, 8 to 9 leagues.

24. Donald E. Chipman carefully assesses Cabeza de Vaca's route in "In Search of Cabeza de Vaca's Route across Texas: An Historiographical Survey."

25. Frederick W. Hodge, ed., "The Narrative of Alvar Nuñez Cabeca de Vaca,"

in Hodge and Lewis, *Spanish Explorers in the Southern United States, 1528–1543*, 92n2.

26. The Abbé Jean Cavelier, brother of the French explorer, described a journey taken from the French settlement near present-day Matagorda Bay during the summer of 1685. On the trip La Salle, his brother, and a small number of French troops accompanied friendly Indians to visit a village area that was fortified with small towers erected at intervals. According to the Abbé Cavelier, they found fastened to a post the arms of Spain engraved on a copper plate dated 1588. The local Indians also showed La Salle hammers, an anvil, two small pieces of an iron cannon, a small bronze cannon, spearheads, old sword blades, and some volumes of Spanish comedies (Isaac Joslin Cox, ed., *The Journeys of René Robert Cavelier, Sieur de La Salle*, vol. 1, 273). See also Robert S. Weddle's suggestion about La Salle's trip in *The French Thorn: Rival Explorers in the Spanish Sea, 1682–1762*, 29, 30.

27. For a brief sketch of the life of Martín de Zavala, see Israel Cavazos Garza, *Diccionario biográfico de Nuevo León*, vol. 2, 532–533.

28. Gerhard, *The North Frontier*, 109–110.

29. The following description of Nuevo León's Indians is based primarily on information found in chaps. 3–16 of Genaro García's 1909 edition of *Historia de Nuevo León* (22–71); information about the same natives found in chaps. 6–8 (33–41) of the *Historia* is covered in Campbell, "The Coahuiltecans and Their Neighbors."

30. An *encomienda* was the assignment of a specific Indian band or community to a Spanish landowner. The assignee (the *encomendero*) received the right to work the Indians in return for introducing them to the Spanish work ethic and Catholicism. Peter Gerhard assesses the institution in Nuevo León: "Surely in no part of Spanish America was there a greater abuse of this institution [*encomienda*] than here [Nuevo León]. Carvajal arrived with considerable experience as a slave hunter in the province of Huaxteca, and the pattern he imposed varied little under his successors. The Indians were hunted like animals and chained together until they could be sold or put to work by their *encomendero*" (*The North Frontier of New Spain*, 345). For a more extensive description of the *encomiendas* in Nuevo León, see Eugenio del Hoyo, *Historia del Nuevo Reino de León (1577–1723)*, 433–441.

31. Gerhard, *The North Frontier*, 344, 345. In his *Discourses*, De León refers to twenty-eight Indian tribes. Most were residents of the immediate area, and some are included in Chapa's lists of Nuevo León tribes.

32. De León et al., *Historia*, 34.

33. Robert A. Ricklis reports that Indians on the lower Texas coast near the Rio Grande first used the bow and arrow ca. A.D. 1000 and illustrates examples of

Perdiz and other arrow points with harpoon features as described by De León. "Prehistoric Occupation of the Central and Lower Texas Coast: A Regional View," *Bulletin of the Texas Archeological Society* 66 (1995), 283–287.

34. John R. Swanton, *Source Materials on the History and Ethnology of the Caddo Indians*, 155–156.

35. Peyote is found in a wide area that extends from present-day Rio Grande City in Starr County north to Webb County in Texas and south of the lower Rio Grande to Guachicil. See Omer C. Stewart, *Peyote Religion: A History*, and George R. Morgan and Omer C. Stewart, "Peyote Trade in South Texas."

36. See Campbell's entry "Akokisa Indians" in *NHOT*, 1:76.

37. See E. James Dixon, *Quest for the Origins of the First Americans*. A recent archeological study of a rock shelter in the Calsada region, about 30 miles south-southeast of Monterrey, indicates that there were humans in Nuevo León as early as 10,000 to 12,000 years ago (C. Roger Nance, *The Archaeology of La Calsada: A Rockshelter in the Sierra Madre Oriental, Mexico*).

38. See William B. Griffen, "Southern Periphery: East," 334–335.

39. Hodge, "Cabeca de Vaca," in *Spanish Explorers*, 88.

40. Ricklis estimates that ceramic pottery was widely used among tribes in southern Texas by ca. A.D. 1250–1300 and on the Central Texas coast slightly earlier. Timothy K. Perttula, et al., "Prehistoric and Historic Aboriginal Ceramics in Texas," *Bulletin of the Texas Archeological Society* 66 (1995), 195.

41. Gerhard, *The North Frontier*, 353, 354.

42. Campbell, *The Indians of Southern Texas*, 181.

43. The Spanish government's effort in the seventeenth and eighteenth centuries to incorporate the native population into the formal Spanish legal system and the role of the *protector de Indios* is described in Charles R. Cutter, *The Protector de Indios in Colonial New Mexico, 1659–1821*.

44. The 1675 diary of Fernando del Bosque covering his expedition from Monclova across the Rio Grande is found in Bolton, *Spanish Exploration*, 291–309.

45. The topographic maps cited for locations in Mexico were prepared by the Estados Unidos Mexicanos, Secretaría de Programación y Presupuesto, Carta Topográfica, 1:250,000 *Monclova*, G14-4; *Piedras Negras*, H14-10; *Nuevo Laredo*, G14-2; and the Instituto Nacional de Estadística, Geografía e Informática, Carta Topográfica, 1:250,000, *Nueva Rosita*, G14-1; *Reynosa*, G14-5; *Linares*, G14-11; *Monterrey*, G14-7; *Concepción del Oro*, G14-10; *Rio Bravo*, 14-8; *Matamoros*, G14-6-9-12. The topographic maps cited for locations in Texas are U.S. Geological Survey maps, Western United States, 1:250,000 Series, *Eagle Pass*, NH14-10; *Crystal City*, NH14-11; *San Antonio*, NH14-8; *Seguin*, NH14-9; *Austin*, NH14-6; *Beaumont*, NH15-4; *Palestine*, NH15-1; *Beeville*, NH14-12; *Houston*, NH15-7.

46. In 1915 Bolton concluded that La Salle was killed near the Brazos ("The Location of La Salle's Colony on the Gulf of Mexico," 3n8). This conclusion was confirmed by other Texas historians, including William E. Dunn (*Spanish and French Rivalry in the Gulf Region of the United States, 1678–1702*, 35n2) and Carlos E. Castañeda (*Our Catholic Heritage in Texas, 1519–1936*, I, 196–198). In contrast, Robert S. Weddle speculates that La Salle was killed east of the Trinity (*NHOT*, 4:82). An examination of Henri Joutel's unabridged and untranslated journal in French of La Salle's 1684–1687 expedition to Texas, which includes information on the daily distance and direction traveled on La Salle's final journey, establishes that La Salle was assassinated near the Brazos (called "la rivière aux Canots" by the French), as correctly reported by Bolton and Dunn (Margry, *Découvertes*, III, 260–335). I am preparing for publication an English translation of Joutel's unabridged journal.

47. De León's diary of the trip is found in Walter J. O'Donnell, "La Salle's Occupation of Texas," 12–13.

48. For a brief account of Tonti's trip from the Great Lakes to visit the Caddos on the Red River and those near the Trinity, see Francis Parkman, *La Salle and the Discovery of the Great West*, 464–467.

49. Margry, *Découvertes*, III, 260–386.

50. Ibid., 387–464. See also Charles B. Heiser, Jr., "Ethnobotany and Economic Botany," vol. 1, 199–206; Bruce D. Smith, *The Emergence of Agriculture*, 183–205.

To the Devout Reader

1. Carlos Esteban (or Charles Estienne) was the French author (1504–1564) who wrote *Dictionarium historicum, geographicum, poeticum*—which Chapa paraphrases as "Vocabulario histórico y geográfico"—1596 edition, Paris. For further biographical information, see *Enciclopedia universal ilustrada europeo-americana* (Madrid: Espasa-Calpe), vol. 22, 951.

1. The History of Nuevo León from 1650

"Concerning the History of the New Kingdom of León from the year 1650 onward."

1. Israel Cavazos Garza cites this reference as evidence that Chapa was the author of the *Historia* because Chapa arrived in the province in 1650. See Juan Bautista Chapa, *Historia del Nuevo Reino de León de 1650 a 1690*, ed. Israel Cavazos Garza, 40.

2. Martín de Zavala served as governor of Nuevo León for thirty-eight years, from

1626 to 1664. For a list of the governors of Nuevo León from 1582 to 1851, see Thomas C. Barnes, Thomas H. Naylor, and Charles W. Polzer, *Northern New Spain—A Research Guide*, 106–107.

3. Chapa includes the Tacuanama Indians in his list of tribes who had lived within 10 to 12 leagues of Cerralvo (Chapter 28).

2. Indians Attack Alonso de León's House

"Of how the Indian, Cabrito, head of the band, collected ten nations of Indians and attacked the house of the Chief Justice, and the rest that happened."

1. According to Captain De León, the Icaura Indians spoke the same language and had the same customs as the Inquero and the Ayancura. Capitán Alonso de León, Autor Anónimo, and General Fernando Sánchez de Zamora, *Historia de Nuevo León*, ed. Genaro García, 169. In the middle 1600s, the tribe lived in the Papagayos Mountains between Monterrey and Cerralvo.

3. Governor Zavala Requests the Establishment of Two Presidios

"Of how Governor Don Martín de Zavala, due to the extensive disturbance in the land, obliged the Viceroy to request soldiers to establish two presidios."

1. The Count of Alba was Luis Enríquez y Guzmán, Conde de Alba de Liste y Marqués de Villaflor, who served as the viceroy of New Spain from 1650 to 1653. See Donald E. Chipman, *Spanish Texas, 1519–1821*, 263.

2. The Duke of Alburquerque was Francisco Fernández de la Cueva, Duque de Alburquerque, Grande de España, who served as the viceroy of New Spain from 1653 to 1660. Ibid.

3. The present-day Palmas River joins the Soto la Marina about 60 miles east of Ciudad Victoria before entering the Gulf of Mexico about 100 miles north of Tampico. See the Mexican government map "Ciudad de México" (1:1,000,000), Instituto Nacional de Estadística Geográfica e Informática. In the seventeenth century, the Palmas River was the modern Soto la Marina (Gerhard, *The North Frontier*, 358).

4. Francisco López de Gómara was secretary to Hernán Cortés and was his biographer. The significance of Gómara's comprehensive narrative of the Spanish conquest, published in 1552, is noted in Weddle, *Spanish Sea*, 125. The anonymous author's ability to translate Italian into Spanish was cited by Cavazos Garza as evidence that the Italian Chapa was the author of the *Historia* (Chapa, *Historia*, ed. Cavazos Garza, 48).

5. An *adelantado* was an individual responsible for the conquest of new lands for the Spanish Crown. The expense of outfitting expeditions, transporting settlers,

and establishing towns or posts was paid by the individual. He became governor of the area, received title to large tracts of land, and was assigned a certain percentage of the income generated from the province. He also distributed land and water rights and assigned Indians to *encomenderos* (Barnes et al., *A Research Guide*, 131).

6. The Spanish concept of Indian "reduction" means reducing the native population to a fully cooperative (not rebellious) state.

7. The astrolabe was the most common device used by seventeenth-century explorers in New Spain to determine latitude. An angle measurement of the sun at noon read with the instrument was interpreted with tables that gave a correlation between the angle measurement, the day of the year, and the distance measured in degrees and minutes from the equator. See Robert S. Martin and James C. Martin, *Contours of Discovery*, 50–51. Chapa's comment that they did not have a reliable astrolabe was repeated when readings of latitude were taken on the 1686 and 1689 expeditions.

4. The Events after 1653

"In which the events later than 1653 are followed."

1. According to Israel Cavazos Garza's note (51n2) in his edition of Chapa's *Historia*, Labradores was founded around 1638 by Juan Francisco de Escobedo, and in 1829 the village was renamed Galeana. See the Mexican government map *Concepción del Oro*, G14-10.

5. Punishment of Indians Who Committed the Murders

"Of how, by a certain ruse, the Indians who committed the murders described in the last chapter were punished."

1. Matehuala was located approximately 30 leagues east-northeast of the city of Zacatecas near the Nuevo León–Nueva Galicia provincial boundary. For a brief history of the ore-processing center dating from 1649, see Gerhard, *The North Frontier*, 81–83.

2. According to Chapa, the Hualahuis lived near Cadereyta in the seventeenth century (Chapter 28). Captain De León reported that the tribe captured and sold Indian children to the Spaniards and also engaged in raids against the Spaniards in southern Nuevo León (Alonso De León et al., *Historia de Nuevo León, con noticias sobre Coahuila, Tejas, y Nuevo México*, 169).

3. According to Israel Cavazos Garza, the San Cristóbal mission became the Villa de Hualahuises in 1825 (Chapa, *Historia*, ed. Cavazos Garza, 54n4. See also the map *Linares*, G14-11).

6. Captain Alonso de León Represents Governor Zavala
before the Royal Council

"Of the good negotiation that Capt. Alonso de León brought from the Council for the governor of the kingdom."

1. A *cédula* is a decree or general title used to identify a variety of Spanish documents. In this instance, it emanated from the king, as *cédulas* often did (Barnes et al., *A Research Guide*, 134).
2. A *marco* was a quantity of gold or silver equal to 7.4 ounces (ibid., 75).
3. The region more than fifty leagues north of Monterrey may have included present-day eastern Hidalgo, Starr, Zapata, southern Webb, and western Jim Hogg counties, although no specific statement was made that the area north of the Rio Grande was explored.
4. The Plata (or Silver) Mountains cannot be identified with the information given.
5. The Order of Santiago is a Spanish religious and military order created by King Fernando II of León in 1158. The phrase is translated here as the Order of Santiago, although the "Order of St. James" is used in some translations (*Simon & Schuster's International Dictionary*, 1497).
6. The Royal Audiencia was the judicial and legislative council that administered royal affairs over a large geographic area of the New World. Judicially, it was subordinate only to the Council of the Indies (Barnes et al., *A Research Guide*, 132).
7. The Council of the Indies was the governing body immediately under the king. It was established and given the rank of a "royal and supreme" council in 1524 (ibid., 59).
8. Juan de Leyva y de la Cerda, Marqués de Leyva y de Ladrada, Conde de Baños, served as viceroy from 1660 to 1664 (Chipman, *Spanish Texas*, 262).

7. Other Military Action in Nuevo León

"Of the other military occurrences which took place in this kingdom."

8. Indian Nations of the North

"Of how the nations of the north began to rise up and commit murders and robberies, both in this kingdom and on the roads out of Zacatecas and Sombrerete."

1. Although the term "sargento mayor" means a major, or the third in command of a regiment, the position was often filled by a nonprofessional in the frontier areas (Barnes et al., *A Research Guide*, 138).
2. The Tlaxcalteca had been brought into northern New Spain from Central Mexico, where the tribe had been allied with the Spaniards in the conquest

of the Aztec Indians in the early sixteenth century. The tribe came to Nuevo León to settle, help pacify the local Indians, and engage in exploration with the Spaniards. See Thomas N. Campbell's entry "Tlaxcalan Indians," *NHOT*, 6:510.

3. That the "land of the enemy (the Cacaxtles)" was more than sixty leagues (about 156 miles) from Monterrey suggests that the party may have reached the area near present-day Eagle Pass or may have crossed the Rio Grande into the area near the Nueces River where the Spaniards found the Cacaxtle during the expedition conducted two years later. The tribe ("Catzale") was also mentioned in connection with mission activities in Coahuila in the early 1670s by Francis B. Steck, "Forerunners of Captain De León's Expedition to Texas, 1670–1675," 7.

4. For an excellent study of the Cacaxtle Indians, see Campbell, *The Indians of Southern Texas*, 173–184. The Cacaxtle were likely among the tribes that Captain De León identified as "Indians of the north." The tribe apparently survived the Spanish reprisals in the 1660s because in 1693 Salinas Varona reported meeting some Cacaxtle ("Cacastees") along with some Ocana and Piedras Blancas about 3 leagues south of the customary crossing of the Rio Grande (on May 9), and the governor encountered them ("Cacastle") again at the Indian trade ground near the customary Colorado crossing in present-day Fayette County on May 27. On July 3, during his return trip, Salinas Varona identified hills in southern Medina County as the hills of the Cacastles. See William C. Foster and Jack Jackson, eds., "The 1693 Expedition of Gregorio de Salinas Varona to Sustain the Missionaries among the Tejas Indians," 283n48, 294, 308.

5. That the expedition lasted five months suggests that the Spanish troops had difficulty locating and encircling the tribe, which had acquired horses in earlier raids. The size of the expedition was comparable to that sent to rout the French from Fort Saint-Louis in 1689. The exercise was in the field more than twice as long as the 1689 expedition. See T. N. Campbell's assessment of the expedition in *The Indians of Southern Texas* 175–178.

9. The Death of Governor Don Martín de Zavala

"How Governor Don Martín de Zavala died; his good government and the talents with which he was endowed."

1. Agustín de Zavala served as governor of Nuevo León between 1611 and 1615. See Barnes et al., *A Research Guide*, 106.

10. The Government after Governor Zavala's Death

"Of how Señor Viceroy installed this government due to the death of Governor Don Martín de Zavala."

1. Antonio Sebastián de Toledo, Marqués de Mancera, was the viceroy of New Spain from 1664 to 1673 (Chipman, *Spanish Texas*, 263).

11. Developments in 1665

"Of several occurrences that took place in the year 1665."

1. The Bobole (Babol) Indians were residents of northeastern Coahuila and parts of the present-day Texas counties of Maverick, Dimmit, LaSalle, and Webb, the area into which the expedition marched. See Campbell, "Coahuiltecans and Their Neighbors," vol. 10, 353, 355. On May 29, 1675, Fernando del Bosque met some Bobale Indians hunting bison near the Rio Grande (probably in Maverick County). See Bolton, *Spanish Exploration*, 305, 305n2.

2. The Indian custom of playing a flute during battle was noted by Governor De León on July 10, 1686, on his expedition to the mouth of the Rio Grande (Chapter 30). According to studies in volume 10, *Southwest*, in *HONAI*, the flute was used by Indian tribes of the Southwest for numerous purposes, including as a musical instrument (109, 247, 287, 313) and for dances (302).

   In addition to playing flutes, according to De León, Nuevo León musicians rubbed notched rhythm sticks and rattled rock-filled gourds to accompany the musical beat for community dances. Some of these musical instruments apparently had been in use for centuries by natives on the lower Pecos and Rio Grande (as well as in other parts of Texas). Cheryl L. Highley reports evidence of similar instruments from the Middle Archaic period (ca. 2500 B.C.–400 B.C.) excavated at the Loma Sandia project, the Cueva de la Candelaria site in northeastern Mexico, and sites in the lower Pecos region. Anna Jean Taylor and Cheryl Lynn Highley, *Archeological Investigations at the Loma Sandia Site (41LK 28)*, vol. 2, 649–662.

12. Other Developments in 1665

"In which other events of the same year are treated."

1. For a full consideration of the role of the *alcalde ordinario* in northern New Spain, see Charles R. Cutter, *The Legal Culture of Northern New Spain, 1700–1810*, 82–99.

2. The author's reference to Genoa was cited by Cavazos Garza as an indication that the anonymous author was Chapa, whose baptismal records and other documents trace his family to the Italian village of Albisola, a few miles from Genoa (Chapa, *Historia*, ed. Cavazos Garza, 14).

13. Two Other Strange Occurrences

"Of two other strange occurrences that took place in this kingdom."

1. Saint Isidor was born in Seville (or Cartagena) around 560 and served as arch-bishop of Seville. He died in 636 (*Enciclopedia universal ilustrada, europeo-americana*, 2062–2064).

15. Developments in the Province in 1667

As Chapter 14, entitled "In Which Occurrences and Prodigies That Have Taken Place in Various Parts of the World Are Considered" records Chapa's account of unusual events that occurred outside Nuevo León and that were reported by third parties, the material is not included in this translation. To avoid confusion, the chapter number 14 is skipped, and we proceed with Chapter 15: "In which the matters of the kingdom are continued."

1. For a short history of the reign of Carlos II (1665–1700) and the roles of the queen mother, Mariana, and young Carlos, see John Lynch, *Spain under the Habsburgs*, vol. 2, 258–275.

16. The Indians of the North Continue Their Incursions

"Of how the Indians of the north continued making incursions into this kingdom."

1. Chapa mentions the Tetecuara (Tetacore) on several occasions. The tribe report-edly resided primarily in northern Coahuila in the late seventeenth century. See "Tetecore Indians," in *NHOT*, 6:268. On June 12, 1675, Fernando del Bosque found some Tetecore with over 100 Bobosarigame a few leagues north of Mon-clova (Bolton, *Spanish Exploration*, 307).

2. As the name suggests, the Pelones were described as bald. As Captain De León explained in his first *Discourse*, some Indians in Nuevo León wore their hair long while others had their hair removed. The name Pelones was applied to several different tribes. See entry "Pelone Indians," *NHOT*, 5:132.

17. Tetecoara Indian Attack

"Of how there was news that the Tetecoara Indians tried to enter this kingdom by way of El Alamo."

1. The present-day Mexican town of Alamo, located on the Río Alamo, is ap-proximately 31 miles, or 12 leagues, from the city of Cerralvo. The fact that the measured distance on contemporary maps is identical to Chapa's estimate supports the view that distances recorded by De León and Chapa are generally reliable and that the customary league of 2.6 miles was used.

2. The Cuauguijo Indians had not been previously mentioned nor are they in-cluded in the list of tribes in northeastern Mexico compiled in *HONAI*.

3. The Catujane (Catujano, Catujan) Indians were frequently identified in seventeenth-century Spanish documents that pertain to northern Nuevo León and Coahuila. See "Catujano Indians," *NHOT*, 1:1043; *HONAI*, vol. 10, 356.

4. The distinct mesa is depicted on the Mexican government maps *Nueva Rosita*, G14-1, and *Monclova*, G14-4. William E. Dunn notes that De León first attempted to locate a villa in the new province of Coahuila at the "Mesa de los Catujanes," but a location on the Nadadores was selected instead (*Spanish and French Rivalry in the Gulf Region*, 85n6).

5. Artaxerxes was any of several kings of ancient Persia; Artaxerxes I and II ruled between about 465 and 358 B.C. (*Webster's New World Dictionary of the American Language*, 2d ed., 78).

18. Success in Capturing the Indians

"Of the good success that was had, both in the Villa of Saltillo and in this kingdom, in capturing the enemies."

1. Mazapil was the jurisdiction adjacent to and southwest of Nuevo León. By 1554 Spaniards had reached Mazapil, and by 1568 silver deposits had attracted miners. The Guachichiles and Zacatecos almost destroyed the location in 1573. Because Indians were unavailable, African slaves were brought to the area to work the mines. For a brief history of the area see Gerhard, *The North Frontier*, 108–110.

19. The Request from the Municipal Council of Monterrey to the Governor

"In which the request from the Municipal Council of Monterrey to the Governor is set down."

1. Of these eleven Indian tribes, the Aguata, Tepehuane, Tacuanama, and Guinaimo were included in Chapa's lists of Indians living in Nuevo León (Chapter 28). The Borrado are described as living in Nuevo León or the border area between Nuevo León and Coahuila (*HONAI*, vol. 10, 331). The remaining tribes have not been otherwise identified but are included in Thomas N. Campbell's comprehensive list of tribes that lived in Nuevo León (*HONAI*, vol. 10, 357).

2. Pedro Camacho's people may have referred to mestizo servants or possibly to Indians who were a part of Camacho's *encomienda.*

3. Spaniards used carts as one of the principal modes of transportation to move heavy loads over the roads or paths in northern New Spain in the seventeenth century.

20. The Opinion of Fray Francisco de Ribera

"In which the opinion of Fray Francisco de Ribera is set down."

1. According to Genaro García, *tlatole* is an Indian (*mexicana*) word describing a person who is boastful (De León et al., *Historia*, 262).
2. Bartolomé de las Casas's *Conquest of the Indies* was published in 1645. See Antonio Palau Dulcet, *Manual del librero hispano-americano*, vol. 3, 246. Las Casas was one of the principal critics of the Spanish treatment of Indians and was also a former *encomendero* and a Dominican friar and bishop. See Charles Gibson, "Spanish Indian Policies," *HONAI*, vol. 4, 97.
3. Joseph de Acosta's *Moral History of the Indies* was first printed in Seville in 1590 (Dulcet, *Manual del librero hispano-americano*, vol. 1, 56). For a contemporary assessment of the Jesuit scholar's contribution, see Karl W. Butzer, "From Columbus to Acosta: Science, Geography, and the New World," 557–558.
4. Father Manso is Fray Tomás Manso de Contreras, who served as procurator-general of the Franciscans in New Mexico between 1630 and 1656, when he was appointed bishop of Nicaragua. As procurator, Manso was charged with the financial and temporal care of the order. A summary of Manso's career is found in the *New Mexico Historical Review*, vol. 5, 189–191.

21. Fray Ribera's Opinion Continues

"In which the opinion of Father Rivera is continued."

1. Padre Antonio de Remesal wrote the *History of Chiapas and Guatemala* in 1619 (*Diccionario de Historia Eclesiástica de España*, vol. 3, 2075).

22. The Governor Submits This Opinion to the City of San Luis Potosí

"Of how the governor submitted this opinion to the city of San Luis to other theologians, and the reply that they gave, and what the aforesaid instructor then added."

1. The title means that the person was a *licenciado*, one who had earned an academic degree (Barnes et al., *A Research Guide*, 136).

23. Other Skirmishes That Took Place in Nuevo León

"In which the wars that took place in this kingdom are continued."

24. A Great Uprising in the San Antonio Valley

"Of the great uprising of the valley of San Antonio."

1. A *fanega* of corn represented about 101 pounds (Barnes et al., *A Research Guide*, 73).

25. Don Domingo de Pruneda Is Appointed Governor

"In which it is related how this governorship was bestowed on Don Domingo de Pruneda."

1. Santander was a community located about 15 leagues from the Gulf Coast and about the same distance south of the Conchos River. See map *Nuevo León in 1768* in Gerhard, *The North Frontier*, 347.

26. The Administration of Don Domingo de Vidagaray

"Of the government of Don Domingo de Vidagaray, and how short a time that he lived in it."

1. According to Israel Cavazos Garza, Juan de Echeverría was born in Bilbao, Spain. He married Doña Juliana de Cepeda, daughter of Captain Ambrosio de Cepeda. He was named governor on October 20, 1681. See Chapa, *Historia*, ed. Cavazos Garza, 115n14.

27. Juan de Echeverría Is Appointed Governor

"Of how the Señor Viceroy, Marquis of La Laguna, bestowed this government on Juan de Echeverría."

1. The Huaxteca Valley included the coastal area south-southeast of Monterrey in the general vicinity of the Palmas River. For a brief history of the area, see Gerhard, *The North Frontier*, 358–368. Donald E. Chipman reviews the history and describes the area north of Pánuco toward the Palmas River in *Nuño de Guzmán and the Province of Pánuco in New Spain, 1518–1533*, 158–164.

28. A List of Indian Nations That Were in Nuevo León but Have Vanished

"In which the nations of Indians who were in this kingdom, and have been obliterated, are set down."

1. Captain Alonso de León mentions that the Tepehuan executed a series of raids in Nuevo León beginning in 1633. Although Chapa includes the tribe in his list

of Indian nations that had lived near Monterrey, modern authorities report that the original homeland for the Tepehuan was present-day western Durango (*HONAI*, vol. 10, 306, 331).

2. Chapa (or the copyist) named this tribe twice in his list of Indian nations that lived near Cadereyta.

3. The description of an area 200 leagues in latitude and longitude refers to the original boundaries of the Nuevo Reino de León commencing at a point near present-day Tampico, as described in Carvajal's contract with the king; the same boundary description was included in Zavala's grant (Gerhard, *The North Frontier*, 348).

29. Indian Nations Added by the Spaniards

"In which other nations, which now are added to the Spaniards, are set down."

1. The number of Indian nations Chapa names is as follows: in Chapter 28 he names 47 tribes near Monterrey, 43 tribes near Cadereyta, and 70 tribes who lived within 10 to 12 leagues' circumference of Cerralvo. In Chapter 29 he lists 90 (not 88, as he counted) tribes that had been recently gathered from Indian communities that were located up to 125 miles from Monterrey. Chapa records a total of 250 tribes.

30. The Death of Governor Juan de Echeverría and the Administration of Governor Alonso de León

"Of the death of Governor Juan de Echeverría; entry and administration of Governor Alonso de León."

31. The Beginning of the Marquis of San Miguel de Aguayo's Administration as Governor of Nuevo León

"Of the entrance of the Marquis of San Miguel de Aguayo into this government."

1. Patos was a town located about 10 leagues west of Saltillo. According to Cavazos Garza, the community was established before 1580 and currently is known as General Cepeda (Chapa, *Historia*, ed. Cavazos Garza, 123n16). See map *Monterrey*, G14-7.

2. Tomás Antonio de la Cerda y Aragón, Conde de Paredes y Marqués de la Laguna, served as viceroy from 1680 to 1686. See Chipman, *Spanish Texas*, 264.

3. The Zacatil Indians are not included in Chapa's list of 250 nations that lived in Nuevo León. The identification of a Zacatil village may have referred to a village

of Zacatec Indians brought into Nuevo León from the area around the city of Zacatecas, which was named for the tribe. (*HONAI*, vol. 10, 337–341.)

4. This reference confirms that Juan Bautista (spelled Baptista in the manuscript) Chapa served on De León's personal staff during the 1686 expedition.

5. The reference to "my Indians" suggests that the party may have been moving through the area of De León's own *encomienda*. The note on July 2 suggests that the tribe was perhaps the Caumane.

6. As described by De León, the San Juan River runs due north from the river crossing along the route traversed. See map *Río Bravo*, G14-8.

7. The Caurame Indians apparently lived in the region east of the San Juan River, but Chapa does not include them in his lists of tribes living in Nuevo León. De León's party again passed the friendly Indian encampment on July 24 during the return trip. See *HONAI*, vol. 10, 356. See also Martín Salinas, *Indians of the Río Grande Delta*, 95.

8. The Indian custom of playing a flute to support a tribe during hostile encounters was reported during the battle with the Cacaxtles in Texas in 1665 (see Chapter 11).

9. When used to measure depth, an estado equals approximately 7 feet, or 2.33 varas, whereas an estado in linear measurements equals about 2 varas, or between 5 and 6 feet. See Charles W. Polzer, Thomas C. Barnes, and Thomas H. Naylor, *The Documentary Relations of the Southwest: Project Manual*, 39.

10. According to the Mexican government map (1:250,000), *Matamoros*, G14-6-9-12, the correct contemporary reading of the latitude at the mouth of the Rio Grande is approximately 25°57′. The defective astrolabe was apparently the same troublesome instrument that was used when Captain Alonso de León took a reading on the 1653 expedition to the mouth of the Palmas River (see Chapter 3) and that was used again to take readings on the 1689 expedition.

11. The cornstalk that was brought to shore probably originated from an Indian village located south of the discovery area. Experts believe that agriculture was practiced at that time in the coastal area in present-day Tamaulipas (Gerhard, *The North Frontier*, 358–359). In response to Cabeza de Vaca's report that corn-meal was brought to him soon after he crossed the Rio Grande, Nance has noted that the report is not surprising, as "maize horticulture is recorded for southern Tamaulipas in early historic times" (*The Archaeology of La Calsada*, 2–3). Coastal surface currents move north toward Texas along the Tamaulipas coast.

12. According to Cavazos Garza, the dry marsh or estuary is the same location where the port of Refugio was established. The area today is occupied by the city of Matamoros, Tamaulipas (Chapa, *Historia*, ed. Cavazos Garza, 131n17).

13. The Pajarito was a well-known tribe that lived in the lower Rio Grande area. Members of the tribe entered the mission at Camargo in the middle eighteenth century. See Salinas, *Indians of the Rio Grande Delta*, 102–103.

32. The Continuation of Governor Aguayo's Administration

"In which the occurrences of heretofore are continued."

1. The ford was probably near the mouth of the San Juan River, located about 20 leagues from Cerralvo.
2. The "large salty river" was probably modern Baffin Bay, and the point of contact was likely near the Kenedy-Kleberg county line. The assertion that the party reached the seacoast is inaccurate; they probably reached modern Laguna Madre. Massanet, who was not on the trip, reports that the troops reached a river that forms at its mouth a lake that they were unable to pass (Bolton, *Spanish Exploration*, 354).
3. Melchor Portocarrero Lasso de la Vega, Conde de Monclova, served as viceroy from 1686 to 1688 (Chipman, *Spanish Texas*, 264).
4. According to Cavazos Garza, the location of the San Antonio Valley was the same as the present-day city of Hidalgo, Tamaulipas. See map *Linares*, G14-11.

33. Governor Alonso de León Captures a Frenchman Living among the Indians

"Of how Governor Alonso de León, governor of the Province of Coahuila, sent to request help from the governor of this kingdom, and of how he captured a Frenchman who was among the Indians."

1. The settlement of Coahuila was later called Santiago de la Monclova. De León settled the new community in 1687, and Chapa assisted him. Earlier attempts to establish a community (called Almadén) had collapsed. Gerhard, *The North Frontier*, 325–334, gives a brief history of the location.
2. The Frenchman was Jean Géry. Authorities have given different answers to the question of whether the Frenchman arrived in Texas from Canada or with La Salle. The fact that he said he arrived through present-day Pass Cavallo (and correctly identified its location) and identified "Monsieur Philipe de la sala," and the fact that he knew so well the area and the Indians near La Salle's settlement seems to resolve that issue in favor of his having arrived with La Salle, as he testified.

34. The French Prisoner Explains Why He Lived with the Indians

"Of how the French prisoner declared the cause and motives of having gone to the Indians."

1. A Capuchin was a Franciscan friar of an austere branch established in 1526 by Matteo de Bassi in Italy (*Webster's Third New International Dictionary*, unabridged, 334).

2. In *Wilderness Manhunt*, 139–142, citing original documents, Robert S. Weddle describes the several interrogations of Géry. The interrogation in Monclova on June 7, 1688, conducted by Governor Alonso de León, was translated into English by Walter J. O'Donnell, "La Salle's Occupation of Texas," 9–12.

35. His Excellency Orders an Expedition to Locate the French Settlement

"Of how His Excellency, seeing the Frenchman, resolved that a journey should be made to discover the settlement of the French."

1. An *expediente* was a file of documents pertaining to a specific issue or event (Barnes et al., *A Research Guide*, 135).
2. The Caldera River route probably refers to the road from Monterrey that followed generally the route of the modern Nuevo León Highway No. 1 to the village of Candela, and then turned west along the Candela River toward Monclova. See *Monterrey*, G14-7 and *Monclova*, G14-4.
3. Parral was located in present-day central Chihuahua. For a short history of Parral, see Gerhard, *The North Frontier*, 216–219.
4. Gaspar de Sandoval Silva y Mendoza, Conde de Galve, served as viceroy from 1688 to 1696 (Chipman, *Spanish Texas*, 264).

36. Governor Alonso de León Discovers the French Settlement and the Bay of Espíritu Santo

"Of how Governor Alonso de León discovered the settlement of the French and the Bay of Espíritu Santo."

1. The list of men on the 1689 expedition was not included in the AGN version of De León's expedition diary translated and annotated by Elizabeth H. West, "Governor Alonso de León's 1689 Expedition Diary," 199–224.
2. The list confirms that Chapa accompanied De León on the 1689 expedition.
3. *Tochomite* is a word derived from the Aztec "tochtli," meaning rabbit, and "omero," meaning hair. It was a kind of yarn used by Indian women for their embroidery and hair ornaments (Francisco J. Santamaría, *Diccionario de Mejicanismos*, 1064). Highley notes that native rabbit-fur robes (missing from the Loma Sandia site) were found at the Cueva de la Candelaria and the lower Pecos River sites. Taylor and Highley, *The Loma Sandia Site*, vol. 2, 659.
4. Bison were reported on the south side of the Rio Grande by several expedition diarists. See Foster, *Spanish Expeditions Into Texas*, 236-237. Bison had roamed the lower Rio Grande for centuries, as climate and grass conditions permitted. Solveig A. Turpin summarizes reports on the excavations of numerous prehis-

toric bison remains at sites on the lower Pecos River (about fifty leagues north-northwest of De León's Rio Grande crossing location), including the remains of a large number of bison dated ca. 8000 B.C. excavated at the Bonfire Shelter site. "The Lower Pecos River Region of Texas and Northern Mexico," *Bulletin of the Texas Archeological Society* 66 (1995), 544.

37. The Expedition Continues

"In which the expedition is continued."

1. The crossing was at or near the ford later called Paso de Francia, the one De León had used the year before. The same fording area was used by expeditions that crossed the river near San Juan Bautista after the post was established.

2. In his diary account on April 3, De León apparently refers to Chapa as "el autor," or the author. The governor wrote, "These tables, the author [Chapa?] says, he took from the *Arte de Navegar*, by the Maestro Medina" (Bolton, *Spanish Exploration*, 391). It is difficult to imagine whom De León was calling "the author" if it was not Chapa, who assisted the governor in the use of the astrolabe and tables on both the 1686 and 1689 expeditions.

3. The Guadalupe River crossing was at the ford later referred to as Vado del Gobernador. See Foster and Jackson, "The 1693 Expedition of Governor Salinas Varona to Sustain the Missionaries among the Tejas Indians," 291n70.

4. Santiago de Valladares was established in 1688 and is known today as Candela, Coahuila, according to Cavazos Garza. See Chapa, *Historia*, ed. Cavazos Garza, 144n21; and map *Monclova*, G14-4.

5. The other guide, Juanillo, was a Papul Indian whom Massanet brought on the journey.

6. According to Massanet, the Emet and "Lava" (Cava) Indians were at the encampment (Bolton, *Spanish Exploration*, 359).

7. The Toxo (Toho) and Toaa (Tohaha) Indians were at the second encampment, according to Massanet (ibid.).

8. Jean Géry could converse not only in the Coahuiltecan dialect of the Rio Grande Indians but in Sanan, the language of the Toho. See LeRoy Johnson and T. N. Campbell, "Sanan: Traces of a Previously Unknown Aboriginal Language in Colonial Coahuila and Texas," 206–207.

9. Massanet wrote that this was an Emet village (Bolton, *Spanish Exploration*, 360).

10. Assuming De León's party was at a location about 12 miles east of the Guadalupe crossing (as stated in the diary account), the correct reading would be approximately 29°5′. De León reported 28°41′ in his diary. As the measured distance between 28° and 29° north latitude is approximately 68 miles, a deviation of 34′ (as reported by De León) suggests an error of approximately 37 miles.

38. Arrival at the French Settlement

"Which deals with how they reached the settlement of the French, and what form it had."

1. An arroba was approximately 25 pounds. See Barnes et al., *A Research Guide*, 74.
2. The almud is a dry measurement equivalent to about 4.2 quarts (ibid. 69).
3. It is very unlikely that the cornstalks found south of the mouth of the Rio Grande originated from modern Lavaca Bay. The prevailing current along the Gulf Coast near the mouth of the Rio Grande is toward the north. More likely, floating material (such as cornstalks) moved up the coast from the Huaxtec settlements north of Tampico, where crops were cultivated at the time (Gerhard, *The North Frontier*, 358–359).
4. The route taken by the party first veered southwest and circled several creeks (including present-day Placedo Creek) and returned in a southeast direction back to Lavaca Bay to camp near present-day Magnolia Beach. As indicated on the contemporary map *Beeville*, NH14-12, the party took the most convenient route by not crossing numerous creeks where they entered the bay.
5. The entrance was to Matagorda Bay (present-day Pass Cavallo), where Géry accurately reported the arrival of La Salle's vessel. See map *Beeville*, NH14-12.
6. Although Chapa's manuscript clearly records that Géry said he arrived with "Monsieur Philipe de la sala," the name was mistakenly published in 1909 by Genaro García as "la Gala" rather than "la sala" (De León et al., *Historia*, ed. García, 333). García's mistake has been repeated in subsequent reprints of Chapa's *Historia*, including Cavazos Garza's 1991 edition (150).
7. The Guadalupe enters San Antonio Bay at a point farther south and west than "the southern part" of Matagorda Bay (map *Beeville*, NH14-12).
8. The creek (probably present-day Placedo Creek) was later called Canoe Creek by De León (Bolton, *Spanish Exploration*, 420).
9. The Indian courier had traveled over 500 miles in the ten-day period, running from the Emet camp near modern Shiner in Fayette County to northeastern Houston County and back to the bay.
10. For Robert S. Weddle's translation of the letter, see *Wilderness Manhunt*, 193.

39. The Discovery and Naming of the San Marcos River

"Of how a large river was discovered, and was given the name San Marcos."

1. The correct reading of the latitude near the mouth of present-day Lavaca River is approximately 28°45′.
2. The "San Marcos" was the present-day Lavaca River. The distance given from the creek northeast to the large river (6 leagues) and from the mouth of the river

to the mouth of the creek (1.5 leagues) fits with the measured distance between Garcitas Creek and the Lavaca River at the two locations. The following year De León called the present-day Colorado River the San Marcos, thinking it was the upper stretch of the river he had named the year before. The name San Marcos was used for the Colorado by Spanish explorers through the first half of the eighteenth century.

3. For Robert S. Weddle's translation of the verse, see *Wilderness Manhunt*, 187–188.

4. Presumably these nineteen tribes plus the four (not five) nations mentioned near the Rio Grande crossing lived in the 240-mile area between present-day Maverick and Victoria counties. The Cuba (Cava), Emot (Emet), and Pataoo (Patao) appear to correspond to tribal names mentioned by other colonial period writers. See Appendix B.

5. None of the Indian tribes Chapa identifies as living in *encomiendas* in Nuevo León—the Ayancuara, Pantiguara, Ayanguara, Saguimaniguara, Maguipama-copini, Guciacapo, Bayaguera, Agustiguara, and Payamiguara—were included in his lists of Indian nations in chaps. 28 and 29.

40. Governor Alonso de León Locates the Two Frenchmen

"How Governor Alonso de León made a sally to look for the two Frenchmen, and brought them back."

1. Fire was a central element in the religion of the Tejas. Bolton describes the ceremonial significance of fire and the importance of the fire temple in *The Hasinais: Southern Caddoans as Seen by the Earliest Europeans*, 143, 150–152.

2. The report of an attack of smallpox killing more than 100 French settlers seems exaggerated, but their number had been reduced significantly from the 200 or so when La Salle first landed to about 35. The loss is not fully explained by desertions, accidents, and fatigue, and Henri Joutel and other narrators repeatedly mention that a fever struck La Salle and a number of his companions. See references in Pierre Margry, ed., *Découvertes et établissements des Français dan l'ouest et dans le sud de l'Amérique Septentrionale, 1674–1754*, vol. 3, 120–534.

3. The quintal is a weight measurement approximately equivalent to 101 pounds (Barnes et al., *A Research Guide*, 73).

4. Transcripts of the declarations made by the French captives (L'Archevêque and Jacques Grollet) appear in O'Donnell, "La Salle's Occupation of Texas," 15–21. Henri Joutel described the two captives when they were with La Salle's party. L'Archevêque was a Frenchman from Bayonne who had enlisted at Petit Goave (present-day Haiti). He was among the five men who plotted to kill La Salle, but

later he befriended Joutel. Joutel identifies Grollet as Grolet, a resident of the La Rochelle area who deserted La Salle in East Texas and was living with the Tejas when Joutel's party arrived in the early spring of 1687. Both men decided to remain with the Tejas rather than join Joutel's party on its march to Canada and return to France.

5. María de Jesús de Agreda has been a subject of interest to many Spanish colonial historians. The most comprehensive recent consideration of this nun and her connection to Texas and the Southwest is by David J. Weber. Weber reviews the church stories about her flight, "transported by the aid of the angels," to New Mexico from the convent at Agreda near the Ebro River in Spain. María de Agreda apparently later repudiated much of what she had told church officials about her travels in space. Weber suggests that her fasting (induced in part by the disease anorexia mirabilis) perhaps induced her visions (*Spanish Frontier*, 99–100).

41. Uprisings in Nuevo León in 1689

"Of the unrest that took place in the Kingdom of León that same year, 1689."

1. The tribe is not included among the 250 tribes Chapa lists in chaps. 28 and 29. The Janambre lived in present-day Tamaulipas and in South Texas below the Nueces River (*HONAI*, vol. 10, 331).

42. The Exploration and Settlement of the Río Blanco

"Of the exploration of the Río Blanco and its settlement."

1. General Zamora's material on the Río Blanco area in the southern part of the province is not included in Cavazos Garza's 1990 edition of Chapa's *Historia* and is not included in this translation.

43. The Exploration of the Province of the Tejas Continues

"In which the new occurrences of the exploration of the province of the Tejas [Indians] are continued."

1. The soldiers sent from Parral to join De León may have been detained because the governor of Nueva Vizcaya, Don Juan Isidro de Pardiñas y Villar de Francos, protested the viceroy's order that the soldiers be sent to De León and insisted that they were urgently needed in Nueva Vizcaya to combat local enemy Indians. See Governor Pardiñas's October 18, 1688, report to the Conde de Galve in Thomas H. Naylor and Charles W. Polzer, *The Presidio and Militia on the Northern Frontier of New Spain, 1570–1700*, 575–578. De León's detailed report is

carefully analyzed by William E. Dunn, *Spanish and French Rivalry in the Gulf Region of the United States, 1678–1702*, 113–114.

2. Massanet gives an account of the conflict in Saltillo with the Parral soldiers assigned to De León's expedition (Bolton, *Spanish Exploration*, 370–372).

3. The latitude reading near the head of Lavaca Bay is approximately 28°40′. See map *Beeville*, NH14-12.

4. La Salle took Pierre Talon from his family at the French settlement in January 1687 to live with the Tejas and learn their language (Cox, ed., *The Journeys of La Salle*, vol. 2, 99).

5. "Pedro Muñi" was Pierre Meunier, age 20. For an excellent account of the young Frenchman, see Robert S. Weddle's entry in *NHOT*, 4:649.

6. *Atole* is a gruel made of corn pounded into a flour and mixed with milk or water (*Diccionario de la Lengua Española*, vol. 1, 148).

44. The Journey to the Tejas Continues

"In which the entry among the Tejas is continued."

1. *Pinole* is a dry powder made with powdered corn and sugar. See *New Revised Velázquez Spanish and English Dictionary*, 518.

2. The enigmatic Indian Tomás lived in El Parral, a mining community in central Nueva Vizcaya, over 700 miles from the Tejas governor's village. Long-distance travel and exchange between tribes in West Texas and Indians living in Central and East Texas were not new. Apparently during the Late Archaic period (ca. 250 B.C.– A.D. 750), Indians from the Trans-Pecos region and South Texas traveled east to hunt bison on the lower Colorado River, more specifically near the shallow rock-ledged river crossing north of La Grange in Fayette County. See analysis of artifacts from Site 41FY362 in the Rabbs Creek basin by Steven M. Kotter and Leland C. Bement in Kotter et al., *Final Report of the Cultural Resources Investigation at the Cummins Creek Mine, Fayette County, Texas*, 131–162.

3. The Frenchmen included La Salle's companion Henri de Tonti. For a summary of the movements of Tonti's party along the Mississippi and into East Texas between 1685 and 1691, see Weddle, *The French Thorn*, 98–100.

45. The Expedition to the Tejas Concludes

"In which the expedition to the Tejas is concluded."

1. A discussion of the two graves is found in Weddle, *La Salle*, 214n13.

2. La Salle's party constructed a tree bridge over the Angelina River during its two visits to the Tejas in 1686 and 1687. See Joutel's account of La Salle's party in Margry, *Découvertes*, 387.

3. Chapa repeats De León's reading. See Bolton, *Spanish Exploration*, 417. The latitude reading is off the mark by over two degrees, or over 130 miles. The correct reading for the Tejas community area west of the Neches River, according to map *Palestine*, NH15-1, is approximately 31°33′.

Appendix A. Governor Alonso de León's Revised 1690 Expedition Diary

1. The title of the AGN version of De León's 1690 diary translated by Herbert E. Bolton is "Itinerary of the Expedition made by General Alonso de León for the Discovery of the Bahía del Espíritu Santo and the French Settlement" (Bolton, *Spanish Exploration*, 388). The title of the revised diary was changed to note that Captain Salinas Varona accompanied De León. This change and other additions referenced in the notes suggest that the captain's hand may be found in this revision.

   In his brief introduction to De León's 1689 and 1690 expeditions, Bolton notes that he possessed three transcripts—one from the AGN of Mexico, the second from the AGI at Seville, and the third from Genaro García's collection. Although he selected the AGN version to translate, Bolton claimed that García's version was generally the most complete (ibid., 352).

2. The Coahuila River was the present-day Monclova River. The AGN manuscript erroneously records that the party marched 8 leagues on March 27. The correction in the distance traveled on that day is typical of the instances in which the García version corrects mistakes in the AGN version.

3. The Baluartes (bastions) are the mountain ridges through which the Nadadores River flows. On Fernando del Bosque's expedition in 1675, he described the same mountain ridges as "sharp peaks of rock, like sugar loaves" (Bolton, *Spanish Exploration*, 292).

4. The campsite called Alamo (cottonwood) was also noted on De León's expedition on March 25, 1689 (ibid., 388n4).

5. The Frenchman's Indians were the four or five tribes that acknowledged allegiance to Jean Géry and that De León had met the previous year at the same location, a few leagues south of the Rio Grande.

6. The creek called Caramanchel (modern-day Comanche Creek), which is Spanish for a public bar (*Diccionario de la Lengua Española*, vol. 1, 270), was named on this expedition and was cited by name and crossed on every seventeenth- and eighteenth-century expedition into Texas that forded near Paso de Francia.

7. Zarco (or Sarco) was the name given to the modern Leona River by De León on April 5, 1689 (Bolton, *Spanish Exploration*, 392), but on Terán's 1691 expedition, Massanet called it the Río Frío (Mattie Austin Hatcher, "The Expedition of Don Domingo Terán de los Ríos into Texas," 53). In this version of the diary, De

León used the name Sarco on his trip eastward but, strangely, used Massanet's name for the same stream on his return trip. Bolton does not attempt to identify the Sarco or the Hondo rivers in his annotations to the AGN version, although he does try to identify other rivers named in the diary.

8. The reference to the settlement of Indians to which a Frenchman had come probably refers to the Indians with whom Géry was living when he was captured. Massanet, who was not on the 1688 expedition to capture Géry, named the Indian tribes with Géry as the Mescal, Yorica, Chomene, Machomen, Sampanal, Paquachiam, Telpayay, and Apis (Bolton, *Spanish Exploration*, 356).

9. The AGN version does not mention that Salinas Varona was along on this side trip. This is the type of information about the movement of specific personnel that the revised version provides.

10. The creek is called the Chapa River in the AGN version of the diary, but in this version, De León omits any reference to the name Chapa or to the construction of a bridge, and he refers to the stream as a creek. In 1693 Salinas Varona used the name Chapa to identify the same creek (present-day San Miguel), located about 5 leagues east of the Frio crossing. See Foster and Jackson, "The 1693 Expedition," 288.

11. In 1689 De León had named the stream (the present-day Atascosa River) the "Arroyo del Vino." Bolton recognized that Robalos Creek was the same as Arroyo del Vino, but he did not attempt its present-day identification (*Spanish Exploration*, 408n1).

12. The fording area was at or near the Conquista Crossing on the San Antonio River. It is depicted on the Texas General Land Office map *Karnes County*, compiled and drawn in 1870 by F. H. Arlitt.

13. In his annotations to the 1689 De León diary, Bolton incorrectly suggests that Arroyo del León (Cibolo Creek) was the San Antonio River. See Bolton, *Spanish Exploration*, 394n1. This mistake was made earlier by West, "Governor Alonso de León's 1689 Expedition Diary," 210n1.

14. Arroyo Salado, today called Salt Creek, is a tributary of upper Coleto Creek in DeWitt County. See map *Seguin*, NH 14-9.

15. The ford of the Guadalupe was likely the same used by De León in 1689. The crossing was later identified as Vado del Gobernador on Manuel Agustín Mascaró's 1807 map. See Jack Jackson, "Father José María de Jesús Puelles and the Maps of Pichardo's Document 74," 332–333, fig. 3.

16. This description of the direction from the Guadalupe crossing (near Cuero in DeWitt County) to the bay as being toward the "southeast" is significant because it corrects the misstatements of the direction in De León's 1689 account and in the 1690 AGN version.

17. The ford of the present-day Colorado (called the Maligne by the French and the San Marcos by the Spanish) was likely the same crossing area near modern-day

La Grange in Fayette County that La Salle used in 1686 and 1687 and that De León visited in 1689, when he rode north from the Guadalupe to meet the Tejas chieftain and the two Frenchmen.

18. The Tejas Indians used the area east of the Colorado as their hunting grounds, although the area was apparently shared with other friendly tribes who lived in the region. The Colorado served as a boundary separating the tribes who lived and hunted on the west side of the lower Colorado from the Tejas and associated tribes that usually remained on the east side of the river. See Henri Joutel's description of the Colorado (or Maligne) as a boundary river marking the tribal territories of local Indians in Cox, *The Journeys of La Salle*, vol. 2, 114–115.

19. This version of De León's diary gives the itinerary not only of De León's party but also of the supply party that occasionally was left behind and followed a different route. The account of the separate itinerary of the supply party is not included in the AGN version of the diary translated by Bolton; however, this version contains an incomplete description of the direction taken on May 7.

20. Jesús, María y Joseph de Buena Vista was the present-day Monument Hill, across the Colorado from La Grange. During the period of Anglo colonization, the hill was referred to simply as "María."

21. Pierre Talon was captured in northeastern Gonzales County.

22. Río del Espíritu Santo—called the Rivière aux Canots by the French and sometimes also called the Colorado by the Spaniards—was the modern Brazos River. In his testimony in Mexico City later that same year, Meunier (who was at the assassins' camp at the time of La Salle's murder) said that La Salle had been killed near the Río del Espíritu Santo or the Brazos (see AGI, México, 61-6-21). Bolton confirmed Meunier's report ("The Location of La Salle's Colony on the Gulf of Mexico," 173) but Weddle (I believe mistakenly) places the assassination of La Salle east of the Trinity. See *NHOT*, 4:82.

23. The meeting occurred near Bedias Creek. An area about twenty-five leagues south, along the lower Brazos, was apparently under Caddoan influence several centuries earlier. See the analysis of ceramics and other artifacts in grave goods by Grant D. Hall, *Allens Creek: A Study in the Cultural Prehistory of the Lower Brazos River Valley, Texas*, 267–309.

24. This version omits material included in the AGN version relating to the clergy's activities among the Tejas. Also, certain place names differ between the two diaries; see Bolton, *Spanish Exploration*, 415–417.

25. The names of these tribes are not included in the AGN version of De León's 1690 diary. However, Father Massanet wrote that their party found the Emet, Tohaha, Toho, Cava, and other tribes near the Colorado crossing (Bolton, *Spanish Exploration*, 384). Chapa's identification of the Sana and Cantona tribes at the Colorado ford is significant. Both tribes are recognized as residents principally of the region between the lower Guadalupe and the Colorado. See Thomas N.

Campbell's entries "Sana Indians" and "Cantona Indians" in *NHOT*, 5:792 and 1:962–963. La Salle's chronicler, Henri Joutel, also listed the tribes that lived toward the west and northwest of the Colorado (called the Maligne by the French); Joutel's list also included the Tohaha and Toho (Tohau). See Margry, *Découvertes*, vol. 3, 288, 289. It should be noted that the tribal names listed in Cox's edition of the 1714 English translation of Michel's abridgement of Joutel's journal are seriously flawed (*The Journeys of La Salle*, vol. 2, 114–115, 145–146). William W. Newcomb, Jr., has questionably concluded (citing Cox) that the Cantona and the French-identified tribe called Canohatino are probably a single ethnic group ("Historic Indians of Central Texas," 23–24).

26. De León's party and the supply party split near the ford of the Colorado in Fayette County. The supply party proceeded south along the old Indian trail to return to the Guadalupe campground in DeWitt County; De León's small party moved south-southeast toward Matagorda Bay. De León's party followed approximately in the reverse direction the route from the Colorado crossing to the bay that La Salle's party in 1687 had taken from the French settlement to the same crossing of the Colorado (Margry, *Découvertes*, vol. 3, 260–297).

27. The Thoó (Toho, Toaa, or Tohan) was the same tribe that De León met near the Colorado crossing on the 1689 expedition (Bolton, *Spanish Exploration*, 363) and the same tribe that La Salle's chronicler, Henri Joutel, listed as living west of the Colorado (Margry, *Découvertes*, vol. 3, 288).

28. The Cooc (Coco) was a local tribe found living on both sides of the lower Colorado. In his footnote on this tribe, Bolton mistakenly renders the name in the manuscript as "Cóoé" rather than Cóoc, the spelling that seems clear in the summary list of tribes encountered on the expedition as recorded in the Yale University library manuscript that was used in both Bolton's annotations and in this translation. See Bolton, *Spanish Exploration*, 420n1. Authorities are divided on the question of the tribe's connection with the Karankawan tribes found near the Matagorda and San Antonio bay areas. See *NHOT*, 2:184–185, and *HONAI*, vol. 10, 360. Jean Louis Berlandier writes that the Cocos and Karankawas spoke different languages (*Journey to Mexico during the Years 1826 to 1834*, vol. 2, 382). This band of Coco was found about 80 miles north of Matagorda Bay, the area where the Karankawa Indians traditionally resided. The confusion is aggravated by editor Fritz Leo Hoffmann's suggestion that the friendly Coco (seen by De León on June 19 in northwestern Colorado County) was the same tribe as the feisty Caocossi (encountered on San Antonio Bay, 100 miles south, while recovering the French children three days later) (Francisco de Céliz, *Diary of the Alarcón Expedition into Texas, 1718–1719*, 101n138).

29. The Naaman was the largest tribal group De León reported. Massanet includes the Manam in his list of tribes who lived near the Guadalupe. See Massanet to viceroy, Sept. 1690, AGI, Mexico, 61-6-21, 75–84.

30. The Caisquetebana Indians were not identified by the same name on any subsequent Spanish expedition. See Thomas N. Campbell's entry "Caisquetebana Indians," *NHOT*, 1:892.

31. The stream was modern Garcitas Creek, where La Salle's French settlement had been located. De León's route from the Tejas villages in East Texas to the former French settlement was the same route that La Salle followed in his 1686 and 1687 journeys from his settlement to visit the Tejas Indians (called the Cenis by the French). They both crossed the Trinity (so named by De León but called the Cenis River by Joutel) about 10 to 12 leagues west of the main Tejas settlement, crossed the Brazos (called the equivalent of Colorado by local Indians, the Espíritu Santo by the Spaniards, and the Canoe by the French) near its junction with the Navasota, and apparently crossed the Colorado (called the San Marcos by the Spaniards and the Maligne by the French) near present-day La Grange. De León records traveling south approximately 42 Spanish leagues between the Colorado crossing and the French fort; Henri Joutel (with La Salle in 1687) recorded traveling northward approximately 43 French leagues between the same two points. De León and La Salle identified the same Indian tribes (the Cantona, Toho, and Tohaha) on the west side of the modern Colorado near the crossing.

32. Canoe Creek was likely present-day Placedo Creek or one of its larger tributary creeks.

33. The small bay was San Antonio Bay. The Cascosis may have been a name used for a Karankawan band that lived near San Antonio Bay. Bolton cites the tribe as the Cascossi, a reasonable, but I think incorrect, reading when one examines the name as written in the manuscript both in the diary entry and in the closing summary list of tribes. Governor Alarcón met several members of a tribe called Caocose on his visit to Matagorda Bay in 1718. See Céliz, *Diary of the Alarcón Expedition*, 66. Editor Hoffmann says the Caocose were probably the same tribe as the Coco and Cabeza de Vaca's Capoque, which he considers to be a branch of the Karankawas (ibid., 101n138). De León had probably encountered the Cocos on the nineteenth, nearer the area where the tribe was later encountered.

34. The history of the Talon family, including the children, is extensively covered by Weddle in *Wilderness Manhunt*, 253–266.

35. The governor probably used the ford of the Guadalupe that was later called Vado del Gobernador, the same crossing he used on his 1689 expedition and that Governor Salinas Varona used on his 1693 expedition. See Foster and Jackson, "The 1693 Expedition," 291n70.

36. This is the second reference to the campground near modern Salt Creek; the first was made on April 22.

37. The Toho (Thooé) are likely a band of the same tribe whom De León met in

Fayette County, near the Colorado River, on June 18. See De León's list of tribes at the close of the diary in which he notes that he had met the tribe twice. Massanet identified the same tribe at the second Indian encampment that he and De León visited in northern Lavaca County on the 1689 expedition. This Toho encampment was in Atascosa County, approximately 12 leagues west of the San Antonio River crossing. This was the area in which De León's remuda was spooked on both his 1689 and 1690 expeditions and represents the only reported sighting of an Indian encampment between the Frio and San Antonio rivers on any Spanish expedition into Texas in the seventeenth century.

38. The AGN version of the diary (Bolton, *Spanish Exploration*, 422) does not mention that the Hondo (Frio) River stopped. Because the modern-day Frio does have stretches in which the water flow is primarily or entirely subterranean (in the dry summer months), De León may have meant that the stream went below ground.

39. Las Cruces was not identified as a ford in the AGN version of the diary. It is the location (near present-day Frio Town) where De León found petroglyphs on April 6, 1689 (Bolton, *Spanish Exploration*, 392) and where Terán forded the Frio in 1691 on his march east toward modern-day San Antonio (Hatcher, "The Expedition of Don Domingo Terán," 13).

40. The rain delay was De León's justification for sending the AGN version of the diary to the viceroy before the expedition was completed. Consequently, the AGN version, translated by Bolton, does not contain entries for the conclusion of the expedition march from the Rio Grande to Monclova, as does this version.

41. The ponds are likely the campsite that was used, but was not identified by name, on April 1. Governor de León probably camped at the same ponds in 1689; see Bolton, *Spanish Exploration*, 389.

42. The Indian tribes listed were all named along the route except the Mojoman; no explanation is given as to when or where this tribe was encountered. The Mojoman are not identified in *HONAI*. Listing the names of each Indian tribe seen on the expedition at the end of the diary was not common. The AGN version does not include a comparable list. Governor Salinas Varona was the only diarist who provided such a summary, at the close of his 1693 diary. See Foster and Jackson, "The 1693 Expedition," 310. Having the name of the tribes written twice, once in the diary text and again in summary fashion at the close of the diary, is very helpful in determining the spelling that the author intended for each tribal name.

Bibliography

Archival Sources

Archivo General de Indias (AGI), Seville
Archivo General de la Nación (AGN), Mexico City
Bancroft Library (BL), University of California at Berkeley
Beinecke Library, Yale University, New Haven
Center for American History, University of Texas at Austin
Library of Congress, Manuscript Division, Washington, D.C.

Published Sources

Acosta, Joseph de. 1962 [1590]. *Historia natural y moral de las Indias*. Ed., with commentary by Edmundo O'Gorman. Mexico City: Fondo de Cultura Económica. Facsimile ed. with English commentary and anthology by Barbara G. Beddal. Valencia: Hispaniae Scientia, Albatross Ediciones, 1977.

Alessio Robles, Vito. *Coahuila y Texas en la época colonial*. Mexico City: Editorial Porrúa, 1978.

Barnes, Thomas C., Thomas H. Naylor, and Charles W. Polzer. *Northern New Spain—A Research Guide*. Tucson: University of Arizona Press, 1981.

Berlandier, Jean Louis. *Journey to Mexico during the Years 1826 to 1834*. Trans. Sheila M. Ohlendorf, Josette M. Bigelow, and Mary M. Slandifer. 2 vols. Austin: Texas State Historical Association and the Center for Studies in Texas History, University of Texas at Austin, 1980.

Bolton, Herbert E., ed. *Spanish Exploration in the Southwest, 1542–1706*. New York: Charles Scribner's Sons, 1916.

———. *The Hasinais: Southern Caddoans as Seen by the Earliest Europeans*. Ed. Russell M. Magnaghi. Norman: University of Oklahoma Press, 1987.

Butzer, Karl W. "From Columbus to Acosta: Science, Geography, and the New World." In *The Americas before and after 1492: Current Geographical Research*, guest ed. Karl W. Butzer. *Annals of the Association of American Geographers* 82 (September 1992), 543–565.

Campbell, Thomas N. "The Coahuiltecans and Their Neighbors." In *Handbook of North American Indians*, vol. 10, ed. Alfonso Ortiz, 343–358. Washington, D.C.: Smithsonian Institution Press, 1983.

———. *The Indians of Southern Texas and Northeastern Mexico: Selected Writings of Thomas Nolan Campbell*. Austin: Texas Archeological Research Laboratory, University of Texas, 1988.

Castañeda, Carlos E. *Our Catholic Heritage in Texas*. 7 vols. Austin, Tex.: Von Boeckmann-Jones, 1936–1958.

Cavazos Garza, Israel. *Diccionario biográfico de Nuevo León*. 2 vols. Monterrey: Ediciones Minas Viejas, 1984.

———. *Historia de Nuevo León by Juan Bautista Chapa*. 2nd ed. Monterrey: Centro de Estudios Humanísticos, Universidad Autónoma de Nuevo León y Gobierno del Estado, 1961.

———. *Historia del Nuevo Reino de León de 1650 a 1690 by Juan Bautista Chapa*. Monterrey: Gobierno del Estado de Nuevo León, 1990.

Céliz, Francisco de. *Diary of the Alarcón Expedition into Texas, 1718–1719*. Ed. and trans. Fritz Leo Hoffman. Los Angeles: Quivira Society, 1935.

[Chapa, Juan Bautista.] *Historia de Nuevo León con noticias sobre Coahuila, Texas y Nuevo México, por el Capitán Alonso de León, un Autor Anónimo y el General Fernando Sánchez de Zamora*. Ed. Genaro García. Mexico City: Bounet, 1909.

Chipman, Donald E. "In Search of Cabeza de Vaca's Route across Texas: An Historiographical Survey." *Southwestern Historical Quarterly* 91 (October 1987), 127–148.

———. *Nuño de Guzmán and the Province of Pánuco in New Spain, 1518–1533*. Glendale, Calif.: Arthur H. Clark, 1967.

Cox, Isaac Joslin, ed. *The Journeys of René Robert Cavelier, Sieur de La Salle*. 2 vols. New York: A. S. Barnes, 1905.

Cutter, Charles R. *The Legal Culture of Northern New Spain, 1700–1810*. Albuquerque: University of New Mexico Press, 1995.

———. *The Protector de Indios in Colonial New Mexico, 1659–1821*. Albuquerque: University of New Mexico Press, 1986.

Davenport, Harbert, ed. "The Expedition of Pánfilo de Narváez by Gonzalo Fernández Oviedo y Valdez." *Southwestern Historical Quarterly* 26 (October 1923), 120–139; 26 (January 1924), 217–241; 27 (April 1924), 276–304; 28 (July 1924), 56–74; 29 (October 1924), 122–163.

De León, Alonso, et al. *Historia de Nuevo León, con noticias sobre Coahuila, Tejas y Nuevo México*. Ed. Genaro García. Mexico City: Bounet, 1909.

Dixon, E. James. *Quest for the Origins of the First Americans*. Albuquerque: University of New Mexico Press, 1993.

Duaine, Carl L., comp. and trans. *Caverns of Oblivion*. Corpus Christi, Tex.: Privately printed, 1971.

Dulcet, Antonio Palau. *Manual del librero hispano-americano.* 7 vols. Barcelona: Librería Anticuaria, 1923-1927. 2nd ed., 28 vols. Barcelona: Antonio Palau, 1948-1977.

Dunn, William E. *Spanish and French Rivalry in the Gulf Region of the United States, 1678-1702.* Austin: University of Texas, 1917.

Espinosa, Fr. Isidro Félix de. *Crónica de los colegios de propaganda fide de la Nueva España.* Ed. Lino Gómez Canado. Washington, D.C.: Academy of American Franciscan History, 1964.

Fittig, James E. "Regional Cultural Development, 300 B.C. to A.D. 1000." In *Handbook of North American Indians*, vol. 15, ed. Bruce G. Triggen. Washington, D.C.: Smithsonian Institution, 1978.

Foster, William C. *Spanish Expeditions into Texas, 1689-1768.* Austin: University of Texas Press, 1995.

Foster, William C., and Jack Jackson, eds. "The 1693 Expedition of Governor Salinas Varona to Sustain the Missionaries among the Tejas Indians." Trans. Ned F. Brierley. *Southwestern Historical Quarterly* 97 (October 1993), 264-311.

Gerhard, Peter. *The North Frontier of New Spain.* Rev. ed. Norman: University of Oklahoma Press, 1982, 1991.

Gibson, Charles. "Spanish Indian Policies." In *Handbook of North American Indians*, vol. 4, ed. Wilcomb E. Washburn, 96-102. Washington, D.C.: Smithsonian Institution Press, 1988.

Gómez Canedo, Lino, ed. *Primeras exploraciones y poblamiento de Texas (1686-1694).* Monterrey: Instituto Tecnológico y de Estudios Superiores, 1968.

Griffen, William B. "Southern Periphery: East." In *Handbook of North American Indians*, vol. 10, ed. Alfonso Ortiz, 329-342. Washington, D.C.: Smithsonian Institution Press, 1983.

Grove, Jean M. *The Little Ice Age.* London and New York: Methuen, 1988.

Hall, Grant D. *Allens Creek: A Study in the Cultural Prehistory of the Lower Brazos River Valley, Texas.* Research Report No. 61. Austin: Texas Archeological Survey, University of Texas at Austin, 1981.

Hammond, George P., and Agapito Rey. *The Rediscovery of New Mexico, 1580-1594.* Albuquerque: University of New Mexico Press, 1966.

Hatcher, Mattie Austin. "The Expedition of Don Domingo Terán de los Ríos into Texas." *Preliminary Studies of the Texas Catholic Historical Society* 2 (January 1932), 10-67.

Hedrick, Basil C., and Carroll L. Riley. *The Journey of the Vaca Party: The Account of the Narváez Expedition, 1528-1536, as Related by Gonzalo Fernández de Oviedo y Valdés.* University Museum Studies. Carbondale: Southern Illinois University, 1974.

Heiser, Charles B., Jr. "Ethnobotany and Economic Botany." In *Flora of North America, North of Mexico.* New York: Oxford University Press, 1993.

Hodge, Frederick W., and Theodore H. Lewis, eds. *Spanish Explorers in the Southern United States, 1528–1543*. Reprint. Austin: Texas State Historical Association, 1990.

Hoyo, Eugenio del. *Historia del Nuevo Reino de León (1577–1723)*. Monterrey: Publicaciones del Instituto Tecnológico y de Estudios Superiores de Monterrey, 1972.

Jackson, Jack. "Father José María de Jesús Puelles and the Maps of Pichardo's Document 74." *Southwestern Historical Quarterly* 91 (January 1988), 317–347.

Jackson, Jack, and William C. Foster. *Imaginary Kingdom*. Austin: Texas State Historical Association, 1995.

Johnson, LeRoy, and T. N. Campbell. "Sanan: Traces of a Previously Unknown Aboriginal Language in Colonial Coahuila and Texas." *Plains Anthropologists* 37 (August 1992), 185–212.

Kotter, Steven M., et al. *Final Report of Cultural Resource Investigations at the Cummins Creek Mine, Fayette County, Texas*. Studies in Archeology 11. Austin: Texas Archeological Research Laboratory, University of Texas at Austin, 1991.

Lawson, Merlin P. *The Climate of the Great American Desert*. Lincoln: University of Nebraska Press, 1974.

Lynch, John. *Spain under the Habsburgs*. 2 vols. New York: New York University Press, 1984.

Margry, Pierre, ed. *Découvertes et établissements des français dans l'ouest et dans le sud de l'Amérique Septentrionale, 1674–1754*. 6 vols. Paris: Maisonneuve, 1876–1886.

Martin, Robert S., and James C. Martin. *Contours of Discovery*. Austin: Texas State Historical Association and the Center for Studies in Texas History, University of Texas at Austin, 1982.

Morfí, Juan Agustín de. *History of Texas, 1673–1779*. Ed. and trans. Carlos E. Castañeda. 2 vols. Albuquerque: Quivira Society, 1935.

Morgan, George R., and Omer C. Stewart. "Peyote Trade in South Texas." *Southwestern Historical Quarterly* 87 (January 1984), 269–287.

Nance, C. Roger. *The Archaeology of La Calsada: A Rockshelter in the Sierra Madre Oriental, Mexico*. Austin: University of Texas Press, 1992.

Naylor, Thomas H., and Charles W. Polzer. *The Presidio and Militia on the Northern Frontier of New Spain, 1570–1700*. Tucson: University of Arizona Press, 1986.

———. *Pedro Rivera and the Military Regulations for Northern New Spain, 1724–1729*. Tucson: University of Arizona Press, 1986.

Newcomb, William W., Jr. "Historic Indians of Central Texas." *Bulletin of the Texas Archaeological Society* 64 (1993), 1–63.

Nunley, Parker. *Archeological Sites of Texas*. Austin: Texas Monthly Press, 1989.

O'Donnell, Walter J. "La Salle's Occupation of Texas." *Preliminary Studies of the*

Texas Catholic Historical Society 3, no. 2 (April 1936), 5–33.

Perttula, Timothy K., et al. "Prehistoric and Historic Aboriginal Ceramics in Texas." *Bulletin of the Texas Archeological Society* 66 (1995), 175–235.

Polzer, Charles W., Thomas C. Barnes, and Thomas H. Naylor. *The Documentary Relations of the Southwest: Project Manual.* Tucson: University of Arizona Press, 1977.

Ricklis, Robert A. *The Karankawa Indians of Texas: An Ecological Study of Cultural Tradition and Change.* Austin: University of Texas Press, 1996.

———. "Prehistoric Occupation of the Central and Lower Texas Coast: A Regional View." *Bulletin of the Texas Archeological Society* 66 (1995), 265–300.

Salinas, Martín. *Indians of the Rio Grande Delta.* Austin: University of Texas Press, 1990.

Santamaría, Francisco J. *Diccionario de Mejicanismos.* 3rd ed., 1978.

Schroeder, Albert H., and Dan S. Matson. *A Colony on the Move.* Salt Lake City: School of American Research, 1965.

Simmons, Marc. *The Last Conquistador: Juan de Oñate and the Settling of the Far Southwest.* Norman: University of Oklahoma Press, 1991.

Steck, Francis B. "Forerunners of Captain De León's Expedition to Texas, 1670–1675." *Preliminary Studies of the Catholic Historical Society* 2, no. 3 (September 1932), 5–32.

Stewart, Omer C. *Peyote Religion: A History.* Norman: University of Oklahoma Press, 1987.

Swain, Susan H. "Mexico and the Little Ice Age." *Journal of Interdisciplinary History* 2 (Spring 1981), 633–648.

Swanton, John R. *Source Materials on the History and Ethnology of the Caddo Indians.* Bureau of American Ethnology, Bulletin 132. Washington, D.C.: Smithsonian Institution, 1942.

Taylor, Anna Jean, and Cheryl Lynn Highley. *Archeological Investigations at the Loma Sandia Site (41LK28),* vol. 2, Studies in Archeology 20. Austin: Texas Archeological Research Laboratory, University of Texas at Austin, 1995.

Turpin, Solveig A. "The Lower Pecos River Region of Texas and Northern Mexico." *Bulletin of the Texas Archeological Society* 66 (1995), 541–560.

Tyler, Ron, ed. *The New Handbook of Texas.* 6 vols. Austin: Texas State Historical Association, 1996.

Weber, David J. *The Spanish Frontier in North America.* New Haven, Conn.: Yale University Press, 1992.

Weddle, Robert S. *The French Thorn: Rival Explorers in the Spanish Sea, 1682–1762.* College Station: Texas A&M University Press, 1991.

———. *Spanish Sea: The Gulf of Mexico in North American Discovery, 1500–1585.* College Station: Texas A&M University Press, 1985.

————. *Wilderness Manhunt.* Austin: University of Texas Press, 1973.

————, ed. *La Salle, the Mississippi, and the Gulf.* College Station: Texas A&M University Press, 1987.

West, Elizabeth H., trans. "Governor Alonso de León's 1689 Expedition Diary." *Texas State Historical Association Quarterly* 8 (January 1905), 199–224.

Index

Indian tribes with variant names are indexed under the name found in Appendix B.